Views from the English Community

edited by Tony Linsell

Athelney

Published 2005 by

Athelney
1 Providence Street
King's Lynn
Norfolk, England

British Library Cataloguing-in-Publication Data. A catalogue record for this book is available from the British Library.

ISBN 1-903313-03-1

For

Cyning Meadowcroft

&

Michael Knowles

Both have made a very special contribution

to the cause of an English Parliament

Contents

Acknowledgements

My thanks to all the contributors to this collection. In particular I am grateful to T.P. Bragg for his help and good humour in preparing the manuscript for publication.

Contributors

It should be made clear that the contributors to this book represent a wide spectrum of political views. It is certain that each of them disagrees with many of the views expressed here by one or more of the other contributors. Yet, despite that, they share a common *we* sentiment, a sense of Englishness that unites them. There is one exception to this, Veronica Henderson, who has worked and lived in England for many years but is still very Scottish.

You may be surprised to learn that three of the contributors to this book have a well-to-the-left political background – Militant Tendency, Anti-Nazi League, Social Workers Party, and that sort of thing. I mention this because it might be thought by some that a book of this kind is bound to be Rightwing – whatever that means. Two of the *Lefties* feel uncomfortable being labelled nationalists but that is what they are. I hope they come to warm to it in the same way as do Irish, Scottish, and Welsh nationalists. The third of them relishes the label and looks to Ho Chi Minh for inspiration –*a great man and great nationalist*. As for the other contributors, some are Conservatives and one comfortably wears the label Liberal-Democrat. Others I wouldn't care to pigeonhole. A few I barely know.

Several of the contributors advocate an English Parliament, as do former Labour Ministers Tony Benn and Frank Field. The Conservative MP David Davis once openly supported the idea of an English Parliament. Perhaps, if he becomes leader of the Conservative Party, David Davis will change that party's policy and present an English Parliament as being a way of strengthening the Union.

In view of the fact that politics moves on in spurts and some statements can become dated, please note that all of the contributions to this book, except the introduction, were written before August 2004.

Mak Norman lives in Sussex with his wife Katrina and his daughter Ottylia.

He spent his twenties in a three-piece rock band and has fond memories of being on the road in Canada, reading the Anglo-Saxon Chronicle onboard the tour bus. Not very rock 'n roll, but then Mak had already become sensitive to England's identity problem as a small boy while watching the 1966 World Cup. "The sight of England fans waving the union flag sparked a type of *cultural envy* - even more so in the *Home Internationals*".

In his thirties he began studying Anglo-Saxon heathenism, which exposed an exciting and dynamic dimension to Mak's definition of English ethnicity. Other interests include traditional English Folk Song, Old English language and creating fairy stories for his daughter.

Mak's Czech wife once asked him, "Why do children's television programmes in England predominantly promote other cultures, but do not include English fairy stories, folk song or folk dance, like you would see in the Czech Republic - even something simple like how to make Toad in the Hole?" He looked and saw that she was right. Perhaps foreigners in England are more aware of what is being done to the English and less inhibited than the English in voicing an opinion on the matter. Maybe they have a fresh eye, and the knowledge that they would not tolerate such things in their homeland.

Mak shows to great effect (especially in his *English frogs go 'croak'*) how a gentle and humorous approach can often be more effective than a full frontal assault.

Raymond Tong was engaged in African education in Nigeria and Uganda from 1950 to 1961. From 1961 to 1982 he worked for the British Council in South America, India and the Middle East; his last overseas post being British Council Representative in Kuwait. Besides educational books with Cassell and Evans brothers, he produced a travel book with Cassell and nine collections of poems, the most recent being *Crossing the Border*, published by Hodder and Stoughton, and *Selected Poems* published by the University of Salzburg Press. His poems have also appeared in a great many anthologies, periodicals and magazines.

Oliver Postgate is best known for having made a multitude of small films for what is often referred to as *the golden age of Children's Television*. The worlds that he created cannot be said to be overtly English but they are undoubtedly part of an established English tradition of original story-telling.

Ian Holt is a member of the Campaign for an English Parliament and works in various ways for English causes. He lived for many years in London where he became involved in the activities of the Campaign for an English Parliament. Ian has now returned to live in Gloucester.

Edmund Wainright has a wide and deep knowledge of things Anglo-Saxon. His book, *Tolkien's Mythology for England*, provides much information about the English and Scandinavian mythology, literature, and attitudes that inspired Tolkien.

Rohan is an apt bye-name selected by me – it is from the name given by Tolkien to the heroic English of Middle-Earth.

"I was educated at the expense of members of one of the UK's leading trade unions and of members of the Labour Party in the ways of *Devout Episcopalian and Non Conformist Christian Socialist One World Multiculturalist Lumpen Proletariat Environmentalist Conservationist Feminist Revolutionaries.*"

Rohan, who is Anglo-Saxon/Ethnic English (self-description), attended university in "the Socialist Republic of South Yorkshire", as was, and then went onto qualify as a Solicitor of the Supreme Court. Rohan is in private practice and specialises in the areas of commercial, business and corporate law.

If when you read Rohan's contribution you find yourself frowning or bewildered, you should perhaps instead be smiling. In writing this piece, Rohan has adopted a Left/liberal mindset and employed the jargon that goes with it. Those readers who are familiar with the techniques and perceptions of the Left have a better chance of understanding what Rohan is doing. Some of what is written is *true*, some is the product of viewing history through ideological spectacles. In other words, much of it is mockery.

Rohan is a contributor to www.theanglo-saxons.co.uk.

Roy Kerridge has been a freelance writer since leaving school in 1959. He is a contributor to *The Spectator* and *The Daily Telegraph*. His latest book, *From Blues to Rap*, was published in 2004 by Finbarr International. His contribution to this collection is a short story with an English atmosphere.

The Rev. John Lovejoy was born in East Dulwich, London. After National Service he read theology at King's College, London, and then was ordained to the Anglican Church ministry. John served ten years in the North East of England before going overseas, to Nigeria, Italy, Algiers, and North West Australia. While in Australia he had the chance to get acquainted with the Aboriginal population and see the results of cultural disintegration among them. Returning to England, John was shocked to see the signs of cultural disintegration among the English, and especially the young. John's book, *The Deculturalisation of the English People* was published in 2000. He is a founder member of Steadfast.

In recent years he has become an Orthodox Christian and now lives in Newcastle upon Tyne, where he writes for Steadfast and helps promote the interesys of the English community.

T.P. Bragg is a founder member of *Steadfast* and is its editor. He stood as an English Democrats Party candidate in the 2004 Euro-elections. T.P. is a musician and writer. His novel *The English Dragon* was published in 2001. He has had many short stories published – some prize winners.

He read English and American literature at Warwick University and then taught English in the Czech Republic.

T.P. likes to play guitar, flute, and drums. He also sings and writes songs – his album *"Fields of England"* was released in 2004. His contribution *Grandfathers* is a lyric from *Fields of England*, which is a collection of songs that reflect the concerns of contemporary England and the English. Details of his recordings can be obtained from storehousestudios@aol.com or Storehouse Studios, 17 Higher Elmwood, Barnstaple, Devon EX31 3SG

T.P. puts a great deal of time, effort, and especially soul into *the struggle*. He is married and has a young son.

Veronica Henderson is an accomplished cellist who has worked and lived in England for many years but is still very Scottish. It is perhaps because of this that she is able to help the English understand the importance of folk-culture. Her contribution points to the way institutions in England and Scotland promote, or fail to promote, the identity and culture of those countries and its people.

Robert Henderson is a History & Politics graduate (Keele University) who has divided his working life between private industry and the civil service. He has written for various political magazines including *Right Now!* and *Steadfast*. Originally from Cheshire, he has lived in London for the past thirty Years.

Robert Henderson has a direct and aggressive style – no prisoners taken. The CRE did not reply to his letter (*Dear Mr Phillips*), which should surprise no one. I know many people who have written to the CRE but not one of them has received a reply. Perhaps being English is a handicap when dealing with what many regard as a racist organisation.

The letter to the CRE mentions housing associations which restrict tenancies to Blacks and Asians. Good news – application has been made for the registration of The Ethnic English Housing Trust.

Richard Todd is involved in several projects which promote the interests of the English community, including the quarterly journal *Steadfast*. He has a general interest in all things English and has a love of English culture.

Robert Alfred Sulley was an RAF Air Traffic Controller, during the Berlin Airlift 1948-49. He later joined a research group at Imperial College of Science & Technology, London, which designed and developed the UK's fourth digital computer. After thirty years he retired from Imperial College and became a professional water-colourist.

When Robert wishes to promote the English cause he introduces into the conversation the question, *Are you English?* It never fails to give him the opportunity to challenge common misconceptions and make the other person think about their identity – what does Englishness mean

Robert is a patron of the Campaign for an English Parliament and a founder member of the English Democrats Party.

Richard Chambers is a student at Keele University. Only a few decades ago students challenged the ideological status quo, today they help enforce it. Most politically active university students are like the Red Guards of the Chinese Cultural Revolution – earnest, blinkered, and intolerant of opposition to state ideology. Like the Red Guards they accept and regurgitate the tired and flawed dogma they are fed by the state, yet think themselves radical in doing so. Fortunately, there are some, like Richard, who, in a moderate and very English way, are prepared to challenge the ideological establishment.

Ken Howman is a seventeen year old student who lives in Norfolk.

Edward Canfield is an anti-EU campaigner and former member of the UK Independence Party (UKIP). He now believes that, "anti-EU campaigners must oppose the construction of an authoritarian European Empire or super-state by returning to the politics of English democratic radicalism and in doing so to proudly affirm our identity and ethnicity as English. The British ruling elite has betrayed our people so often and so outrageously that we dare no longer give our loyalty to it".

9

P Scrivener has in her contribution tended to use the term *White* instead of *English* because those agencies of the British state that collect and use statistics do not recognise the English as a nation/ethnic group, instead the English are included under the label White-British. This obsession with race, which permeates the British state and the way it collects and presents statistics, makes it difficult not to use the terms Black, White, and Asian.

When asked for information about herself, she replied, "Has always detested injustice."

Tony Linsell is a political activist. He played a part in founding the Campaign for an English Parliament, *Steadfast*, and the English Democrats Party (no longer a member). His *An English Nationalism* was published by Athelney in 2001. He is a graduate of the London School of Economics.

Introduction

The main thread in this book is a very brief sketch of the history of the English people. The greatest emphasis is on the origins of England and the English. The reason for this approach is that every nation needs a clear sense of who they are, where they are from, and where they belong. Yet the early period is the one about which the English people are most confused, which is not surprising given the deliberate policy of those who govern us to strip us English of our communal identity and the communal loyalties that spring from it. Instead they want us to identify with, and be loyal to, the British state and the ideology it promotes. A fine example of the propaganda employed was to be seen on Channel 4, 20th September 2004. It was the final part of *Britain AD*. This programme serves as a comic example of how multiculturalists go about attacking and undermining English national identity. The strategy is simple; they seek to show that the English do not exist. *What Anglo-Saxon migration? Englishness is merely an invented identity – a fashion statement – something concocted by Bede.* We are not English at all, but British. And to lend support to this they wheeled on Robin Cook, MP, who conjured a form of words that lent support to the idea that English national identity is without historical substance and that we are British, members of a longstanding and vibrant multicultural society. Why ask Robin Cook for his opinion – what authority can he bring to the argument? The short answer is none. He is a Scotsman who is rightly proud of his Scottish identity and did what he could to bring about the creation of the Scottish Parliament. As for Francis Pryor who wrote the book and presented the programme, I can only hope that he comes to see that *Britain AD* had more to do with politics than history, and that a serious history programme would not end with an advertisement for multiculturalism. In an article in *BBC History* September 2004, he is reported as saying, "I must confess that I am not an Anglo-Saxonist, nor even a specialist in early medieval history..." Those words should have been written on his forehead so that those watching the programme could have given such credence to his theories as they deserved.

Fortunately, the instinct for national identity is deep and enduring, so despite our communal enemies having complete control of the institutions of the state, which includes education (at all levels), the English continue to assert their identity. We should give thanks for historians like Simon Schama and David Starkey.

I feel gloomy about what is happening to our country and people but I am very optimistic about the way an English resistance is in the making. Capable people are coming forward with the skills, energy, and determination that are essential to a successful campaign for the revival of English fortunes. Other ethnic groups have a very long start on us in promoting their culture, interests, and needs but they will soon find us alongside them demanding recognition and asserting our rights.

The principal aim of this book is to set the record straight – to establish our roots and mark out our territory. It is, if you like, a brick through the glass house of those who would prefer that we English meekly melt away. The people propagating anti-English propaganda will eventually come to see that we English are not going to tolerate their insults any more than other ethnic groups would. Perhaps these historical revisionists should make programmes which argue that the Atlantic slave trade or the Jewish holocaust never happened. Ideally the writers and presenters should not be expert on the subjects. Let them see what would result from such insults.

Missionary Work

Tony Linsell

I never cease to be amazed at how ignorant most English people are of their communal origins and history. It is strange that this should be so in an age when the British state encourages the members of every other ethnic group to embrace and celebrate their culture and identity. It is perhaps due to the lack of a perceived strong and clear national English identity that many English people search their family tree hoping to find someone with a positive identity of which they can be proud. An Irish grandfather or great-grandfather fits the bill nicely but it really doesn't matter what nationality they are, as long as it isn't English. Then, with the encouragement of those who detest any positive expression of Englishness, they can claim – no boast – that they are ¼ or ⅛ Irish, which is of course infinitely preferable to being ¾ or ⅞ English. This sort of thing doesn't just happen in England. In Australia there are the noisy Irish-Australians who jump at every opportunity to insult English-Australians, i.e. the vast majority. Such is the propaganda that few Anglos are willing to admit to being English-Australians and instead try to find an Irish or other ancestor. The result is a very large number of English-Australians, with English names, indulging in Pom-bashing. When I was a lot younger, I wondered why the Anglos didn't retaliate and call the Irish-Australians *bogtrotters* or the like, but then it dawned on me that such name-calling is infantile.

One of the extraordinary things about those who take such pride in being 25% Italian, or whatever, is that in other circumstances they are often the first to deny that national identity has anything to do with ancestry. Instead they promote the notion that anyone born in England is English, or more extraordinary still, that anyone living in England is English. So, on the one hand you can claim to be Irish if you have an Irish grandparent (and officially represent Ireland in a sport), which means that Irishness is deemed to be *in the blood*. On the other hand, if you claim that Englishness is determined by ancestry (i.e. that the English are, like the Irish, an ethnic group) then you risk condemnation for not being *inclusive* – a mortal sin. It only requires a little thought and the application of common sense to see that membership of a nation/ethnic group, and the sense of community and belonging that comes from it, depends on very much more than where you happen to live or are born. If I had been born while my mother was travelling in Japan I would not be Japanese, and if I went to live in Scotland I would not become Scottish.

Due in large part to the deliberate and relentless promotion of alternative identities and loyalties, we are witnessing the decline of what was once a confident and positive English nation. Much missionary work is needed to turn things around, and it will not come from the British state or its governing elite, which see Englishness as a problem – a competing identity. It is for each of us to be a missionary and do what we can to show our fellow English that they do not have to apologise for being English or for defending their birthright. We also have to provide, as best we can, the cultural information that helps shape our sense of who we are and where we belong. Much of that information is to be found in the contributions to this book.

'Tell me a story Daddy!'
A grownup's view of children's programmes

Mak Norman

Once upon a time, animal characters in storybooks were based on our indigenous creatures such as Peter Rabbit and Toad of Toad Hall. Early television continued with warm rustic themes such as *The Wooden Tops* and *Rag Tag & Bobtail*. In the 1960s *Noggin The Nog* and *Pogles Wood* came to our screens with wonderful tales conjured from our myths and our landscape. These traditional formats made our land a magical place where children could exercise their imagination.

Having been a father for the past three years I have been disappointed at what children are presented with today. In fairness there are some programmes which are good (*Angelina Ballerina* gets my 4 star rating) but there is also a plethora of children's programmes which are decidedly odd.

Children's – sorry – *Kids'* satellite channel CBBC, includes stories featuring a blue cow as well as a Big Red Dog called Clifford. Clifford is not only red, but also the size of a six bedroom detached house. Gone are the pastoral settings of our fair land, the caddish fox and the wise old owl. Now you are more likely to see monkeys, zebra and bizarre character creations.

When *Teletubbies* first arrived it was indeed revolutionary. It was also accused of dumbing down children's viewing. But Teletubbies went on to set a trend that others followed. *Bahboo, Fimbles, The Hoobs* and *The Tweenies* all imitated the addictive traits of *Teletubbies*. All contain a psychedelic splash of garish colours which visually smack you around the face. Then there is a catchphrase which is repeated endlessly. A phrase ideally requiring no translation for the sake of overseas franchises, e.g. 'Eh Oh'!

It's clear that television companies feel the need to constantly change and move forward in order to retain viewing figures. Perhaps then, *new* ideas are considered more important than *good* ideas.

Although the barrel of real quality children's television programmes never ran completely dry, *real tales* have been replaced by mass-produced tales that are the creative equivalent of a cheap but well marketed lager.

Today's children's programmes for under-5s are often strangely abstract. Those of us who are 40+ will remember the magic and warmth of *Tales of the Riverbank* and the wonderful Johnny Morris in *Animal Magic*. There are no longer gentle programmes like these.

To my surprise, many parents can't wait to move their tots up to the next level of viewing. While I am buying old videos of *Bagpuss* and *Ivor the Engine* for my daughter, many of my daughter's little friends have already made the jump up to films like Disney's *Nemo*, a film best suited to older children.

Once introduced to the visual impact of modern animation and heavy product marketing, a child's attention span for simple tales must be affected. From there on I feel that children are encouraged to do less with their imagination and instead they learn to respond to action and effects only.

Sadly I do not see the quality children's television that I experienced as a child - there is just more of it. Children can gawp at the TV from 5.30 am through to 8 pm. Gone are the days when it was 'Watch with Mother' and children actually did. Now it's bung on a DVD and keep 'em quite for a while.

I also suspect that there is a sinister 'pc' influence on some of today's programmes and that we are seeing the manufacture of programmes which aim to appeal to a multi-ethnic, multi-cultural mass-market. I conclude this because the common trend for under 5s children's programmes is to have bizarre multi-coloured characters, belonging to no particular place or culture.

Perhaps we should be grateful that our traditional and once familiar characters are not wrenched from their cultural setting and placed before a *non-cultural specific* background. They would suffer in the same way that Asian or Afro Caribbean characters would if set amidst a traditional English, rural, fairyland setting - they would appear incongruous. Nobody's fault, it's just a fact that our traditional tales are born from a two-thousand year marriage between English/European folklore and our north European landscape. That's why there are no zebra in *Wind in the Willows* or a crocodile in *Little Red Riding Hood*.

Could it be that modern abstract and multi-coloured themes have been created so that all ethnic groups can fit in nicely and no one need feel excluded? If so, a rich seam of English and European tradition is being abandoned in the search for inclusivity.

When my daughter is read the traditional stories written by The Brothers Grimm, Hans Christian Anderson and Beatrix Potter, I lead my little girl into our folk pool of imaginings. This is what makes these tales so precious. They are rooted in our tradition and our culture and capture a magic that stays with us for life.

Now nothing is safe from the prying interference of the politically correct. Even our old favourite Humpty Dumpy is accused of being an unresolved and negative tale. It has been suggested that he be pieced back together at the end of the rhyme.

As we know, Humpty Dumpty is born anew each time the rhyme is told. It is not meant to be a moral exercise in fair play for two year olds. Similarly the wicked Queen must never regret poisoning Snow White, nor should the big bad wolf ever lose his taste for pork.

During 2004, a two-page feature appeared in a national paper celebrating 30 years of Bagpuss. It centred on Emily Firmin who appeared in the series at the age of seven and whose father Peter created the 'fat, furry cat puss'. The feature stated that Bagpuss was voted best children's series of all time in 1999. Emily is quoted as saying that she could understand why Bagpuss had become a classic, because it had such a dreamy and bewitching feeling to it.

And in a nutshell, that is precisely what is missing today. Children's programmes are often clinical, technical and professional pieces of work, but they do not bewitch.

I for one do not trust the thinking of children's TV programmers. Whether tomorrow's child turns out to be happy ever after is down to each parent. The early formative years are so important and *real* children's tales are vital. I suppose it's a case of 'they just don't make 'em like they used to'.

Afterword

I recently came across Oliver Postgate's website containing an article which lends some support to my thoughts. It follows here with the kind consent of Oliver Postgate.

Alongside the artist Peter Firmin, Oliver Postgate wrote, filmed, and voiced the stories of Noggin The Nog, Ivor The Engine, Pogles Wood, The Clangers, and Bagpuss.

Allow me to direct you to his website.

www.oliverpostgate.co.uk

Stamp Issues
Raymond Tong

When I first began collecting stamps
my magpie instincts were always attracted
by the large, brightly coloured colonials
with exotic names like the Congo and Togo.

I was very scornful of British issues,
feeling my country should do better
than those small, mono-coloured stamps
decorated only with the king's head.

When I asked my father why they were
so dull and unimpressive he told me
it was because a secure and powerful country
has no need of large, resplendent stamps.

He said a weak, yet aspiring country
will often take every opportunity
of attracting attention, rather like a cockerel
puffing himself out and loudly crowing.

Fifty years later, buying the latest
special issue of large, brightly coloured
British stamps, I feel strangely troubled,
recalling my father's simple explanation.

Does children's television matter?

Oliver Postgate

Certainly, when we started in 1957, the TV Company I was hoping to work for clearly didn't give a toss about children's television. Well, no, it did, just. It tossed about a hundred pounds a programme to spare programme directors and told them to cobble something together. So when Peter Firmin and I made our first film series about a Welsh railway engine who wanted to sing in the choir, we received about ten pounds a minute for the finished films.

Today, on the rare occasions I watch children's programmes on television, many of which cost more than a thousand times as much to make, I can see how profoundly lucky we were.

Lucky?

Yes, for two reasons. One was that because the TV Company looked on children's television as small-time stuff, it sensibly gave a free hand to the very sensible head of the children's department whose sole purpose was to get programmes that were fun, interesting and cheap. The second reason was that because we didn't have the money for elaborate equipment we had to rely on the basic hand-writing of animation, laboriously pushing along cardboard characters with a pin. Thus we were thrown back on the real staple of television: telling and showing a good story, carefully thought out and delivered in the right order for stacking in the viewer's mind. Come to think of it I must have produced some of the clumsiest animation ever to disgrace the television screen, but it didn't matter. The viewers didn't notice because they were enjoying the stories.

Also we were lucky enough not to have time or money for lengthy conceptual meetings. All we could do was try to turn out two minutes a day of film that was fun to watch and hope to pay the bills. It was a happy time.

Then, in 1987 the BBC let us know that in future all *programming* was to be judged by what they called its *audience ratings*. Furthermore, we were told, some U.S. researchers had established that in order to retain its audience (and its share of the burgeoning merchandising market) every children's programme had to have a *hook*, i.e., a startling incident to hold the attention, every few seconds. As our films did not fit this category they were deemed not fit to be shown by the BBC any more. End of story - not only for Peter and me - we had had a very good innings - but also for many of the shoestring companies that had been providing scrumptious programmes for what is now seen as 'the golden age of children's television'.

Those days are long gone. Today making films for children's television has become very big business requiring huge capital investment, far beyond the reach of small companies, and that has inevitably brought with it a particular poverty from which we never suffered.

Poverty?

Yes. In our time we had been able to found great kingdoms of mountains, ice and snow in our cowsheds. In Peter's big barn we commanded infinities of Outer Space, starred it with heavenly bodies made from old Christmas decorations and made a moon for the Clangers.

Now, today, burdened with the search for the millions of pounds which they have to find to fund their glossy products, the entrepreneurs have to lead a very different sort of life. They must hurtle from country to country seeking subscriptions from the TV stations to fund the enormous cost of the films. Each of these stations will often require the format of the proposed film to be adapted to suit its own largest and dumbest market. They have to do this because, for them, children are no longer children, they are a market. With so many millions at stake the entrepreneurs know that the bottom line must be 'to give the children of today only the sort of things that they already know they enjoy'. They have to do this because they fear that if they don't the little so-and-so's might switch channels and the Company could lose a bit of its share of the lucrative merchandising market.

They do have another difficulty. Because originality can't be bought off the shelf, (and even if it could it would be too risky to consider with so much money at stake), the competition for quality-of-content, has gone by the board. In its place there has evolved what could be called a competition for quality-of-method. This requires small armies of technicians and artists to spend their time seeking ever more astounding ways for the heroes to zap their foes. That is where the huge money goes: on high technology and on the clouds of pundits who confer at length in costly comfort about motivations, targeting and market strategies.

Behind them, in the manner of mass-market publishers, the nail-biting money-people peer anxiously over their shoulders to try and locate some content, some past sure-fire formula that they can re-vamp and use again.

All this is perfectly ordinary - the demise of small companies and with it the elimination of integrity is just the predictable result of trying to turn a small craft into a massive industry. It is sad of course, because crud is always crud, however glossily and zappily it is produced, but that is just part of a general trend in human commerce, part of the way things are going today.

So does it matter?

Yes it does! The Head of Acquisitions at the BBC outlined the Corporation's policy in a recent radio programme. She told us:

The children of today are more used to the up-market, faster-moving things ...

and that

... in today's hugely competitive schedule we are up against about another twelve to fourteen children's channels and we have got to stand out.

As a policy that is, in my considered view, almost criminally preposterous. Firstly, because it isn't true. There is no such thing as *the children of today*. Children are not *of today*. They come afresh into this world in a steady stream and, apart from their in-built instincts, they are blank pages happily waiting to be written on.

Secondly, because it simply isn't true that children have to have what they are *used to*. They do want programmes that are new to them, programmes that are original and mind-stretching. They just aren't being offered them.

Let me give you an example. As part of the same radio programme one of our old film series: *Noggin and the Firecake*, was shown to a primary school. It was heavy stuff, clumsy and slow by *today's standards*, but my goodness how eagerly the children followed and enjoyed it! At the end they could gleefully recount whole sections of the story, and when asked if they would like more they shouted with one voice: "YES!"

Lastly, the policy is tragically preposterous because there is simply no need or reason for the BBC to *compete and stand out*. It is a publicly funded body and it should know that feeding the minds of young people is a serious loving responsibility. We ourselves have passed this responsibility on to the BBC and it has no business leaving it to the mercies of a money-grubbing market.

Finally, let me offer you the following serious thought. Suppose, if you will, that I am part of a silent Martian invasion and that my intention is slowly to destroy the whole culture of the human race. Where would I start?

I would naturally start where thought first grows. I would start with children's television. My policy would be to give children only the sort of thing that they *already know they enjoy* like a fizzing diet of manic jelly-babies. This would no doubt be exciting, but their hearts and their minds would receive no nourishment, they would come to know nothing of the richness of human life, love and knowledge, and slowly whole generations would grow up knowing nothing about anything but violence and personal supremacy. Is that a fairy-tale? Look around you.

English Names for English Children

Tony Linsell

Dear Jacqueline,

It was a pleasure to meet you again at Anne's birthday party, and learn of your pregnancy. News of that kind is rare these days and especially pleasing.

Having spoken to you about names at the party, I want to make it clear that I am not suggesting you necessarily use Old English names like Alfred or Alfwynn (female), but merely look at the names to see how they were constructed and perhaps see something you can modify. There is a list of names in *The English Elite* - enclosed. Tolkien used the same method when he created the names of the Riders of the Mark – the men of Rohan – in *Tolkien's Mythology of England* - also enclosed.

If I had gained my interest in early English history 30 years ago, it is likely that my children would have been given different names. Many of my friends and acquaintances have a strong sense of English identity and they naturally look for English names for their children, just as the Scots, Welsh, and Irish tend to use Scottish, Welsh, and Irish names. While one friend has gone for the full-bloodied Old English names Hereward and Leofric (known as Leo), most have used names like Edmund, Edward, Elliot, Edwin, Alden, Dunstan. As you will have gathered, usable Old English girls names are rare, although in Victorian times there was a great interest in Anglo-Saxon history, and names like Edith and Agatha were common. Fashions change and the names of one age sound odd in another. When I was about 10 years old I first met a man named Eadric, and didn't give his name a second thought because I had no preconceptions. Because I am used to it, Eadric seems a good and distinctive name, as was the man who had it.

Some people have used Old English names as inspiration for invented names. (Vanessa is after all a name *invented* by Jonathan Swift, 1667-1745.) Others have moved forward in time and, like Tolkien in *The Lord of the Rings*, used names with foreign roots but which have been adapted and made English, e.g. Tom and Sam. Other examples of the kind are Jack and Harry. Girls names have flourished in recent centuries, and looking through my family tree I see names like Eleanor, Jane, Ginny, Blanch, Jess, Rose, Elsa, Elizabeth, Alice, Emma, Hayley. Some of these names, such as Blanch, are given as being of Old French origin, which mostly means they are of Germanic origin, the Franks being a Germanic people.

I like the idea of people looking at Old English names because it shows, in most cases, an awareness of national identity and the importance of preserving it. Even if none of the Old English names are used, toying with the idea might lead to later and more conventional English names being used. So I offer you the name-lists as places from which to start afresh and perhaps reassess or confirm options you have already considered.

Have fun

Tony

The English Elite, Donald Henson, Anglo-Saxon Books, 2001

English names from 10/11ᵗʰ century documents with modern English versions. Female names are underlined

Ælfgar	- Algar/Elgar	Ælfgeat	- Elliot	Ælfmær	- Elmer
Ælfnoð	- Allnatt	Ælfred	- Alfred	Ælfric	- Aldrich
Ælfsige	- Elsey	Ælfstan	- Allston	Ælfward	- Allward
Ælfwig	- Elvey	Ælfwine	- Alwin	Ælfwold	- Elwood
Ægelberht	- Allbright	Ægelfrið	- Alfrey	Ægelmær	- Aylmer
Ægelnoð	- Allnatt	Ægelric	- Etheridge	Ægelward	- Aylward
Ægelwig	- Alaway	Ægelwine	- Aylwin	Blacman	- Blackman
Brihtmær	- Brihtmore	Brihtsige	- Brixey	Brihtwine	- Brightween
Bruning	- Browning	Brunwine	- Brunwin	Burhred	- Burrett
Cenric	- Kerrich	Cild	- Childs	Coling	- Colling
Cyneward	- Kenward	Cypping	- Kipping	Deorman	- Dearman
Dodda	- Dodd	Duning	- Downing	Dunna	- Dunn
Dunstan	- Dunstan	Eadgar	- Edgar	_Eadgyð_	- _Edith_
Eadmund	- Edmund	Eadred	- Errett	Eadric	- Edrich
Eadward	- Edward	Eadwig	- Eddy	Eadwine	- Edwin
Ealdgyð	- _Aldith_	Ealdred	- Aldred	Ealdwine	- Alden
Earnwig	- Arneway	Eastmær	- Eastmure	Garwulf	- Gorrell
Goda	- Good	Godcild	- Goodchild	_Godgyfu_	- _Goodeve_
Godleof	- Goodliffe	Godric	- Goodrich	Godwine	- Goodwin
Goldman	- Goldman	Goldstan	- Goldstone	Goldwine	- Goldwin
Hearding	- Harding	Hereward	- Hereward	Hwateman	- Whatman
Leofa	- Leaves	Leofgeat	- Levet	Leofric	- Leveridge
Leofsige	- Lewsey	Leofward	- Livard	Leofwine	- Lewin
Leofwold	- Leavold	Lyfing	- Levinge	Manna	- Mann
Norðman	- Norman	Ordgar	- Orgar	Ordric	- Orrick
Osgod	- Osgood	Osmær	- Osmer	Osmund	- Osmond
Oswold	- Oswald	Sæfara	- Seavers	Sæman	- Seaman
Sæward	- Seward	Sæwold	- Sewell	Selewine	- Selwyn
Sideman	- Seedman	Sigered	- Sirett	Spracling	- Sprackling
Swetman	- Sweetman	Wihtgar	- Widger	Wine	- Winn
Wuduman	- Woodman	Wulfgar	- Woolgar	Wulfgeat	- Woolvett
Wulfgyfu	- _Wolvey_	Wulfmær	- Woolmer	Wulfnoð	- Woolnoth
Wulfric	- Wooldridge	Wulfsige	- Wolsey	Wulfstan	- Woolston
Wulfward	- Woollard	Wulfwig	- Woolaway	Wulfwine	- Woolven

Tolkien's Mythology for England: A Middle-Earth Companion
Edmund Wainwright, Anglo-Saxon Books, 2004

Riders of the Mark

The following is a selection of the names from Rohan, with their standard Old English equivalents and meaning (like genuine Old English names, they are often composed of two separate words):

Aldor	*ealdor*	elder, leader
Baldor	*bealdor*	prince, leader
Brego	*brego*	champion, hero
Brytta	*brytta*	distributor (usually of treasure)
Ceorl	*ceorl*	yeoman, freeman
Deor	*deor*	brave, bold, fierce
Deorwine	*deor, wine*	dear + friend
Dernhelm	*dyrne, helm*	secret + helmet
Dunhere	*dun, here*	highland + warband
Elfhelm	*ælf, helm*	Elf + helmet
Elfhild	*ælf, hild*	Elf + battle
Elfwine	*ælf, wine*	Elf + friend
Eomer	*eoh, mære*	horse + famed
Eomund	*eoh, mund*	horse + hand, protector
Eorl	*eorl*	hero, war-leader
Eothain	*eoh, þegn*	horse + retainer, servant
Eowyn	*eoh, wynn*	horse + joy
Erkenbrand	*eorcen, brand*	splendid + flame
Fastred	*fæst, ræd*	firm + advice
Fengel	*fengel*	leader, receiver of treasure
Folca	*folc*	tribal muster, army, people, folk
Folcred	*folc, ræd*	folk + advice
Folcwine	*folc, wine*	folk + friend
Fram	*fram*	effective, purposeful
Frea	*frea*	lord, beloved one
Frealaf	*frea, laf*	lord + survivor
Freawine	*frea, wine*	lord + friend
Frumgar	*frum, gar*	first + spear
Galmod	*galmod*	wanton, destructive
Gamling	*gamol*	aged
Garulf	*gar, wulf*	spear + wolf
Gleowine	*gleo, wine*	song + friend
Goldwine	*gold, wine*	gold + friend
Grima	*grima*	mask, face-plate on helmet, disguise
Grimbold	*grim, bold*	grim + bold

Guthlaf	*guþ, laf*	battle + survivor
Haleth	*hæleð*	hero, warrior
Hama	*hama*	garment, covering
Harding	*heard*	hardy, brave
Helm	*helm*	helmet
Herefara	*here, fara*	army + traveller
Herubrand	*heoru, brand*	sword + flame
Hild	*hild*	battle
Holdwine	*hold, wine*	trustworthy + friend
Horn	*horn*	horn
Leod	*leod*	prince, leader
Leofa	*leofa*	beloved, dear
Thengel	*þengel*	prince, prosperous person
Theoden	*þeoden*	folk-leader, ruler
Theodred	*þeod, ræd*	folk + advice
Theodwyn	*þeod, wynn*	folk + joy
Walda	*wealda*	wielder, ruler
Widfara	*wid, fara*	wide + traveller
Wulf	*wulf*	wolf

Afterword

Jacqueline and her husband Malcolm called their daughter Abigail Louise. Ah well, win some lose some. Abigail is a Hebrew name, and Louise is French.

When my late wife used the Web, she often went by the name Etheldreda, a modern variant of it being Audrey.

P. Scrivener, a contributor to this book, has a daughter named Frith – an Old English word meaning *Peace*. Another contributor researched names in the University of Sussex library and came up with Ottylia – Otty for short – and has a son named Alfie - Alfred. The German name *Ottilia* means fortunate heroine. The Old English *Ottile* means wealthy one. Other Old English girls names are Freo, Rowena, and Elfen. Two additional Old English boys names are Finn and Lee.

An example of using *The Lord of the Rings* as an inspiration for names is Rohan, after the heroic English of Middle-earth.

One of the saddest things about the decline in the English birthrate and the greater likelihood of English women *marrying out*, is that English family names are being lost. The war memorials throughout England have upon them long lists of English surnames, many of which are dead or near extinction.

A good website for first names is
www.askoxford.com/dictionaries/name_dict/?view=uk

The Rejection of the English

Ian Holt

Sadly there are many English people who reject their English identity. It is all too easy to think of them as self-haters. But is this true? Is it not the unpleasant case that such people hate their country and its culture and traditions rather than themselves? After all, if they hated themselves that much, they would do something suicidal to end their pain. No, the fact is that they hate and reject England and their English identity. This trend cannot be entirely ascribed to post-imperial guilt since the Scots were as heavily implicated in British imperialism as the English, if not more so. Yet most Scots rejoice in their Scottish identity. Besides, there is only so much mileage you can get out of post-imperial guilt. Those who hanker after guilt as if it were a narcotic, are not satisfied with the British Empire; they need fresh supplies of the stuff from around the world. Most of the rejectionists are not imperial guilt trippers. They have other axes to grind.

George Orwell spoke of "other patriotism". By that he meant that there were people whose patriotic feelings were displaced onto another country of which they were not citizens. He mentions in this context the intellectual Left in England whose *other patriotism* was focussed on the old Soviet Union. This was a phenomenon that well outlived Orwell and seemed to affect the middle and upper classes, from whose ranks came such luminaries as Philby, Burgess, Maclean and Blunt. In the interests of balance and accuracy, it should never be forgotten that in the thirties there were a number of well-born and well-placed Englishmen who entertained similar feelings about the Third Reich and Mussolini's Italy. Many of our most enthusiastic Europhiles suffer from *other patriotism*, and even Margaret Thatcher, who was very mush a British patriot, was drawn to a form of *other patriotism*, the locus of her OP being the USA.

With a lot of English people *other patriotism* takes the form of intellectual francophilia. This is on two levels: an agreeable fantasy about the French way of life being full of good wine, haute cuisine and joie de vivre; and a conviction that France is in every way superior to England, culturally, politically and socially. The first is very seductive and is not too far removed from the idea of the good life and the dreams realised by many English people of living in a villa in Spain or Portugal or in the part of Italy that John Mortimer has dubbed Chiantishire. The second, however, indicates a total lack of belief in the culture, institutions and way of life of England. Is France really that much better than us at everything? Certainly there is a great deal of envy because French leaders stand up for their country's interests, which includes actively preserving French culture and its way-of-life. In this they are unlike our own apologetic and useless political leaders who take every opportunity to promote every culture but our own. But no true Englishman, however much he may admire and even envy the way other nations have preserved their cultural landscape, would attempt to wear another nation's cultural clothes as if they are his own.

This francophilia is primarily intellectual and is far removed from the *Costa Geriatrica* syndrome whereby elderly and not so elderly English people take up residence on the Costa del Sol. These expats are not interested in Spanish culture and rarely bother to learn the language (more fool them, I say). They are primarily motivated by sunshine and a lower cost of living in which tobacco and alcohol, among other things, are cheaper than they are in England. In fact they retain their Englishness intact, watch English television via satellite and, indeed, form what amounts to English colonies in Andalucia's not so green and pleasant land.

There are many English people who stay in England and pursue their *other patriotism* under the guise of celebrating *diversity*. There is of course much to be gained from investigating and enjoying various aspects of other cultures. But the more the *other patriots* clutch at the baubles of other cultures, the more they become distanced from their own cultural traditions. Yes, sample *other* music, dress, religion, and food but also be aware of, celebrate, and keep alive our distinctive English traditions. If we did this, we would see fewer *other patriots* and the ever stranger *other identities* they adopt.

The most amusing group of English *other patriots* are what have been described as *cardiac Celts*. These people imagine that they are Celts. Their celtophilia is based on romantic tales about Caractacus, Boadicea and King Arthur. There is also a large dollop of faux druidry involved. It is worth pointing out that the Celts themselves are very elusive. However, this has not deterred inventive romantics from crediting them with the building of Stonehenge and the creation of Druidry. Virtually everything we know about the Druids comes from Roman writers like Caesar and Tacitus - as does our knowledge of Caractacus and Boadicea. The Arthurian legends, unknown in England until the eleventh century, have found a place in the national consciousness thanks to Malory and Tennyson among others; so much so in fact that a sub-myth has grown up in which Arthur has become the hero king who defends England against the Anglo-Saxons (how about that!). Caractacus and Boadicea have also had the treatment from people as diverse as Dryden and Elgar. So a romantic view of a brave warrior people led by heroes and inspired by druids has grown up. To be fair, these pseudo-Celts have little sympathy with the Roman Empire, but, of course, their prime target is their own people, the English. They argue that the Roman occupation was a temporary phenomenon, whereas the English conquest and settlement was permanent, the Celts (Britons) being either slaughtered or driven to Wales, Cornwall or Brittany. There is a lot of truth in that too! However, what truth is there in their belief that the Britons were in any sense Celts?

In fact this is the heart of the issue as far as the *other patriots* are concerned. Whether they are francophiles swilling Beaujolais while holidaying in a peasant cottage in Normandy and resolutely forgetting about 1940 and the plumbing, or middle class fantasists milling around Stonehenge in druidic robes and dreaming of the *Once and future king*, they have rejected their English heritage and adopted another. This rejection is not based on post-imperial guilt. The reason for it is often much more basic than that. It is because they have identified with a culture that has a strong anti-English thread running through it.

The English are the descendants of the Anglo-Saxons who settled lowland Britain and, for the most part, displaced the Britons, many of whom migrated to the already Celtic Gaul (Britons went to what then became Brittany). The centuries long mistrust and enmity between England and France itself is partly an Anglo-Saxon - Celtic rivalry in which the Anglo-Saxons (English) have almost always come out on top, with the exception of 1066 when Britons from Brittany fought on the side of the Normans. Little did those Britons realise that they were helping to create the British state that would end the independence of the Welsh kingdoms and absorb them.

Anti-Anglo-Saxon bias is not just the result of the so-called *Celtic twilight* which has been the wellspring of so many bad plays, novels, sub-Wagnerian operas etc. It is also inspired by an aversion to anything Germanic. So, the knowledge that the Angles, Saxons and Jutes who formed the English nation were Germanic, not to say German, sets the whole Hitler thing into play in the minds of these people. To proclaim one's Englishness, therefore, is for them tantamount to giving a nazi salute and signing up to nazi beliefs about race and eugenics.

The fact is that there are English people, already predisposed toward francophilia or Celtic fantasies, who also abhor the idea of having remote ancestors who were Germanic. These influences merge and encourage some English people to reject their true identity and adopt another. That is sad, but it is their choice. They are perfectly entitled to choose whatever identity suits them. They are not entitled to choose anyone else's identity for them. If they wish to abandon their English heritage, that is up to them, but they have no right to criticize those of us who cherish our Englishness.

The Blood and Bone of England
Ian Holt

I am of the blood and bone of England,
Son of her soil, child of her weary womb.
I can hardly be less than what I am,
To try to be more would be to presume.
Mine is the voice of the folk, unheeded,
That screams its pain unheard in the darkness.
Mine is the heart full of grief and anguish
For what they are doing to my mother.
Mine is the soul that burns with injustice
At the degradation heaped on her head
By those unworthy to bear her fair name.
And mine is the hand that will avenge her
Because her blood sings in my arteries.
Mine is the duty and mine the burden
To stand full-square with my beloved mother
In the hour of her greatest trial.
Woe to the knave who betrays fair England;
A curse on those who reject their mother.
Eternal torment to the murderers
Who would carve her up for their own foul ends.

Migration-Myths and Magic
Edmund Wainwright

In the turmoil of Britain after the Roman legions departed, King Arthur led his people to victory over the barbarian invaders and freed England from the Saxon hordes forever.

This is a familiar image, one we have seen in the cinema and heard in stories from childhood. Britain is crumbling into ruin until one man steps forward and rallies his people, teaching them to fight back against oppression. It really needs a Mel Gibson or Sylvester Stallone to carry it off – someone with a self-image so inflated that it can bear the weight of the fate of nations. What difference does it make if it is not totally accurate, if pedantic historians would disagree with some of the detail?

The problem lies in the fact that this scene is not merely inaccurate in its detail – it is wholly wrong from start to finish. A full dissection would require a whole book to analyse the assumptions behind the picture presented, but I hope to show in what follows where some of the misconceptions lie, and to suggest why they have arisen.

The Quest for Arthur

To start with, we have the famous – nay, legendary - King Arthur champion of England. *Legendary* is probably the most appropriate word to use of this figure, although *mythical* would be a good second choice. Put simply, this character does not belong in history at all. There are no records of his existence, no inscriptions to his honour, no poems praising his valour, no mentions in the monastic records of the time. The oldest references to him are in the early medieval Welsh tales collectively known as *The Mabinogion*, where his role appears to be that of the leader of a band of remarkable folk-tale characters. Like Odysseus or Jason, he is the central figure on a mission around whom adventurers and heroes congregate – men and women whose stories are far more interesting than his. His name is a hook on which to hang a skein of tales. Nowhere is this Welsh *Arthwr* called 'king'; this is not surprising, as that is an English title.

The mention of 'records of the time' brings us to the next question: which time? Roman withdrawal from Britannia is believed to have taken place within a year or two of 410 AD – that is to say, the Roman authorities withdrew their troops and left the Britons to defend themselves. It is not clear whether they stopped collecting tax from Britannia until later, but in the tradition of authoritarian regimes everywhere, they probably felt that they could go on taking the tax income without actually providing the corresponding public services.

In the context of the early 5th century, Roman power and Rome itself are curiously misleading ideas. The reader thinks of smart legions dressed in scarlet and steel marching out under the Imperial banner to deal with the natives of far-flung provinces (an illuminating presage of the later British version). Actually, 5th century Roman legions were composed almost entirely of peoples from elsewhere: Ostrogoths, Visigoths, Franks, Swabians, Lombards, Huns and Sarmatians; all peoples who would be labelled 'barbarian' by the classical Romans. It was on these peoples that Roman survival depended.

In Britain, the situation is unclear. The lack of records of *Arthwr* and his men might be expected in a time when record-keeping was no longer a priority, and from which one would expect little of what was written down to survive. Yet we do have the testimony of a British writer of that time: Gildas, a cleric, wrote of the chaos of his country and the decadence of its rulers, the great victories won over the invaders and the squandering of the opportunities those victories provided. He does not mention *Arthwr* at all. That alone should sound a warning: that we are dealing with figures from myth and legend, not flesh and blood.

Fifth century Britain is almost outside the historical records. A visit by a Gallic cleric to St. Albans records the presence of bands of marauders in the area. This may be taken as evidence for barbarian invaders, but it might be no more than groups of dispossessed natives who had decided to band together and take what they could.

In any event, the *Arthurian* period saw the fall of the Roman province of Britannia and the rise of a range of new political units. These were the successor states which sprang up in the vacuum left by Roman withdrawal. In the west they were mainly British-speaking and presumably reflected some continuity with the authorities of the Roman state but in the east they held to different languages and customs. They would eventually come to call themselves, after one of the more successful tribes, by the name *Anglisc* or *Englisc*, 'English'.

Archaeology is rubbish (says TV's Professor Mick Aston)

Archaeologists have looked at the process by which lowland Britain became England. Up to the early 20th century there was a presumption that the incoming Germanic migrants from Jutland and the lower Rhine displaced the Britons, either by force or by weight of numbers. The records of the early English specify that the Britons fled from them *swa fyr* 'as (from) fire'. Welsh records of the time – of which there are few – speak of heroic resistance to invasion.

After the First World War and especially after the Second, historians began to look again at the hypothesis of invasion and to try to revise it. Archaeology – then a relatively new discipline, recently rescued from the hands of treasure-hunters and curio collectors – was brought in to cast doubt on the traditional model. Academics began to question the mass movement of folk-groups and to look for other explanations for change.

It was evident that something major and disruptive happened between the late Roman period ending in the early 5th century, and the introduction of Roman Christianity at the very end of the 6th century. Tradition said that the Angles, Saxons and Jutes came over from the Continent and displaced the natives, but this was unpalatable to a generation which had spent most of the last four decades fighting these same Continentals. The shadow of The Hun was everywhere, even in their own ancestral traditions. The evidence of history had to be shown to be wrong, and a lot of effort went into disproving the notion of migration from the northwest Continent to Britain.

For their part, archaeologists seized on the vagueness of the records: deductions about *ethnicity* were made from the evidence of the graves, but this evidence could be tilted to suit the climate of the times.

Anglo-Saxon graves were characterised by a range of properties. Some were cremations, where the body was burnt and placed in an urn or other container with a few objects from the pyre. Others were inhumations, where the body was deposited fully-clothed and often with weapons (for men) or jewellery (for women). A prestigious few were buried in treasure-chambers beneath mounds. Some were just buried without any grave-goods at all. This last group looked like a way out of the migration puzzle: for if the normal Anglo-Saxon inhumation rite involved weapons or jewellery, then the bodies without any such goods were *ipso facto* not AS (Anglo-Saxons).

The possibility that some AS were buried without grave-goods does not seem to have been considered until recently, when the cemeteries of the Continental homeland were re-examined. In fact, some AS were always buried without grave-goods so the hypothesis does not stand. Likewise, there is the certainty that some AS were buried with perishable grave-goods which have simply not survived – sumptuous clothing, for example, could be just as splendid as a shield and spear, but does not normally survive.

Cremation had been practised in Roman times, but the difficulty with AS cremations is that the urns are very ornate and therefore difficult to mistake for anything else. They appear very similar to ones from northern Germany; in fact, some are identical and could have been made by the same potters. To get round this problem, archaeologists proposed that it became very fashionable in post-Roman Britain to be associated with the AS and that theirs became the dominant culture. Then, when Britons died, it became a fashion statement to follow the new trend and be buried like an AS. This trend also extended to other aspects of material culture: buildings erected in AS styles had to be explained as the adoption of Germanic building traditions by British families; the commonplace usage of Germanic styles of brooch and spear and belt-buckle were also presented as the spread of culture, like Coca Cola and Levis in the modern world.

The assumptions underlying this proposed adoption of AS culture *en masse* by the British are rather strange. To demonstrate this, it is necessary to do little more than to compare them with each other.

On the one hand, AS identity was so popular that Britons began burying their dead in perfect replicas of AS cremation urns, against all previous practice, but on the other hand they held tenaciously to their own tradition of unaccompanied inhumation (in AS cemeteries).

On the one hand, AS metalwork forms were so popular that the Britons all converted to wearing Germanic styles of jewellery and weapons; but on the other hand, they continued manufacturing their own traditional forms of metalwork such as feasting cauldrons (examples of which turn up in 7th c. AS burials).

On the one hand, British building traditions were abandoned very quickly in favour of AS ones; but on the other hand, the villa-based economy continued for several centuries.

In Denial

The denial of Germanic migration was founded on a number of principles, specifically

(1) the population of Roman Britain was relatively large, so a small number of migrants could not have replaced it;
(2) the technology to move large numbers of people around did not exist; and
(3) there are no parallels for such a move anywhere else at this time.

These arguments need to be looked at individually, as they appear reasonable at first but actually cannot withstand a closer examination.

(1) Population Size. In fact, there are no secure data for the size of population of late Roman Britain. Experts put the figure at somewhere between 1.5 and 4 million people. Given that the AS did not expel the entire British populace but at first only established dominance on the eastern and southern seaboards (say, from the Solent to the Firth of Forth), the affected British population may have been 2 million at most, and probably considerably less. If this is so, then it is surprising that there is not more evidence for RBs in AS areas.

The probable numbers of AS migrants have never been assessed since there is so little evidence to go on. However, it is not necessary to assume a migration of 2 million AS to outnumber the Britons, because to achieve dominance they need only have been more numerous in the coastal areas of early settlement.

If we assume – as I think we must – that the early Germanic settlements took place under some kind of late Roman or post-Roman control, then the first groups were arranged in militarily sensitive areas to protect strategic sites or corridors. (For example, the people buried at Buckland will have protected Dover, and those at Mucking will have controlled access to London.) Tradition says that when the tax revenues ran out, the British authorities refused to honour their obligations to these military personnel and that this was the reason for the 'revolt' which led to the settlement of the AS. In other words, having been denied the agreed payments, they decided to take land instead. This was in the mid 5th c. By the end of that century, within one or two generations, AS culture was already dominant in the east and south. This rapid dominance needs to be explained.

If the early AS decided to take land instead of gold, they would have taken the land that appealed to them most – that is to say, they would have taken over prime estates and dispossessed the British owners. They must then have established their own way of life – modified for British conditions – and any Britons left on the estates must have had a stark choice of either integration or relocation. Having seized the prime estates, the AS must then have been at an advantage over their British neighbours for access to resources.

Within a hundred years, an original settlement group of 100 AS in an area with a birthrate allowing adult survival of 1.5 (i.e. each couple produces three adult offspring) would have grown over five generations to over 500 individuals (100 ~ 150 ~ 225 ~ 338 ~ 507). Denied access to resources, the British would have likewise had a lower birthrate, allowing adult survival of say 0.8, and over the same timespan an original 100 Britons would have been reduced to almost two-fifths (100 ~ 80 ~ 64 ~ 51 ~ 41). This means that within a century there were more than ten times as many AS in the east as RBs (500 : 40).

Therefore an initial influx of a few thousand AS would by normal reproduction rates have greatly increased the numbers of AS in the country. If the influx lasted for a century, then the numbers become so great as to demand expansion of the settlement area.

Having gained control of the plentiful resources of the eastern and southern coastlands, the AS were well placed to begin the policy of expansion that their increasing numbers dictated. The Britons in the west, not under the same economic and social constraints and with a greater survival of late-Roman organisation, mounted a strong military defence which it would take more than two centuries to overcome. Here, if anywhere, we may find the kernel of truth inside the legends – the historical Arthwr / Artorius.

(2) Transportation. The question of ship movements has been confused by some misconceptions: principally, the notion of the one-way voyage and the capacity of vessels of the time. In essence we do not know how many settlers would have come in a voyage. The Sutton Hoo ship had provision for 40 oarsmen plus a cargo hold, but this may not have been a typical craft of its day – rather, it was probably a royal warship. A safer estimate is in the order of 25 persons in one average ship, with their belongings.

The sailing time from Jutland along the coast of Germany and the Netherlands, then across the Channel to the Thames Estuary is around four days; the duration would be longer if this safest route was used and the ship then sailed north to the Humber or west to the Solent. Equally, in good sailing weather, it could have been shortened by cutting across the open sea. Allowing for some time in port for loading and discharge, re-supplying and waiting for favourable weather for the return, one might think in terms of a round-trip of two weeks from home port to destination and back.

Suitable weather might only be available for the optimum seasons – mid-spring through to mid-autumn, or about thirty weeks of the year.

The numbers of ships available are also unknown but, given that the nations involved were noted for their seamanship, it is likely that several hundred vessels could have been available, of varying configurations and capacities. Assuming for the moment that only one hundred ships were ever used for the movement of people and their belongings to Britain, we have a relatively simple mathematical problem:

Round trip per vessel = 14 days
Sailing season = 210 days (30 weeks)
Trips per ship per season = (210/14=) 15
Passengers per trip = 25
Passengers per season per ship = (25 x 15=) 375
Ships available = 100
Total passengers per season = (375 x 100 =) 37,500

If one assumes that this level of activity was sustained for just 25 years, then the number of persons transported reaches (37,500 x 25 =) 937,500 which is almost enough to engulf the population of late Roman eastern Britain by itself, without factoring in the disparity in reproduction rates mentioned under (1) above.

This does of course assume that ships were always full, always used on round-trip voyages and that the level of activity was constant – all convenient assumptions which are probably inaccurate. The length of the period was in all likelihood not 25 years but closer to 75 (mid 5th c to early 6th), some ships could have held more than 25 people but against these positives one must also assume losses for shipwreck; population reductions due to re-migration (we know that some AS settled in the southern Channel area and were subsumed into the Frankish kingdoms); the numbers of vessels involved depended on the ability of migrants to pay and the relative risks of the voyage versus the reward, and other trading opportunities for the vessels. Some vessels probably remained here and were not further used for movement of settlers. Some of the settlers were engaged in warfare and died before reproducing.

In all, the movement of a million people over a century would have been technically straightforward. Were there a million people waiting to make the trip?

That is a debatable point – the population size of the northern Germanic folk has also never been assessed. What we do know is that the mid-5th c. was a period of immense upheaval across Europe, with large-scale movements of Turkic peoples from the Steppe pushing westwards and driving other folk before them. Roman reports suggest armies numbering tens of thousands, but it is not clear whether that is the number of combatants or the number of persons on the move (i.e. including wives, children, camp-followers and indeed displaced persons fleeing from their path). In this context, the 35,000 persons per season we have conservatively estimated could have made the trip to Britain does not appear unduly large (while freely admitting that surges in demand are likely, rather than a constant, steady trickle).

It is unlikely that the Jutland peninsula and the lands between the Elbe and Weser could have supported such numbers. With marine transgression making habitation impossible, the majority who could do so would have left, of which a proportion would have come to Britain. (Angles also turn up in Central Germany in conjunction with other folk in historical times.) But with a pressure to move being felt across the whole of Western Europe at this time, it is likely enough that many separate groups of settlers would have arrived here. (A few are recorded in AS place-names: Frisians, Franks, Swabians and so on.)

(3) Genetics. Historians and archaeologists have pinned their hopes on the relatively new science of genetics, or specifically the forensic aspects of that discipline, which were thought likely to be able to disentangle the Angles, Saxons and sundry other Germanic migrants of the 4th-6th centuries from the pre-existing population. The results so far have been disappointing, for reasons which should have been obvious. In order to establish two groups which could be genetically distinguished in the modern populations, a recent survey used baseline data drawn from the centre of Ireland and from Norway. However, while these groups could indeed be distinguished, there was no possibility of differentiating between AS and

later (Danish) genetic influx. This is because the population of parts of modern Denmark is cognate with the AS themselves - in effect, Jutland and its closest neighbouring islands became politically part of the Danish territory only once the Angles had transferred their political centres to Britain.

There is also a methodological flaw in using modern populations to evaluate ancient gene-flows, given that the 250 years of the *Viking* period were characterised by invasion (inward flow of Scandinavian genes) and slaving (outward flow of AS and British genes). It is also an unproved assumption that the genetic map of pre-Roman Britain was uniform, when the evidence suggests that the population of the south-east had been exposed to successive settlements from the neighbouring Continental areas for centuries. The notion of a homogeneous *Celtic* Britain is a folly erected by Victorian romantics in search of a respectable ancestry for their nation to put beside those of Greece and Rome.

Modern genetic science is simply too blunt an instrument to use for the task of analysing the genetic history of the modern population, and any results it has produced have been challenged in subsequent research. Possibly future refinements of technique will enable a more accurate assessment to be made, but the present state-of-the-art is unable to deliver firm results.

(4) Parallels for Population Replacement. The evidence for similar shifts in population at this time is not plentiful, but neither is it entirely lacking. A central problem with population movements is that they can be invisible to archaeologists if the material culture (e.g. pottery) changes only slightly (it can be explained through 'increased contact' rather than 'replacement') and they can be invisible to historians if the elite remains in place and therefore the group name does not change.

In eastern Central Europe, for example, a Turkic people from the Steppe established themselves on land previously held by the Goths. Their state lasted down to the modern day as Hungary. To their south, Slavs from eastern Europe established themselves in lands previously held by Italic and Illyrian peoples, in what would eventually become Slovenia and the Yugoslav regions. Displaced Britons crossed the narrow seas to Armorica and established the state of 'Little Britain', *Bretagne*, Brittany.

These examples are merely indicative. We do not know in detail whether the Britons replaced the Armoricans or simply absorbed them. We do not know whether the Armoricans were in a state of collapse and welcomed the bolstering of their resources from their northern kindred, or whether they resented and resisted the British incursion and were fought to a standstill. All we can say is that within a century Armorica was transformed from a Continental Celtic sub-Roman state to an Insular Celtic post-Roman state. Its language changed too, which brings us to the next argument.

The Language Conundrum

There are two models that archaeologists use to represent contact between peoples when one invades another's territory: *elite dominance* and *replacement*.

Under *elite dominance*, a group of invaders arrives, drives off the leaders of the territory and takes over the existing structure. This is approximately what happened with the British colonisation of India, where the majority of the population continued as before but positions in the upper strata of society were filled by British men and women. In post-Roman contexts, this is the situation with the Franks, a Rhineland Germanic people who moved into gallia (Gaul) and settled there. They formed an elite and actually replaced the natives only in the areas of their first invasion – the northeast corner of France and Belgium. Within a century, they had become Gallic-speaking post-Roman provincial landowners and were almost indistinguishable from their Gallic countrymen.

Under *replacement* the whole of the existing society is swept away and a new order is erected by the conquerors. If elements of the pre-existing population remain, they learn very quickly to adapt to the new way of life, or they are reduced to a people living on the margins of society. This is what happened with the European colonisation of North America, where most existing structures were removed and replaced by European ones. Native Americans, where they survive at all, are either low-class members of the new Euro-centric society, or they eke out an existence on lands allocated to them because the settlers do not want them.

The *favourite* model for the AS takeover is of course *elite dominance* – a small group of incomers assumes power but nothing really changes much for the average inhabitant. Continuity of population – the sacred doctrine of the right-thinking modern historian and his archaeologist chums – must be demonstrated.

When we look at the linguistic evidence we see something rather curious, though. Under *elite dominance*, the languages of the conquered remain – maybe adding a few words from the language of the conquerors, but generally staying much as they were. This is the situation in the Indian sub-continent, where English remains the language of government but the Indian population continues to speak an array of different languages, augmented by handy English words. This is also the model for the Norman invasion of England: the upper strata of society changed, but among the majority of folk the only linguistic effect was an influx of new words which, characteristically, the AS used to augment their vocabulary, so that 'chair' meant something different from 'stool', 'table' from "board' and 'carpenter' from 'woodworker'.

Under *replacement*, the languages of the natives usually dwindle. They lack political importance and only continue in use while there are enough speakers to sustain them. This can be turned round artificially – Cornish and Hebrew are extinct languages which have been re-invented for political, religious and cultural reasons, but in neither case is there continuity from the ancient world. They are self-conscious attempts to distance their speakers from those around them, groups they see as threatening.

So what is the position in Britain? Most of the island speaks English now, of course, but what was the position 1500 years ago? Can the records of Old English throw any light on the matter?

There are two areas to look at in OE records which can throw light on language contact between OE and British (Old Welsh). One is place-names and other geographical words, as these are usually difficult to displace. Once a market has a name known to a lot of buyers and sellers, it is difficult to replace that name with another. Once a river has a name known to sailors and fishermen, imposing a new one is not easy. As one would expect, many – indeed most – river names even in eastern England have a British or Roman origin, and many of the larger places do too: Thames, Humber; Dover, London, Leeds, Lincoln, Colchester, York. Geographical words such as *cum* (coombe) 'steep-sided valley', *dun* 'hill-top settlement' are also taken over from British.

But in the records of OE generally, as they have come down to us, there is an embarrassing silence. British words are simply not there in any quantity. In fact, while OE may have a recorded vocabulary of around 25,000 words, the input from British is an embarrassing dozen words or so, including *brocc* (brock) 'badger' and *crompeht* (crumpet) 'savoury yeasted bread'.

The implication seems to be that there were very few Britons living alongside the AS, according to this evidence. This view is supported by place-names such as 'Walton' which may reflect OE *weala tun* 'village of the Welsh', implying that British (Welsh) survival was unusual and could be used to name the settlement. Therefore, from a linguistic point of view, the Welsh input seems to be minimal – not a scenario that could be accepted by modern historians, so a variety of explanations have been devised to account for this. The commonest these days is acculturation: the records of British are slight because the Britons adopted AS speech as well as material culture. This looks promising at first sight: look at parallels in South America and Asia where the native languages have been abandoned in favour of Spanish, French or English. The problem is that in most cases it is only the official language which changes – the language of government – and the native languages continue in use among the ordinary folk as before. In fact, when we look for examples of total language change without substantial population change, we fail to find any. Even in the modern world where suppression of a native language may have been official policy for generations (as in British-dominated Ireland, or Russian-dominated Poland) the native language always survives if it has enough speakers to sustain it, and those speakers maintain contact with each other. In the case of British, it actually did survive: Welsh continues to be spoken in Wales today, Cumbria retained traces of Welsh vocabulary into the last century, and Cornish only died out in the 17th c. Breton – British transported to the Continent – is also still very much a living language. (In fact, English has dominated the world for two centuries but has still not managed to eradicate its closest neighbour or continue its sweep westwards the last hundred miles to the Irish Sea.)

The fact that so little British penetrated OE suggests that the languages were not in close contact, which is hard to explain if acculturation was the method by which OE replaced British. Even with rapid acculturation, a whole generation must grow up whose parents spoke the old language even as it adopted the new one.

No retreat, no surrender

So how can we square this circle? How can it be that so many archaeologists and historians are totally convinced that the AS were only ever a dominant minority when the facts are far from clearly in support of this idea? If you read archaeological reports, one thing comes through very clearly: the better the human remains are preserved, the less exact the interpretation. Archaeologists used to make simple equations (beads and brooches = female burial; spear and knife = male burial) but closer analysis of skeletal material has shown that some graves contain skeletons with female traits which are accompanied by male grave-goods, and vice versa. To avoid this probem, the trend is now to write about 'gender' rather than 'sex', which is to say that the skeleton appears to be Sex A and the grave-goods suggest Sex B, so rather than choose between these alternatives it is easier to simply state that the appearance of Sex B has been assumed by (or assigned to) a person of Sex A, and that this is a personal choice.

This is reasonable up to a point, but we must suspect that all it really is intended to do is to allow archaeologists a means not to answer the question of whether they have a male or female burial. Skeletal remains offer only 90% certainty of sex in even the best preserved material, so the question cannot be given a Yes/No answer. Likewise with age – there are skeletal indications of age, but these can vary with diet and other factors to mislead the observer. Status is sometimes very evident – gold, weapons, jewellery and so on – but in perishable materials its evidence is no longer there.

So in effect archaeologists follow a line of reasoning: "We have a body here; we don't know if it's male or female; we don't know if it's young or old; we don't know if it's high or low status, but all we can say is that it's definitely not AS."

To summarise: the AS tradition says that the AS came to Britain and drove off or conquered the Britons. The British records say much the same thing. The Breton tradition says that people sought safety from the AS across the sea. The linguistic evidence points overwhelmingly towards population replacement. Only the archaeology is open to question: it is one of the most exasperating things about archaeology that it can rarely, if ever, answer the questions put to it. All that can be established is a balance of probabilities.

If a grave contains a Saxon saucer brooch, one might infer that the grave is that of a Saxon, but archaeological thinking insists that that this is not so. All that can be said is that the person buried was given a certain type of brooch by the people who buried her (or, indeed, him – since gender is open to interpretation too). No assumptions about ethnicity, age or sex can be entertained, and speculation is discouraged.

Now, if archaeologists would confine themselves to the facts and say that this grave may or may not be that of an Anglo-Saxon, then that would be fine (if a little indecisive). But many archaeologists build from that premise: we have thousands of graves with Anglian, Saxon and Jutish grave-goods, but we cannot say for sure that any of them are actually the graves of Angles, Saxons or Jutes. Therefore, there is *no* evidence for Angles, Saxons or Jutes in England. QED.

They manage to say this with a straight face – most of the time – but one wonders how much longer this state of affairs can last.

The Anglo-Saxon Migration to Britain

Tony Linsell

5th Century

By the end of the fourth century Germanic tribes were spread far and wide across Northern Europe. Their societies had developed in different ways and they often fought each other, but they had much in common. The migrations and wars of that time resulted in the break-up of some tribal alliances and the creation of others, with the result that new loyalties and new elites were formed. For example, at the end of the first century there is no record of the Saxons and Franks but by the fifth century they were two of the most powerful confederations of tribes in Northern Europe.[1]

The early fifth century was a time of great importance for the Germanic tribes who had by that time taken control of nearly all the territory on the east bank of the Rhine and held most of the north bank of the Danube. There had been several military successes against the Romans in the east but in the west there had been no recent breakthrough. Now, however, there was a period of turmoil which may have been started by a new wave of migration and invasion from the east. For whatever reason, this was a period when many of the Northern European peoples sought new land to settle.

If the Northmen were to migrate to the south and west, they would have to cross into the territory of the Roman Empire and overcome the military might of Rome. It became apparent that this would require an alliance, which came into being in 406 when a force of Vandals, Swabians, Burgundians and Alans gathered on the east bank of the Rhine. They launched their attack across the river and fought their way through the enemy defences and broke them so that when the fighting was done they had the whole of Gaul before them. In an attempt to re-establish control the Romans withdrew troops from Britain but they were unable to recover their position in Gaul.

During the breakthrough, the Asding, King Godegisel, was killed but his son took command and led the Vandals into Gaul and then into Spain. In 429 they crossed to North Africa and captured Carthage and forced the Romans to formally cede a large part of that territory to them. The Vandals landed in Sicily and forced further concessions from the Romans. After a period of peace, a new wave of

---

[1] In *Germania*, 98AD, Tacitus mentioned the tribes that later became part of the Saxon confederation but not the Saxons as such. Ptolemy mentions the Saxons in his *Geography*, c.150 AD, and is thought to have based much of his work on information from a Roman naval expedition 150 years earlier. In other words, it is not known when the confederation began but it is probable that it started with a small group of tribes, including the Aviones and Reudingi, and was situated between the southern end of the Jutland peninsula and the Elbe. Saxon expansion after that was probably due to a mixture of voluntary membership and conquest. Certainly by the time of Offa (4th century), the Saxons were a powerful southern neighbour of the Engle.

activity began around the year 455 with the capture of Corsica, Sardinia and the Balearic Islands. Raids were made on the coast of Spain and Greece, and a landing in Italy culminated in the capture and sacking of Rome.

The Swabians, like the Vandals, moved across Gaul to the Iberian Peninsula where they established their own kingdom. The Burgundians remained in the east of Gaul and eventually created a kingdom with two capitals; one at Lyons and the other at Geneva. The Alans went to Spain and North Africa but gradually lost their identity and became merged with the Vandals who in turn became absorbed into the populations of the conquered territories.

The Alamans and Franks made less spectacular advances into Gaul than the Vandals and other tribes but their gains were to be more long-lasting because they captured and settled land lying next to their existing territory. The Alamans, which means *all men*, were a confederation of several Germanic peoples, the largest group being Swabians.

The Franks were also a mixture, or confederation, of peoples who lived near the Rhine. They did not take part in the events of 406 but were able to take advantage of the disintegration of Roman power in northern Gaul and move into territory adjacent to their own. Their advance was mostly by means of steady migration and settlement rather than sweeping military conquest. Towards the end of the fifth century the Franks became a powerful people and much later one of their kings, Charles the Great (Charlemagne) 742–814, created a great empire. The Frankish population was small compared with that of the Empire they created, and although they gave their name, and much else to France, their separate identity was eventually lost in the large Gallic population.

The victory of 406 dealt a great blow to the Roman position in Gaul and to the Empire as a whole, and it was one from which it never recovered. In the east the Goths moved into Italy and took Rome in 410, and in the extreme west the seaborne raids of the North Sea tribes, known collectively to their enemies as Saxons, probably played a part in the decision of the Romans to abandon Britain.

The success of the various Germanic tribes in following up the victory depended mainly on the size of their population and the extent of the new territory they controlled. The Vandals travelled great distances and made a powerful impact before disappearing almost without trace. The Franks moved into territory adjoining their own and survived as a distinct people for many generations.

A lesson to be learnt from this turbulent period is that there is no long-term survival for a small nation that conquers and lives among a larger nation. A native people who remain on the land, and are more numerous than the invaders, can survive many defeats and long periods of foreign rule. Elites can be overthrown or absorbed into the native population.

When invasion and defeat of the enemy is followed by tribal migration and displacement of the earlier population, the future of the victors is assured. Those who take land, live on it, produce children and govern themselves, are well placed to remain united and strong both in arms and culture.

The Saxons and Frisians

The empathy and loyalty that bind people together as a community varies from time to time and place to place. The Saxons were a mixture of peoples united by a family of warrior kings, while the unity of the Frisians was based primarily on their long history and comparative isolation. The unity of the Engle was in part based on common religious practices. All of these tribes had contact with Britain, the Frisians primarily as traders, the Saxons and the Engle as raiders and as mercenaries fighting for Rome.

The Saxons were a confederation of peoples living in the lands between the lower Rhine and Jutland. When faced with an external threat they united under a family of warrior kings, but in times of peace their unity was not great and many warlords took independent military action. The Saxons took to piracy and coastal raids in much the same way as the Franks. The seafaring exploits of the Franks, and others, during the third and fourth centuries are far more extensive than is commonly believed, and are largely overlooked by those who enthuse about Scandinavian *Vikings*. Franks, Saxons, Engle and other North Sea and Baltic people had well-designed and well-built sailing ships which enabled them to make long-range coastal and river raids, and attack Roman shipping. Eutropius reported that by the mid-280s, the coasts of Belgica and Armorica were infested with Frankish and Saxon pirates.[2] A Roman writer reported that the courage of the Saxons was so great and their seamanship so expert that they welcomed a storm because of the opportunity it gave them to take their enemy by surprise. Saxon and Frankish attacks on the coasts of Gaul and Britain, and on Roman, Gallic and British ships, became so frequent and troublesome that the Romans tried to sweep them from the sea. Despite the considerable resources devoted to the task they were unsuccessful and the attacks continued. The Romans also built strongholds at strategic points on those parts of the coast of Britain and Gaul known as the Saxon Shore.[3]

After the victory of the Germanic tribes in 406 and the withdrawal of Roman forces from Britain, the Saxon war bands increased the frequency and duration of their raids on Britain which in 408 were on such a large scale that they amounted to an invasion. The British leaders appealed to the Romans for help but none was given because the Romans were deploying their forces in trying to regain control of Gaul. It is probable that most of the North Sea tribes took part in the raids on Britain but they became known collectively, by foreigners, after the name of the largest and probably most active group of raiders, the Saxons.

The Frisians were among the first of the North Sea peoples to cross to Britain and settle there. They went as traders and farmers, and settled in the east between the

---

[2] *Dark Age Naval Power*, John Haywood (Anglo-Saxon Books, 1999)

[3] The Saxon Shore may have been so called because: (a) The ports there were involved in trade with the North West Germans; (b) Much of this coastline was settled by *Saxons*: (c) The coast was subject to *Saxon* raids. The purpose of the fortifications probably varied from place to place and time to time. Some perhaps defended places of economic importance or together they might have formed part of an extensive shore defence. See p.47 *Roman Britain*

Thames and The Wash. When the Romans withdrew their forces from Britain the structure they left behind them survived but seems to have gone into a slow but orderly decline. In some places the decline was greater than others. The Roman Empire, like empires before and since, created local governing elites with a vested interest in maintaining trade and other links with the empire. The wealth and power of these elites would have been weakened by the departure of the Romans but they would nevertheless have had sufficient resources to hire military help (mercenaries) to protect their interests. Trade routes once established tend to endure, so it is unlikely that there would have been a sharp break in economic activity. The rich would have continued to buy wine, olive oil and other goods to which they had become accustomed. However, Rome was an imperial power which gained much wealth from the lands and people it ruled. While subservient governing elites from that time to this have gained wealth and power from imperial connections, the people they rule are usually exploited and feel less enamoured with being ruled by foreigners, even if is done through people who are nominally their fellow countrymen. Britons fought to resist Roman rule and unless they were abnormal, they would have welcomed the opportunity to be free of it. So although it is probable that there was no sudden collapse of the Romano-British governing elite, the imperial network upon which their power was founded gradually unravelled. The economic activity that sustained estates, villas and town life dwindled. Eventually it succumbed to locally based economic activity.

Frisian merchants had a widespread trade network which included Britain. They traded with the Britons and some lived in the ports and other towns of eastern Britain where they were able to acquire information about events in that land. It was probably the merchants' cargo ships, knowledge of Britain, and trade routes across the North Sea, that drew them into the movement of settlers to Britain. Frisian cargo ships were better suited than Saxon or Engle warships and coastal traders to the task of carrying baggage and cattle. The early Frisian involvement in seaborne trade and settlement led to their language becoming known beyond their own land. Frisian is closely related to English.

North of the Frisians and Saxons, across the Eider, were the Engle who in the 1st century AD had been united in their worship of Nerthus – the Earth goddess. The Engle had considerable seaborne power but it was mostly projected into the Baltic. To the north of the Engle were the *Eote* (Jutes).

Celts

The Celts were famed as warriors and for various technological and artistic innovations. They were a people belonging to a linguistic, cultural, and probably an ethnic group which had its origins in Central Europe in the Bronze Age - 13th century BC. The Celts consisted of many tribes which over a period of several centuries migrated to various parts of Europe. It is generally accepted that it was about the year 400 BC that the great migration of Celtic tribes began. As they spread out across Western Europe, so their linguistic and cultural traits were adopted by others. This period was in many ways like a relay race where cultural attributes were passed on before the baton carrier became *lost* among the peoples nominally conquered.

The height of Celtic power was in the La Tène period – 5th to 1st century BC.

Although it is often suggested that Druidism has its origins in Celtic culture, its roots are probably in a non-Celtic culture centred in the West of Europe, and possibly the British Isles.

The Celtic tribes greatly influenced the language and physical culture of those they dominated but it seems that their separate ethnic identity was lost. Many of the tribes that had assimilated Celtic cultural attributes, in turn migrated and were subsequently given a Celtic identity because they had become *cultural-Celts*, having adopted elements of Celtic language, art, and technology. In other words, they had a Celtic gloss over their indigenous ethnic traits. Some of these tribes migrated to the British Isles where, as in other parts of Europe, nominally Celtic peoples sometimes overran or came to dominate other *Celtic* peoples.

It was perhaps because these various tribal groupings retained much of their ethnicity, and their Celtic cultural attributes were comparatively slight, that they did not have enough in common to bind them together and make them a *nation*. Such differences would have made it difficult for them to join together in enduring strategic military or political alliances. This lack of unity is commonly blamed for the failure of the various *Celtic* peoples to resist the Romans and Germans.

Britain

It is evident from history that those with the greatest power generally take the best land while the weak have to be content with poorer soils. In the distant past Britain was inhabited by peoples we call *Ivernians* and *Hibernians*, most of whom lived on the fertile and easily cultivated lands of the south and east. They were driven off that land by invading Gaels (*Goidels*) a people who came to Britain from the continent.[4] The Gaels, it seems, were better armed, motivated and organized than the native population, many of whom moved to high ground or into the forests that covered much of Britain. The Gaels were greatly influenced by Druidism, which they perhaps discovered in Britain and adapted and developed it for their own purposes.

After the Gaels came the Britons (*Brythons*) who displaced many Gaels and took the best districts. As Gaels migrated to the north and west, they conquered, or pushed before them, the Hibernians who migrated to the north of Britain and to what is now Ireland.[5] The power of the Britons increased and their control of much of the island that was to be given their name became firmer. As it did so, Gaels moved further north and west, many crossing the sea to Ireland where they occupied the eastern districts while the Hibernians lived in the west. It was only in the very north of Britain and the west of Ireland that the Hibernians were able to preserve their separate identity.

Many of the migrants to Britain from the continent were part of the Celtic language group. There is nothing to suggest that they were part of the Celtic tribe that had sacked Rome. It is more likely their ancestors had been ruled by Celts or been subject to them, or had otherwise absorbed, to varying degrees, elements of

---

[4] Gael now means a person who speaks a Gaelic language, especially a Highland Scot or an Irishman. *Collins English Dictionary*

[5] Hibernia is the Roman name for Ireland.

Celtic culture. Like the Vandals, Celts made a great impact for a relatively short period then disappeared from history having spread themselves thinly, and expended their military and cultural energy. They were absorbed and disappeared into the much larger populations amongst which they settled.

Tribes from Belgica, some of whom were Germanic, crossed the sea to Britain during the period of German and Roman expansion and there were also migrations of other people. The most unusual journey was that made by North African Berbers who arrived in Spain and then sailed to the west coast of Britain where they settled and created a kingdom on the western shore of what is now Wales.[6]

In the north of Britain lived tribes to whom the Romans gave the collective name Caledonians. The most powerful of those people were the Picts (*painted people*). Little is known about them but it has been suggested that they may have been either one of the earliest tribes to migrate to Britain, having entered from the south, or were possibly of Germanic origin, having migrated from Norway via the Shetland Islands.

Like many people of that time the Picts painted their bodies when they went to war but they seem to have developed that custom more than most and had unique tattoo designs. They also had distinctive forms of writing and patterns, both of which they marked on rocks.

The population of Britain consisted of an assortment of tribes who, as far as possible, sought to settle, control and defend territory in a collective way. At times there may have been an inward migration of comparatively small but effective military groups, which defeated and ruled an established population. But it seems probable that most migration was by tribes which consisted of both warriors and settlers – a whole kindred and cultural unit. They sought land for settlement, and once established they increased their territory and power by increasing their population and number of settlements. Displaced people were forced to move on and perish or displace others. Thus, a succession of migrations produced a ripple effect across Britain.

During the periods of European migration, a very large number of people and tribes were on the move seeking land for settlement. A people, or tribe, might number one hundred thousand individuals or more. The migrations gave rise to widespread disturbance and conflict. Some tribes were powerful enough to resist such pressures and to hold their territory but others were driven from their land and sought more elsewhere. It was the custom at that time for individuals to migrate as part of a large group as it made them stronger in defence and attack. It also enabled them to retain their communal and cultural identity.

It was the custom at that time to take captives as slaves (bondsmen), either to keep or to sell on. Another source for slaves were those who were unable to pay compensation (wergild) for crimes committed or damage done. Presumably any skills the bondsman had were made use of. Surplus captives were sold to traders and transported to other districts or countries.

---

[6] The Berbers also settled in Ireland and influenced the development of the Gaelic (Irish) language.

The English and Welsh

The people of the North Sea tribes (Jutes, Frisians, Saxons and Engle) were collectively known as Saxons to the people of Britain. Yet when those North Sea migrants settled in Britain they became absorbed into a common core English identity. Their country became England and their language English. Hereafter they will be referred to as English or Anglo-Saxon.

The non-English population of what is now England and Wales were known to the English as *Welsh* (Old English *wealh*, meaning *foreigner* or *slave*). The Welsh (Britons) were a mixture of peoples who had adopted various aspects of Celtic culture, especially language. The inhabitants of Ireland where known as Gaels. The homeland of the Picts was called Pictland, and roughly corresponded with what is now Scotland.

Roman Britain

The Romans conquered Britain for the purpose of absorbing it into their empire – they extracted minerals (including gold and tin) and exacted taxes. They sought land and people to rule; they were not settlers. Many of the troops employed in the conquest and later defence of Britain were Germanic and their camps were usually in strategic defensive positions either close to, or inside, Roman fortifications. The Roman forts at Brancaster, Burgh, Bradwell, Reculver, Richborough, Dover, Lympne, Pevensey and Portchester were strategic strong points in the Saxon Shore defences, which stretched from The Wash to the Isle of Wight. Norwich and York were important garrison towns and there were German camps guarding the lower Thames (Mucking) and the southern approaches to London (Croydon and Mitcham). Germanic mercenaries were also stationed along the Middle Thames to provide protection for the heartland of Southern Britain.

Some Germanic warriors stayed on in Britain after their term of service as Roman mercenaries ended. They continued to live in or near the settlements that had grown up by the camps and were able to obtain there the goods and services that were being provided locally for the garrisons. They also benefited from the security that such settlements offered. It was in this way that small Germanic communities were created in Britain even before the Romans abandoned it in 410. Many of those communities survived the economic changes following the Roman withdrawal and were strengthened by the arrival of settlers who were seeking new land. The settlement of Britain by North Sea Germans was not a sudden or swift occurrence. It started slowly and carried on for many years at a low level. Then later, when the circumstances where right, it became a great surge.

When the Romans abandoned Britain, those Britons who had benefited from the Roman occupation naturally wished to preserve Roman customs and forms of administration. They had grown accustomed to living in towns and villas, and wanted to maintain the economic and political system that made the Roman way of life possible. They believed the Roman withdrawal was only temporary and that once the legions had re-established the boundaries of the empire on the Continent they would return to Britain and restore the position of their allies and the Church. Their response to Saxon and Pictish raids was to appeal to the Romans for help rather than to attempt to unite and provide their own defence.

Without the Romans the political and economic structures they had created (to meet the needs of the Empire) started to decay, as did the towns, churches and estates that were a part of that society. The partially suppressed separate cultures and identities of the Britons re-emerged, as did the ancient hostilities. As is common when an imperial power declines, there was a struggle for power. Various tribes, local leaders and factions fought each other for dominance.

The Britons managed to unite for the purpose of repelling an invasion of Picts in 410 but after that there was little unity. Many years later a king named Vortigern achieved a position of dominance and became an overlord.[7] The Britons continued to fight amongst themselves and while they did so Engle, Frisians, and Saxons crossed the sea to Britain and steadily strengthened their position in the East and, possibly, in the Thames valley. The lack of unity among the Britons suggests that tribal and ethnic divisions were much greater than is often thought.

The twenty years following the Roman withdrawal were not all ones of war. There were times of peace and prosperity but that comparatively tranquil period came to an end about the year 430 with an outbreak of plague and renewed Pictish attacks. After suffering several defeats at the hands of the Picts, the Britons decided to seek help from abroad. Some still wanted to re-introduce Roman power but Vortigern was opposed to that policy, probably because he thought it would undermine his own position. Instead, he obtained support and promises of funding from British leaders to recruit mercenaries to fight against the Picts. The natural thing to do was to employ the warriors that the Romans had used, so Vortigern sent a messenger across the sea with an appeal for help.

Hengest and Horsa

The messenger from Vortigern arrived at the hall of Hengest and his twin brother Horsa. They were invited to Britain with their companions to protect the Welsh (Britons) and drive out the Picts. The payment would be land and provisions. The offer was accepted and a host of warriors set sail in three longships and landed at a place called Ypwinesfleot (Ebbsfleet, Kent). They took possession of the land that had been given them (Isle of Thanet) and then went north in their ships to fight the Picts who had been attacking the Welsh on land and from the sea. Hengest and Horsa were victorious wherever they went and drove out the Picts and brought peace to the land.

The warriors served Vortigern well for many years and there was peace and prosperity in Britain. Each year they received the food, and other provisions promised them. Their success, and the economic and political stability it helped bring, encouraged more of their fellow countrymen to cross the sea and their number in the east of Britain increased. As the English population in the East increased, so the Welsh began to move away. The movement need not have been far or in all places. A continuing trend involving a few people at any one time can, after a decade or two, have a marked effect - the need for people to live with those of their own kind is very strong. The Welsh probably preferred to withdraw and seek new land rather than live in areas being increasingly populated by people who could not be absorbed into Welsh society and culture, and had no wish to do so. In

---

[7] *Vortigern* might be a personal name or a title.

those early years of settlement, the English probably gained control of territory in the east by a gradual and steady increase in their numbers and expansion of their settlements. The taking of land by one people from another is more often achieved in this way than by military conquest. When the process is gradual, and the will to organise and resist is low, the point eventually comes when the settlers have control of the land and effective resistance by the earlier population is impossible. They are sometimes provoked to fight for their independence but usually their position is by then too weak. More often they drift away to another part of their country and abandon increasingly large parts of it to the settlers who come to regard it as their own and use it as a base for further expansion.

One of the reasons for people to want to move from Northwest Europe to Britain may have been the rising sea level. This may have been due to global warming, which caused flooding and salt contamination of low-lying arable land near seacoasts and river mouths.

Shortly after 440, following a long period of peace, many Welsh leaders complained about the levy being raised to pay Hengest and Horsa. It was felt that there was no longer a need to pay for protection and they refused to make any further contributions – they *welshed on the deal*, which was not something the cheated warriors could be expected to take lightly. Just as in the heat of summer it is hard to recall the biting cold of winter, so in the calm of peace it is hard to recall the turmoil and suffering of war. An assembly of representatives from the Welsh kingdoms withdrew their support for Vortigern and his policy. He had no choice but to inform Hengest that the agreement was ended and the payments would stop.

When Hengest heard that the Welsh were refusing to supply his warriors with the food and other provisions they were due, he went to Britain to assess the situation and to talk with Vortigern, who was facing increasing internal opposition. Hengest offered to fight for the King against his opponents and a deal was struck by which Hengest would receive additional land in Kent in return for his support. Word was sent back across the sea to Angeln ordering them to send more men. When reinforcements arrived Hengest and his twin Horsa led the rebellion and drove away those who wished to overthrow Vortigern. But Vortigern, concerned at his increasing reliance on Hengest and fearing that he was losing the support of his countrymen, turned on Hengest who again sent for more men and told them of the worthlessness of the Welsh and of the excellence of the land. A large force of picked men was assembled and sent across the sea in nineteen ships to help the others.

Hengest and Horsa were said to be the sons of Wihtgils, the son of Witta, the son of Wecta, the son of Woden. Many of the southern kings and all the Northumbrian royal family claimed descent from Woden. Hengest and Horsa fought Vortigern in the place called Aegelsthrep (Aylesford, Kent). Hengest was victorious but Horsa was killed and Oisc succeeded to the kingdom and ruled with Hengest. Two years later Hengest and Oisc fought the Welsh at a place called Crecganforf (Crayford, Kent) and killed four thousand of the enemy. The Welsh abandoned Kent and fled to London in great terror.[8]

---

[8] An account of the early conquest is given in *The Anglo-Saxon Chronicle*.

Hengest fought in many battles in the south and the north of Britain and he put the Welsh to flight through fire and the sword's edge. Hengest and Oisc fought them near Wippedesfleot and killed twelve Welsh lords. One of their own thanes, Wipped, was also slain there. Eight years later the Anglo-Saxons again fought the Welsh and captured innumerable spoils, and the Welsh fled as one flees from fire. The Anglo-Saxons became rulers of their own lands in Britain and the dominant political and military force.

Migration

The warriors who sailed to Britain to fight for Hengest came from three powerful Germanic nations; the Engle, the Saxons and the Jutes. From the Jutes came the people of Kent and the people of the Isle of Wight and the mainland opposite Wight. From the Saxons came the East Saxons and the South Saxons and the West Saxons. From the Engle came the East Engle, Middle Engle, Mercians and all the Northumbrians. Such was the extent of the migration from Angeln to Britain that when it was finished, the country of Angeln stood empty.[9]

Behind the warriors went settlers, who farmed the new land as they had the old. The king of the Engle, his family, companions, and all his people went to Britain. Some went to the lands to the south of the River Humber (Southumbrians) while some went to the lands north of the Humber (Northumbrians). They eventually occupied the East Coast of Britain as far north as the Firth of Forth. Many of the Lowland Scots are descended from the Engle, and their language, Scots, is a dialect of English.

Saxons, Jutes, Frisians and Franks[10] also settled in Britain but the bulk of those groups remained on the Continent. The Engle were probably the most numerous of all the Germanic nations that crossed the sea to Britain. Whatever their numbers may have been, theirs was certainly the core community, culture and identity into which other settlers merged. The English nation spoke English and their country was called England.

It was not unusual at that time for migrations to take place on a very large scale with whole nations moving together as an organised group. For example, in Caesar's *Gallic War* there is an account of how the Helvetii (a Celtic people), who numbered about 263,000, set about preparing for migration. They lived in a large territory north of the Alps between the Rhine and the Rhone but they decided it was no longer suitable for them because, despite its large size, the geographical and political conditions were unfavourable to their aspirations. It seems that several other tribes in the area were persuaded to join the migration.[11]

---

[9] Bede's, *Ecclesiastical History of the English People*.

[10] Franks settled in Kent and their kings had some influence there.

[11] The other tribes were the Tulingi, Latovici, Rauraci, and Boii. This and other information is from *Caesar: The Conquest of Gaul*, Translated by S. A. Handford. (The Penguin Classics, 1951).

The First

England

(the land of the Engle)
at the end of 4th century

Jutes

Jællinge

E
n
g
l
e

N o r t h   S e a

Rendsburg

Eider

M y r g i n g s

Weser

Elbe

Ems

S a x o n s

49

England

Late 5th century

The West Engle were called Mercians
which means 'borderers' or
'dwellers on the march'.

North Engle

Mercians

Lindesey

Middle Engle

East Engle

East Saxons

West Saxons

Jutes

South Saxons

Jutes

ENGLAND

9th Century

Strathclyde

Welsh

Be
r
n
i
c
i
a

Northumberland

Deira

Gwynedd

Powys

Dyfed

Welsh

Mercia

East
Anglia

Northfolk

Southfolk

Essex

Middlesex

Kent

Sussex

Wessex

Welsh

A common feature of migrations was massive baggage trains. The Helvetii prepared by buying all the draught cattle and wagons they could get hold of. They sowed as much of their land as they could with corn so that they would have a good supply for their journey. In addition to grain, each family was instructed to take with it a three-month supply of flour for its own use. It was all highly organised and followed a two-year plan. In the third year they burnt to the ground all twelve of their towns and four hundred villages. All isolated buildings were also destroyed, as was all the grain they were unable to take with them. They then set off with the other tribes on a migration. The total number of people on the move was 360,000, of which 92,000 were warriors.

It is not being suggested that the English did the same as the Helvetii but it is clear that whole nations did migrate in a planned and well-ordered manner. Instead of buying waggons, the English may have bought cargo ships to supplement their own or chartered ships from trading nations such as the Frisians. A well-organised migration could have moved a lot of people, livestock, and baggage in a relatively short time. Perhaps it took place in stages over a number of good sailing seasons. Whatever the method, the idea that the seagoing Germanic tribes of that time did not have sailing ships or were unable to navigate across open sea and had to hug the coast, is outdated.[1]

Another fallacy, and one commonly promoted in schools, is that Anglo-Saxon migration (if mentioned at all) was small-scale and of no special importance, being just another of many similar migrations. This view is promoted primarily for ideological reasons that are dealt with later. For the time being, it is worth noting that the evidence for the migration being very large and very significant is overwhelming. It brought a deep and lasting change in the population, culture and language of lowland Britain. Such an important event in English history should be made known to English children.

The Settlement

In the time of Hengest, new territory was opened up to English domination and eventual settlement. In later times, the threat of force was often there and sometimes used as advances were periodically made in a general east to west direction. As the English population increased it began to displace the Welsh who gradually migrated to areas where they were still dominant. The English advance was marked by changes to place names. The Welsh names for settlements and local features of the landscape were either Anglicised or given new English names. Woods, streams and settlements became known to the English by names derived from the names of the tribe or family who owned the land, or lived on it, or to the use to which it was put, or its physical description. Some woods, hills, and springs were given names that linked them with the gods, for example, Tuesley (Tiw) and Thursley (Thunor) in Surrey, Wednesfield and Wednesbury

---

[1] John Haywood (*Dark Age Naval Power*, Anglo-Saxon Books, 2000) and others have advanced a convincing and widely accepted argument that the shipbuilding and seamanship skills of the North Sea Germans were far in advance of those with which they were formerly credited.

(Woden) in Staffordshire. Harrow-on-the-Hill in its earliest form means *the holy place of the Gumeningas*, the Gumeningas being a tribe.

The names of Romano-British towns and the Welsh names for geographical features, such as large rivers, were retained because they had been learned from the Welsh by the early English settlers. While it is easy to change a local name, it is more difficult to change the name of something known to many people over a wide area. A similar process occurred when the English settled in North America. Indian names were retained for mountains and large rivers but smaller geographical features and settlements were, generally, given English names. More North American Indian words entered the English language during the conquest of North America than Welsh words entered the English language during the conquest and settlement of much of Britain.

The extent to which words from one language enter another during periods of migration and settlement is a good indication as to whether populations became mixed or remained separate. Other than place-names, very few Welsh words have entered the English language. The flow from English to Welsh is also small. This suggests little cultural or other interchange between the two groups.

With the exception of large towns, the place names of a country rarely change while the indigenous population remains on the land. For example, Wales, Scotland, and Ireland were later absorbed into the British state, and the population of those countries now speak English but there are few English place names. The exceptions being mostly in areas where there was early English (Anglo-Saxon) settlement, such as the eastern Lowlands of Scotland, which where once part of Northumberland. The city of Edinburgh probably takes its name from Edwin, king of Northumberland, who captured a settlement there about the year 617.

An important question is the extent to which the Anglo-Saxon population drove out and replaced the Welsh, or Romano-British, population. Those who can best be described as *Celtic* nationalists, tend to be drawn to one of two opposing views on this matter. The first argues that the English drove the Welsh from their land, burning and looting towns and churches as they spread destruction across Britain from one sea to the other. This *barbarian approach* has little to support it because it seems that buildings and parts of towns fell into disuse and disrepair, and did not meet a swift end by fire. The evidence suggests that the Roman way of life and economy started to decay shortly after the Romans left. That process was well under way by the time of Hengest. However, the barbarian approach appeals to those modern day Celtic nationalists who use it to justify the view that the English are a nasty lot deserving the wrath of the gallant Celtic peoples who were defeated by the treachery and savagery of the English. In other words, we are justified in using every means possible in our modern-day fight against the English (e.g. IRA bombs in shops and pubs) because they did nasty things to us.

The second view takes a different and subtler approach. It suggests that the Welsh population, which they mistakenly refer to as *Celts*, remained in place and absorbed the *Saxon* invaders who were small in number and only constituted local ruling elites. In other words, there are no such people as the English, just a mostly Celtic people living in a place called England. Just how a small *Saxon* elite was able to bring about such profound and rapid change in every aspect of society, and at all levels, is never adequately explained. How, for example, do they explain the absence in England during the relevant period of Welsh cemeteries and the large number of Early English cemeteries? It seems that the small ruling elite was able to get the *Celts* to not only change their place names and language but also to build and farm like the English, use English artefacts and in every way adopt an English way of life. The graves and their contents where not English at all, merely *Celts/Britons* who were buried in multi-ethnic cemeteries wearing English dress and accompanied by artefacts in the English style. Likewise, buildings, weapons, literature, etc. were not English but in the style of the small English elite. This line of argument shows the desperately low levels to which some will go in trying to deny our English origins and argue for an inclusive British melting-pot society.

Many of those advocating the absorption theory are engaged in a form of cultural warfare in which history is rewritten in a way that denies the origins of the English and a continuing English ethnic identity.[2] Such propaganda has had much success in recent years amongst young romantics who like to see the *Celts* as nice peace-loving people who lived in harmony with nature. Celts are also often incorrectly credited with being the founders of Druidism and having constructed the ancient earthworks and stone circles of Britain. The need to believe this nonsense springs in part from a search for roots. *Celticmania* has been rolling along unchallenged for such a long time that criticism of it is usually much resented.[3]

Also linked to the absorption theory are those who, for ideological reasons, favour the *continuous waves of migrants* integration and absorption *cultural enrichment* interpretation of English history, which they like to call British history. This approach attempts to demonstrate that the population of Britain has always been ethnically and culturally mixed, and that is something undeniably good, to be welcomed and encouraged.

The population of Britain has indeed been varied but that does not mean that the different groups lived happily together in multi-cultural communities. The various groups were not organised in a way that could cater for people of different cultures. The ethnic groups in Britain, including the English, lived apart and defended their territory and way of life.

A third and more realistic approach is that the creation of the English kingdoms took many generations to complete and took different forms in different places at different times. At some times and in some places the Welsh were defeated and put to flight, some going overseas. Others gradually migrated westwards. During the later western conquests, it is probable that quite a large number of Welsh remained on the land but were absorbed into English society. With the exception

---

[2] The Rev. John Lovejoy calls this sort of thing, *ethnocide*. *The Deculturalisation of the English People*. Athelney, 2000.

[3] If people want to adopt a Celtic identity that is their choice and their business. However, it becomes my business when they use it as a political weapon against my communal roots and history.

of Wales and some western regions (such as Cornwall, Dorset and Cumbria), the Welsh only survived as self-governing communities for a short while in small enclaves situated in forested or hilly areas, e.g. parts of the Chiltern Hills. In most of England, and especially in the lowland areas, the changes were very deep and widespread. The English brought with them a system of law and administration that formed the foundations of the institutions that are still found in Anglo-Saxon societies. The type of agriculture, holding of land, shape of fields, construction of buildings, methods of burial, type of grave goods, place names, religion, trade routes, and language, all changed with their arrival. The evidence for a profound break is overwhelming, whereas the evidence for ethnic, social and cultural continuity in Britain from before the Anglo-Saxon migrations until the formation of England is very slight and not at all convincing. To ignore the broad range of connected evidence for Anglo-Saxon migration and see continuity of population takes the determination and blindness of those who wish it were true.

Research based on the distribution of ABO blood groups supports a large-scale Anglo-Saxon migration. Blood group O is more common in Ireland and the west of Great Britain, while A is more frequent in East Anglia. A blood-type map produced by Kopec (1970) from the records of half a million blood donors, showed a very high incidence of A, and a very low incidence of O, in East Anglia. It also showed the incidence of A decreasing and that of O increasing from east to west and from south to north.

Another study (Roberts et al., 1981) showed that if the gradient is looked at closely it is seen to contain within it a patchwork of gene pools that are, or were, separated by geographical barriers such as mountains, rivers marshes or forests. Where geographical factors were not the cause of the enclaves it must be presumed that they were due to cultural barriers. For example in Cumbria, where there is a high incidence of group O, it is possible to identify areas high in group A which corresponded with Norwegian place names. That such a gradient and patchwork still exists would seem to indicate that one wave of migrants tended to displace an earlier wave who tended to move west or northwest and that the mixing of the population was not so great as to produce an even distribution of blood groups.

In more recent years there has been genetic mapping of the British Isles and Western Europe which reveals much the same as the earlier blood group mapping. Both are of little help in determining the difference between Danish and English (Anglo-Saxon) migration and populations because the people are so closely related.

Some of those who are keen to demonstrate that the population of Britain is homogeneous and has been much the same since the last Ice Age, like to produce genetic maps based on mitochondrial DNA, which is passed on through the female line. Such maps do the job intended and show an almost common genetic inheritance for the whole indigenous population of the British Isles. But, they also show much the same thing for most of Western Europe because mitochondrial DNA reveals a common female ancestor from very ancient times.

A few years ago it was reported that in Somerset the remains of a body more than 2000 years old had been found, and that DNA retrieved from it was a close match with the DNA of a local schoolteacher. It was then suggested that this showed a continuity of population from that time to this. In fact it showed no such thing because the similarity was in mitochondrial DNA. All it showed was that both people had a common female descendant who lived about 35,000 years ago – probably in Central Europe.

A lesson to learn from this is that genetics is increasingly becoming a battlefield, and caution is needed in interpreting DNA evidence. Much depends on what a particular form of genetic evidence is able to prove and how it is used.

For the most part, the Welsh and English seem to have lived apart and retained their own languages and customs. The English and the Welsh were proud of their history, achievements and way of life. They did not praise all gods but their own or tell of the deeds of all heroes but their own or see the worth of any culture but their own. They were confident and noble peoples who had no wish or need to adopt the customs of others.

It is highly likely that there was some trade between the Welsh and English, and that later, during the period of the separate English kingdoms, there were occasions when English and Welsh leaders formed alliances for the purpose of confronting a common Welsh or English enemy. However, it seems that most English people traded with their fellow countrymen in England and with the Germanic peoples across the North Sea.[4] Likewise, the Welsh traded mainly with their fellow countrymen in Britain, and with Ireland, Brittany and the lands that had been part of the Roman Empire.

Brief Outline of Migration 400–1100

Anglo-Saxon settlement and the creation of England occurred in several stages. Their settlements grew up close to Roman garrison towns during the Roman occupation of Britain and most of those settlements remained after the withdrawal of Roman forces from Britain and acted as focal points for later migration. After the withdrawal of the Romans there was a gradual and mostly peaceful settlement of the coastal areas of what is now East Anglia by various Germanic peoples. The second half of the fifth century was a period of steady military conquest and migration, in which the early settlements formed a base and secure bridgehead. The Welsh either migrated from, or were driven from, most of Eastern, Southern, and South-eastern Britain, and at the end of the fifth century the land east of a line from The Wash to the Isle of Wight was in English hands, as were lowland areas north of the Humber. The Welsh managed to halt the advance for a generation at the Battle (or Siege) of Mount Badon where they enjoyed a significant victory over the English and may have recaptured some territory. Where and when the battle took place is unknown but two of several suggested locations are a hill just east of Bath and Bradbury, southeast of Swindon. Suggested dates for the battle range from 490 to 518.

After a generation of stability, in which the English were able to consolidate their position, they advanced once again, but more quickly than before, and drove many of the Welsh into the inhospitable lands on the western fringe of Britain. That last advance, which may have followed an outbreak of plague in the west,

---

4 Baltic trade was still of great economic importance to England 1,000 years later. Indeed it was the search for trade routes beyond the Baltic that led to the creation of the English/British Empire.

was carried out in a series of rapid campaigns that captured large territories. It is likely that a greater number of the Welsh population remained than had been the case in earlier campaigns but those that stayed were gradually absorbed into the advancing English population and their culture.

The Anglo-Saxons went to Britain as heathens and took with them their institutions, their Gods, and the confident and positive outlook on life that their beliefs fostered. More than 150 years after that migration began, Augustine landed in Kent (597) and set in motion the process which saw the nominal conversion of the English people to Christianity. The strategy employed by the Church was *top down*, which meant they converted kings first, usually by offering a political advantage of some kind, and then used the influence of the Church at the heart of the state to impose its ways on the whole population. That process did not involve an abrupt end to one system of belief and the beginning of another, it was instead a gradual take-over of the existing institutions and the adoption and modification of many heathen customs and the suppression of others. The success of the Church was in part due to its ability to adapt to local conditions and to assimilate local customs, folklore and beliefs. In this way the Church preserved and promoted as Christian much that had its roots in the heathen past. This is not to say that the Church was not hostile to the Old Religion or that it did not discriminate against or punish those who indulged in practices which the Church deemed un-Christian. However, it would seem that nothing like the witch burning of later times or the practices popularly attributed to the Spanish Inquisition occurred in England during the first millennium.

The Anglo-Saxon migrants were able to merge into one nation because of their similarities. For the same reason, the Danes and other Scandinavian settlers were absorbed into the English population, culture, and identity. Many parts of Eastern England saw Danish settlement but there was not a mass migration on a scale comparable with that of the English. The Danes in England were comparatively small in number but of considerable significance, although their influence is often overstated. For example, some would have us believe that *Vikings* founded York. It was in fact founded by the Romans and had a large English population when the Danes and other Scandinavians arrived. The later migrants built their own settlement on the edge of York.

An important consequence of the Danish invasions was that it led to the unification of the English under one king. England existed before the time of the Dane Guthrum and King Alfred but it was divided into several kingdoms. After the lowest point in the fortunes of the English and Alfred (849–899) at Athelney (878), the creation of one English kingdom for the whole of England began. All of the fighting, clever planning, and hard work were rewarded when under King Athelstan (893–939), England became a united and powerful kingdom.

The assimilation of the Danes led to small changes in the English way of life and some Danish words were introduced into the English vocabulary. The most important consequence of the linguistic compromises that took place during that period of assimilation was that the English language was simplified. For example, word endings were dropped and word order was changed. These fundamental changes were far more important than the comparatively few additions to English vocabulary.

The Norman invasion, which left its mark on the English language, also had other far-reaching consequences for the English. Whereas Danes eventually joined and fitted in with what they found, the Normans imposed themselves on the English.

The Normans were *Northmen* who, under the leadership of Rolf Ganger, a Norwegian, went to Northwest Gaul in 911 and, after an initial defeat and conversion to Christianity, established the Duchy of Normandy. It might have been because they were so different in appearance from the native population that the Northmen felt able to assimilate Frankish culture and language without it threatening their group identity. When the Normans, lead by Wilhelm, invaded England 155 years later, they formed a comparatively small ruling elite. It was perhaps because of their similarity to the English in appearance that they used their adopted Frankish culture and language as a way of preserving their separate identity. The main influence they had on the English language was to greatly expand its vocabulary by introducing foreign (Norman-French) words. It was this that gave rise to much of the confusion we have in Modern English with, for example, different rules for spelling different foreign loan words. Much is often made of the introduction of new words and *the enrichment of the language* but the other side of it was the loss of many English words.

Because Norman-French was used by the political, administrative, and legal elites, it became entrenched in those areas of activity and among certain classes. However, the English language continued to be spoken and written by the English. In the fourteenth century, Chaucer and others wrote in English instead of French or Latin. The English they used was that of the English people. This suggests an evolving language and literary tradition. There was not a sudden change from Old English to Middle English; one flowed into the other.

Since 1066 there has been no successful and sustained military invasion of England, and until the twentieth century there was no significant migration into England of peoples who could not be absorbed into an English identity.

During the late sixteenth and early seventeenth centuries, English adventurers, explorers and colonists laid the foundations of the English Empire which was later to become known as the British Empire. For the next three hundred years the English migrated overseas and created new communities with English institutions. The way of life and the outlook of those people remained that of English men and women. Even after independence, the political and legal systems of the new states remained, at least for a while, for the most part English in character.

It was natural that the different English communities evolved in different ways and that the descendants of those settlers should identify with their new homeland. However, they are still Anglo-Saxon, a term used in modern times for people of English origin wherever they might live in the world, and whatever their attachment to the country in which they live. This means primarily the Anglo-Saxon people of Australia, Canada, England, New Zealand and the USA. It also includes others of English ancestry wherever they might be. The early period of English history belongs to them all because it is the early history of the Anglo-Saxon diaspora.

Some ask why the English should look to the Continent for their origins and early history. The answer is, because the Engle/Angles provided the core identity into which others were absorbed. It is with them that the origins and early history of the English are to be found.

I am English, my language is English, and my homeland is England – the land of the English. It is therefore not unreasonable for me to trace my communal English identity back through that group of people who have called themselves English (Angles/ Engles), spoken English (Englisc), and named their country England (Anglen/Englalond). That journey takes me back to Offa and Nerthus, not to the Britons or Celts. This is not to deny that some Britons, Danes, Normans and others have been absorbed into the English community and influenced the way it has evolved. The point though is that I am English, not Danish or Norman.

The Day of Reckoning
Raymond Tong

And so the day of reckoning had come.
Nearly everything he had believed in,
or had worked for, would be swept away.

His first reaction was to cut his losses,
to stop speculating about the future
and quietly depart for another country.

It was no good pretending. Earth could show
many cities more fair. Jerusalem
would not be built in this overcrowded island.

Yet where would he go? Wherever he went
there would be the same lack of meaning,
the same anguish and aimless posturing.

In the end he would stay. Accepting
once more the need to compromise
he would assist the bad against the worst.

Showers of Sparks
A Publisher

Dear *Author*,

We are grateful that you offered us the opportunity to publish your book but I feel I should explain why I do not think it suitable. I have no doubt that you will disagree with me but I feel that once you get over the irritation you will find this reply more useful than a polite refusal.

You describe your book as being an in-depth examination of the cultural history of the people of the British Isles. Why then do you not examine the culture of the English, who seem to have no place in your pre-1066 history? There are many topics you completely ignore, such as material culture and mythology/religion, where there are clear links between a large English (Angle) population and their southern Jutland homeland and a wider Germanic society. I get the impression that you do not appreciate the vast size and depth of the swamp into which you are wading.

The view you are evidently trying to promote is that the population of the British Isles in about 2500 BC remained in place and was added to by small inward migrations of related peoples. There is much evidence and many arguments to deploy against this assertion and your statement that the notion that ethnic indigenous Britons remained a substantial part of the population of England "is rapidly becoming established as an incontrovertible fact". All I am prepared to say is that it is very far from becoming established as an incontrovertible fact and you do not produce evidence to suggest anything of the kind.

It has been fashionable since the late 1970s to try, for mainly ideological reasons, to write the English out of history. One of these approaches is that put forward by multiculturalists who promote the idea that the population and culture of the British Isles has over thousands of years been gradually added to and altered by an almost constant influx of immigrants who have enriched British culture and identity. The current influx is merely a continuation of this process, which is making our way-of-life more vibrant – aren't we lucky, and shouldn't we be grateful to them for brightening our dull lives.

A different but similar approach is that put forward by what I will call the Celtic/British/Unionist group. Its purpose is to establish that there is an indigenous British population (a British nation) which has lived in the British Isles for many thousands of years and remained largely untouched by small and occasional groups of immigrants which have been absorbed, almost without trace. According to this view, whether we are nominally English, Irish, Scottish or Welsh, we all inter-related members of the British nation. One of the many curious things about this approach is that despite the insistence that there was no large-scale immigration after, say, the Neolithic period, we are told that in addition to being British we are also Celts. Just how, with so little migration, the indigenous British came to speak a Celtic language and become, as some would have us believe, ethnic Celts, is difficult to explain. Another oddity is that many advocates of this view show a complete lack of understanding of genetics and the help it can give in determining our ancestral and geographical roots.

Something common to both groups is their desire to deny an English ethnic identity. Multiculturalists wish to promote an inclusive Englishness, which at its simplest suggests that everyone who lives in England, or is born in England, is English. This is the view put forward by that great *expert* on the subject, Billy Bragg. I suppose he must be thought an expert by someone because he is often on our television screens giving his simple-minded and absurd opinions on the matter. In giving Billy Bragg so much time to air his views, and no time to others to air contrary views, the multiculturalists, who completely control and dominate the UK broadcasting media, are promoting the idea that the English are not an ethnic group – not a people sharing a common history, culture, ancestry, and communal identity.

The aim of the Celtic/British group is similar. According to them the English are merely that part of the British nation that lives in England. In other words, the English are not an ethnic group but part of a British ethnicity. The *true* or *real* British are deemed to share a common Celtic heritage and ancestry. I came across an example of this only a few days ago in a book that had been sent to me. I give below the first sentence of chapter 1, which sets out *the facts* upon which a mountain of misunderstanding and propaganda are built.

> Chapter 1 A Brief history of England, Britain and the United Kingdom
>
> At the time of the Roman invasion, the land which is now known as England was the domain of the Celts, who were a tall, light-haired race of people from north-western Germany and the Netherlands.

Even a cursory look at the population of what is sometimes referred to as the Celtic-fringe reveals that the population of that area is predominately short and dark-haired. The blue-eyed Irish are, in the main, from the Dublin area, which was settled by Norwegians and English. The remainder of the Irish are mainly dark-haired. The Welsh and the Highland (Gaelic) Scots are mostly a dark-haired, dark - eyed people, while the lowland Scots (of Anglo-Saxon origin) are mostly fair-haired. The explanation for this disparity is that the description of *Celts* being tall and light-haired comes from one source, a Roman writer who was mistaken about the ethnicity of people living along the southern bank of the northern Rhine.

As for the rest of it, the Celts were not a race and they didn't come from northwest Germany or the Netherlands. But none of this matters because that first sentence of chapter one has done the propaganda job intended.

Both Left and Right want to deny that the English are an ethnic group but neither side is able to convincingly deal with the origins of the English, England, and the English language. I have, for example, seen numerous crackpot theories about the English language, including the absurdity that it is a Celtic language. I have seen it suggested that "the ghostly echoes of the ancient Celtic roots" can be detected in modern English yet see no convincing evidence to support this claim. It is noteworthy that those who make such claims apparently have no knowledge of Old English. A recent example of this was a book which, according to the back cover blurb, "would be read with mounting horror by all self-respecting academics and with perplexed fascination by the general public". The blurb also claimed, amongst other things, that historians and archaeologists are out of their depth in the half-light of pre-history. Only the author, it seems, has the wit to see that "most of the entries in the Oxford English Dictionary are wrong, the whole of place-name theory is misconceived", and that "both Old English and Middle English are wholly imaginary academic artefacts". The book was indeed read with mounting horror by self-respecting academics who grappled, while they still had the will to live, with the pseudo-academic gobbledygook. The problem is that some of 'the general public' will be fooled by it and give credence to the claim that there is a conspiracy among self-interested academics to suppress the truth of the author's revolutionary and brilliant insights. Before long this book will be referred to as a source by other crackpots, and so the web of misinformation will grow.

Worse still is the utter tosh dished up in so many television programmes. Recent examples are *The Pagans* (BBC2) and *Britain AD* (Channel 4). The presenter of the first found it strangely difficult to say *Anglo-Saxon* or *English* even though many of the artefacts he showed and the sources he used were English. The second was presented by Francis Pryor, who has confessed that he is not an Anglo-Saxonist nor a specialist in early medieval history, which is only too obvious. Yet he is given the resources to peddle as *new and startling* much the same sort of nonsense that was put out by Catherine Hills in her programme *The Blood of the British* in the 1980s. We are indeed fortunate that Simon Schama did such a good job in his *History of Britain*, which was, for the most part, a History of England.

I am firmly of the view that all historians, and likely all social scientists, have an axe to grind; some do more grinding and produce a lot more sparks than others. In short, there is no such thing as ideologically free history. This is not meant as criticism of historians in particular or social scientists in general but a statement of what I believe to be evident – an observation of human nature. I do not claim to be an exception – showers of sparks fly in all directions

You make several mentions of Tolkien and his works but you do not acknowledge that Tolkien's inspiration came from his knowledge of Anglo-Saxon and Scandinavian culture and history. His love of Old English and Old Norse language and literature is evident in his works. He wanted the English to escape the pseudo-Celtic mythology being thrust upon them (King Arthur and all that) and have a mythology of their own; a mythology rooted in English and related Scandinavian cultures. Tolkien most certainly did not think the English to be Celts.

There are so many points I would like to challenge and so many things I think factually wrong, that my reply could become a long essay – perhaps it already has. I will instead try to keep it short by asking some questions.

1. Why did the English call themselves *English* and give the name *England* to their country? Where did these words come from and what did they mean?
2. Why, when you deal with the matters raised above, are there so many occurrences in your text of the words *Celtic* and *Briton* and so few mentions of *Anglo-Saxon* and *English* (other than as in *English language*)?

Your approach is not, as you imply, part of a new and radical view that challenges the old academic establishment, but one that has in various forms been around since Norman times. Then as now it is a means of promoting Britishness and the legitimacy of the British state. It is, like the Arthurian myths, fundamentally anti-English.

There are from time to time bouts of *Celticmania*, the current revival began in the 1970s. Since then, Anglo-Saxon and Scandinavian designs and patterns have been purloined and labelled Celtic. Even English pagans and witches adopt a romantic cuddly-Celt tree-hugging identity, preferring the Celtic gods, goddess, and calendar to those of their English ancestors. Fortunately, increasing numbers of these *pagans* are calling themselves *heathen* and are looking to Anglo-Saxon history, culture, and religion (what is known of it) for their inspiration. The *Lord of the Rings* films have helped promote an interest in things Anglo-Saxon but unfortunately there are many who think it a Celtic tale. Such misconceptions remind me of the people who on hearing English folk music think it Irish.

You may think all this irrelevant to your manuscript but these things represent confusion in the search for identity. The English have for so long been denied their identity (especially in schools and the broadcasting media) and insulted when they express it, that some of them have looked for a more acceptable/approved identity, and have been vulnerable to the propaganda of liberals who wish to promote various concocted *inclusive* identities, such as *British* or *European* or *citizen of the world*, the ultimate earthly inclusive identity – and the most meaningless. The Right prefer an exclusive *Celtic* and *British* and *White* identity. As for English nationalists, they of course prefer an *Anglo-Saxon* and *English* identity, which like any other communal identity, is exclusive. And so the struggle to promote perceptions of identity goes on, whether it be in popular culture or among academics. I know which ideological group I place you in and you know were I stand.

Some may think our different historical views to be irrelevant to modern life – a silly dispute for those with nothing better to do. On the contrary, we are better placed to understand the unstated perceptions of politicians and the very real modern-day political consequences that flow from them. The *Celtic* v Anglo-Saxon conflict can be seen in the determination of the Scottish dominated Labour government to give the *Celtic-fringe* some degree of freedom from the British state – a Scottish Parliament and Welsh Assembly. England's part in this is to subsidise higher public spending in Scotland and Wales. More vindictive still is the breaking up of England into regions, which weakens it and enables it to be more completely dominated by the British state and its successor the EU. And who have they put in charge of this destruction? Why none other than that brilliant and articulate statesman John Prescott, who happens to be Welsh. For some, the battle goes on.

As for your manuscript, once it gets past the matter of origins and language I agree with much, or even almost everything, you have to say and imply. It seems we will have to agree to differ on origins.

We are grateful to you for having sent the extract from your manuscript but for the reasons given above we decline your kind offer to let us publish it.

Yours sincerely

A. Publisher

Anglo-Saxon Chronicle entry for the year 1066

1066 In this year King Harold came from York to Westminster at the Easter after the Christmas the king died; Easter was on 16th April. Then all through England a sign was seen in the heavens such as no man had seen before. Some men said that it was the star 'comet', which some men call the long-haired star; it appeared first on the eve of the Greater Litany, 24th April, and shone for seven nights. Soon after that eorl Tostig came from across the sea into the Isle of Wight with as large a force as he could gather, and was given money and provisions. And King Harold his brother gathered a shipforce and a landforce greater than any king had gathered before in this land, because he had been told that William the Bastard would come here and strive for the land, just as it happened afterwards. Meanwhile eorl Tostig came into the Humber with sixty ships, and eorl Edwin came with a landforce and drove him out. The shipmen deserted him and he went to Scotland with twelve small vessels. Harold, king of Norway, met him there with three hundred ships, and Tostig bowed to him and became his man. They both went up the Humber until they came to York, and there eorl Edwin and eorl Morkere his brother fought with them but the Norwegians had the victory. Harold, king of the English, was informed of the event; and the fight was on the Vigil of St. Matthew. Then Harold our king Harold came on the Norwegians unawares, and met them beyond York at Stamford with a great host of English folk; and that day a very fierce fight was fought on both sides. Harold Hardrada and eorl Tostig were killed, and the Norwegians that were left were put to flight, and the English fiercely struck them from behind as they chased them to their ships. Some drowned, some were burnt, some perished in various ways, so that there were few left, and the English had control of the battlefield. The king made terms with Olaf, son of the Norwegian king, and the bishop and the eorl of Orkney, and all those on the ships. They went up to our king and swore oaths that they would ever keep peace and friendship with this land, and the king let them go home with twenty-four ships. These two pitched battles were fought within five nights. Then William, eorl of Normandy, came to Pevensey on Michaelmas eve, and as soon as they were prepared, they moved on and built a stronghold at the town of Hastings. This was made known to king Harold and he gathered a great army and came against them at the hoary apple-tree. William came upon them unawares, before they had all gathered ready for the fight. The king, nevertheless, fought very hard against them with those men who stayed with him, and there were many killed on both sides. There king Harold was killed and eorl Leofwine his brother and eorl Gyrth his brother, and many good men. The invaders held the field of the dead as God granted them because of the sins of the people. Archbishop Aldred and the townspeople of London wanted the child Edgar for king, as was his natural right; and Edwin and Morkere promised that they would fight on his side. But though haste was needed, it was put off and grew worse from day to day, just as it all happened in the end. The battle was fought on pope Calixtus' Day, 14th October. Afterwards, eorl William went back to Hastings and waited there to see whether men would submit to him. When he saw that no one would come to him, he went inland with all his army that was left to him, and those who came to him from over the sea, and ravaged all the parts he went over, until he came to Berkhamsted. There he was met by archbishop Aldred, child Edgar, eorl Edwin, eorl Morkere and all the leading men of London. They went, out of need, to submit to him when most harm had been done; and it was most unwise that none had gone before, since God would not change things because of our sins. They gave him hostages and swore oaths to him, and he promised them that he would be a faithful lord to them, yet at the same time he and his men plundered all that they could. On Christmas Day, archbishop Aldred consecrated him king at Westminster. Before Aldred placed the crown on his head William promised Aldred on the book of Christ that if they would be loyal to him he would rule all this people as well as the best of kings before him. Yet he taxed the people very severely. And in the spring he went over the sea to Normandy and took with him archbishop Stigand and abbot Æthelnoth of Glastonbury and the child Edgar and eorl Edwin and eorl Morcar and eorl Waltheof and many other good men from England. Bishop Odo and eorl William stayed behind and had castles built across this land and much distressed the wretched folk and always it became much worse. May the end be good when God wills it.

The Death-Bed Confessions of William of Normandy
as recorded by Orderic Vitalis.

I have persecuted the English beyond all reason. Whether gentle or simple I have cruelly oppressed them; many I unjustly disinherited; innumerable multitudes perished through me by famine or the sword . . . I fell upon the English of the Northern shire like a ravening lion. I commanded their houses and corn, with all their implements and chattels to be burnt without distinction, and great herds of cattle and beasts of burden to be butchered wherever they were found. In this way I took revenge upon multitudes of both sexes by subjecting them to the calamity of a cruel famine, and so became the barbarous murderer of many thousands, both young and old of that fine race of people. Having gained the throne of that kingdom by so many crimes, I dare not leave it to anyone but God . . .

Hereward

Ian Holt

It was a hopeless struggle
That was bound to fail.
He had no choice but to fight
Until there was nothing left.
They holed up in the Fenlands,
Dodging the Norman oppressors.
They fought like English heroes,
The saga heroes of old.
They stood up to the foemen
Who harrowed our beloved land.
A Wake! A Wake! He cried a Wake,
That was England's battle cry.
But the unlawful king won.
We English still bear the yoke.

What the Normans did for us
Tony Linsell

The arrival of the Normans brought an end to what remained of the unity between king and nation. William swore an oath at his coronation that he would rule all his people as well as the best kings had done before him but, as the English Chronicle reports, this did not prevent him taxing the people heavily and generally causing them much distress. Property law was changed so that the king owned all the land in his kingdom and title to it was derived from him. The Normans ruled and the English were ruled. The English paid taxes and the Norman governing elite spent the revenue in England and abroad on projects that served their interests. It was clear that the Normans cared nothing for the English or their interests.

It cannot truthfully be claimed that there was a golden age of English democracy and statecraft in the century before the arrival of the Normans. The power of the state had increased, as had the burdens on the people. The two-way loyalty of the early period was moving towards the one-way upward loyalty of an infant feudalism. The qualifications for kingship had, over the centuries, become more restrictive, making it necessary for a candidate to be a member of a royal family. The witan (council of wise men) originally had the right to select from among the members of the royal family the person thought most suitable to be king but by the eleventh century succession of the eldest son had become normal and the task of the witan was merely to confirm that the proper rules of succession had been observed. The arrival of William rapidly accelerated the trend towards a centralisation of power but the transfer of all land into his ownership probably took the process far beyond anything that would have occurred under an English king.

The alliance between the Norman monarchy and the Roman Church helped to further strengthen the infant British state and enabled a vast amount of wealth to be wrung from the English in the form of taxes and land theft. That wealth financed the building of castles, churches and cathedrals in England and Normandy. It also financed costly wars in the British Isles and on the Continent. The Crusades, like other wars of the time, were not in the English national interest but were fought to further the interests and glory of a foreign governing elite. England, a once rich country was reduced to poverty and exhaustion.

The divorce of the state from the nation was stark and readily apparent in the fact that the language of the state, both written and spoken, became Norman French. As a result, English men and women who went to law, or were put on trial, had their cases dealt with in a foreign language. Instead of being able to speak for themselves in court and make their own case they had to pay a lawyer to do it for them. Trials continued to be conducted in French for many centuries.

The Normans set about destroying English culture and national identity so as to undermine resistance to foreign rule. Six hundred years of English history in Britain was dismissed and replaced with an invented history in which the English were portrayed as barbarian Saxon pirates and invaders, who were defeated by a Christian King Arthur, the saviour of a Romano-British civilisation. Little changed for the English when the Norman kings gave way to the equally foreign Plantagenets.[1] St Edmund, the patron saint of England, was replaced by St George, who if he existed at all was probably a Syrian who had no connection with England. For the English, 1066 was to be year zero.

The Britons, including those called Bretons, who had been allies of the Normans, were treated differently. They were given a manufactured glorious past to substitute for the reality of defeats and decline. The aim was to bolster the self-esteem of the Britons and deny the English a national identity. Political and cultural propaganda is not new and it is a testimony to the effectiveness of Norman propaganda that even now we have misguided Englanders who believe that the King Arthur of legend actually existed and that he was English.[2] There was no *King* Arthur as portrayed in the post-conquest Arthurian fables, which are nothing more than invention heaped on layers of myth. The first mention of Arthur is to be found in Welsh sources dating back to the 9th century. It seems probable that there was a great Welsh heathen warrior with this name but his deeds became the subject of political need and literary fashion. Arthur became a Romano-British leader and then a Christian king, and then his part in the myth becomes secondary to that of Lancelot and Guinevere.[3]

It is understandable that some members of the *Celtic-fringe* should promote the Arthurian myths because it forms part of the anti-English strand that runs through much of their culture and in large part helps define them as nations. In recent times, they have cultivated the myth that they are Celts and have basked in the glory of the cultural and technological achievements of the Celts. It is difficult to see how members of the *Celtic-fringe* can justify their claim; they are certainly not ethnic Celts. Any trace of Celtic culture that exists among those people is probably due to some of their remote ancestors having absorbed elements, including language, of a successful and dominant culture.

---

[1] The Plantagenet period is from Henry II, 1154, to the death of Richard III, 1485.

[2] The following quotation is an example of the mistake and how it is passed on as fact. "The story of this English king and his Knights of the Round Table has inspired a mass of films, novels, and poetry." *The Week*, 15th August 1998. A more recent example is the Channel 4 programme, *Pagans*, August 2004. The presenter said that Arthur emerged as a great warrior when England was subject to *Saxon* invasion. Not understanding, it seems, that England did not exist until the English (his Saxons) gave it their name.

The film, *King Arthur*, released in the summer of 2004 portrayed King Arthur as a fifth century Roman general who crossed the Channel to defend Britain against the Saxons. Nevertheless, according to Christopher Tookey writing in the Daily Mail, the film's pretensions to historical accuracy are "laughable". *The Week* 7th Aug 2004.

[3] The *Arthur – Arturus* - of Welsh legend fought mythological creatures but he may have been based on a real hero. It seems likely that there was a great Welsh warrior with a name like Arthur who fought a series of successful battles against the English, his greatest triumph being the Battle (or Siege) of Mount Badon. That victory appears to have halted the English advance for a generation. Suggested dates for the battle range from 490 to 518.

The device of claiming greatness by association is common throughout history but those doing so reveal ignorance of, or dissatisfaction with, their own real history. Many modern Irish, Scottish and Welsh nationalists know that their history and culture is rich enough without a fake Celtic or Arthurian inheritance. In fact, many of them are embarrassed by those of their countrymen who perpetuate it.

In modern times, the English are once again having their history and culture denied. We have a British governing elite that is hostile to the idea of an English national identity rooted in history, culture, and ancestry. It seeks to undermine Englishness in two ways. On the one hand it does its best to discredit and mock the idea of an English nation. On the other, it tries to *redefine* Englishness in an inclusive way that suits its ideological and political needs. Resistance to this moulding of perceptions is handicapped by the fact that early English history and culture is an area of knowledge that is for the most part the preserve of our universities, where many academics seem to present it as something remote and unconnected with the present.

The final indignity that takes us back to the eleventh century is the process that is transferring to the EU the power to make and enforce law. Once again we will be taxed, judged, punished and ruled by foreigners who have no interest whatsoever in preserving English culture and national identity. Indeed they have an interest in destroying it and replacing it with a concocted European identity that will serve much the same purpose as the manufactured Celtic and British identities.

The English nation survived the Normans and the attempt by the Norman military dictatorship to destroy it. That governing elite crumbled because despite its massive power, it was a small minority of the population and it needed to speak English more than the mass of English people needed to speak Norman French. After several generations of interbreeding between Norman and English, the ancestry of the governing elite was more English than Norman. English eventually became the language of the state but due to snobbery and force of habit French and Latin continued to be regarded as high status languages in government and education, and served as a means of setting the governing elite apart from the masses. One of the demands of the Levellers, made in the *Agreement of the People*, 1647, was that all proceedings in law courts be conducted entirely in English.

Throughout the period of its banishment, the English language continued to be spoken and written, and to evolve. Layamon in the twelfth century wrote in almost pure English.[4] Unfortunately, a large number of French words displaced English ones, and much of the Norman official and technical vocabulary used by the ruling elite remained when spoken and written English were officially re-introduced. As a result, many English words were lost from what was to become Standard English but much of the Old English vocabulary was retained in

---

[4] Layamon, a poet and priest, helped promote an invented history of Britain in *Brut* but at least he did so in English and in an English style. He and others subverted the mythical British history by giving it an English gloss.

regional dialects such as Dorset.[5] Another loss was the English style of alliterative verse, which was replaced with the French rhyming style.

Summary

It is easy to deride those who attach importance to military and political events that occurred nine hundred years ago but criticism usually comes from those who are either ignorant of the importance of those times and the hardships that were suffered or simply couldn't care less. The Normans took control of a highly developed and sophisticated English state and used it to subjugate and exploit the English people. It was the English state that made possible the Doomsday Book which better enabled the Normans to tax the English and raise revenue for the purpose of building castles from which they were able to rule over a hostile population. They destroyed English churches and cathedrals and put up Norman buildings in their place. The larger English towns and their people were soon dominated both physically and psychologically by large buildings that were powerful symbols of foreign rule. The wealth needed to finance the vast building programme, both in England and abroad, came from the English people. Much wealth was moved to the continent where the Normans involved the English in very long and costly foreign wars that were of no relevance or benefit to the English national interest.

Many of the changes that occurred as a result of Norman rule can be summarised as follows.

1. 1066 marked the beginning of the British state and England was its first colony. It was also the beginning of the British class system.

2. The nature of kingship changed from one where the king was a symbol of national unity and a protector of the people and their rights, to one where the king was divorced from the English nation, its interests and wellbeing. The monarch became an absolute ruler and head of state, guided only by his own interests and those of his allies, nearly all of whom were foreign.

3. The king did not just own a private estate but all the land in his kingdom.[6]

4. The rights attached to the ownership of all the land of the kingdom (payments and the provision of services) were transferred to the king and then from him to those of his allies he wished to reward.

5. The state finally changed from one that had originally been created to serve the interests of the nation to one that served the interests of the ruling elite. The English people were treated as an enemy of that elite and had few rights and many duties.

---

[5] William Barnes, the Dorset poet, was very keen on re-introducing Old English words into everyday use and to that end he produced word lists giving English (Saxon-English) equivalents to foreign words. Where he could not find appropriate English words he re-created them, using English root words. If he were alive today he would be promoting the use of plain English. See *The Rebirth of England and English: The Vision of William Barnes*, Andrew Phillips (Anglo-Saxon Books, 1996).

[6] Title to land is still derived from the Crown and reverts to it when title is lost.

6. The language of the rulers became the language of the state and its courts. English was treated as a low status language.

7. The Church in England lost much of its independence. The pre-Norman English Church, which had enjoyed a considerable degree of independence from Rome, came more directly under papal authority and Norman management.

8. The history of the English nation was suppressed and in its place was put a mythical history of Britain in which the Britons played a glorious part and the English became the wicked Saxon enemy.[7] Those who use the word Saxon to describe the pre-Conquest English are helping to perpetuate that myth

9. The history of England was deemed to start in the eleventh century with William being treated as though he were the first king of England. This had the effect of furthering the process, begun when Christianity was introduced into England, of distancing English traditions, culture and learning from Northern Europe and linking them with the Mediterranean world. The attack that took place on English culture and national identity would today be called cultural genocide.

It is evident that many of the changes introduced by the Normans, and much of their propaganda, have endured down the ages. The use of foreign words and phrases are still mistakenly thought to demonstrate intelligence, sophistication and education. As a result, stupid people believe that using long words with foreign roots, instead of shorter English words, will make them seem clever. Clear, simple language usually indicates clarity of thought and is generally more pleasant to the English ear and mind. Saying much with few words is in the tradition of the Old English wordsmiths but the fashion now is to say very little with as many words as possible, and the longer the word the better it is deemed to be.

The English survived the rule of the Normans and other hardships but what happened to the Normans? The only trace to be found of them in England is in the remnants of the landed aristocracy where there are still those who express pride in the belief that their ancestors came over with *The Conqueror*.[8] That they think such a connection reflects well on them says much about them and the teaching of history. The class system in England has been kept alive by those who mistakenly believe that they have Norman blood coursing through their veins.[9] That group of misguided people provided good reason for the reform of the House of Lords, which is in effect the remnant of a Norman institution. This is

---

[7] According to *The Cambridge Guide to Literature in English*, Ian Ousby, CUP 1995, some of Geoffrey of Monmouth's *Historia regum Britanniae* (c. 1135) "bears a remote resemblance to actual events" but "the majority is pure invention".

[8] Duke Wilhelm of Normandy was once better known to the English as *William the Tanner* or *William the Bastard*.

[9] The widely held belief that it is a good thing to have *come over with the Normans* is used by those who peddle (manufacture) bogus family trees and coats of arms. Everyone it seems can be connected to a line of Norman aristocrats and sold a coat of arms with a Latin motto.

not to deny that there are many current and former members of the House of Lords who have a very strong sense of Englishness and are concerned to preserve England and English political and cultural identity. That is more than can be said of a Scottish-dominated British government which is as contemptuous of English rights as were the Normans.

It is unwise to claim too much for early English society but it is probably true that in that time, and especially before the introduction of Christianity, freemen (and women) were freer, and individual and communal rights were greater than after the Norman invasion. The system of justice and the settlement of disputes was built around the idea that an individual belonged to a family and a wider community and was obliged to act in the best interests of both. Kinship brought with it an obligation to protect and assist others in times of need; the closer the relationship, the greater the obligation.

Liberals are given to ridiculing Englishness but in response to one such attack in *New Statesman and Society* (NSS), Sir Richard Body, the then Conservative MP for Holland-with-Boston, replied in a way that expressed the situation rather nicely, even though some might agree with it more in spirit than in detail. After pointing to the libertarian nature of Anglo-Saxon society he went on as follows:

> The Englishness mocked in *NSS* columns belongs to the Normans. Snobbish, conformist, pageant-adoring and hard of heart, the Normans introduced a contrast, which has given England two distinct streams which have mingled uneasily. The civil war saw them clash. The Roundheads were very English; the Cavaliers very Norman. Three centuries on, and the distinction is becoming blurred, but we can discern the true Englishness still. It is not in the City of London, the armed services, the House of Lords, the established church or any other allegedly English institution, for they are in the Norman tradition – conformist, regulated and authoritarian. For true Englishness, we turn to the millions of self-employed businessmen, our public services, the chapels and meeting-houses, the House of Commons and a vibrant, variegated press. The caricature of Englishness is pure Norman.

> For a true specimen of Englishness, I will nominate Michael Foot. It would have been Kingsley Martin if he were still around.

Many more names could be added to the list, including of course Sir Richard Body. Also: Tony Benn, Dennis Skinner, Frank Field, the late Barbara Castle and Enoch Powell.

The English - A view from the Left
Rohan

The ethnic English of England are an ethnic group at law. They are a people who satisfy the legal test in the UK for the existence of an ethnic group. They are a sub-group of, and are the very core of, the Anglo-Saxon peoples of the world. The ethnic English are known by various names. They are the people who refer to themselves as the True, or Authentic, or Real, or Native English, as THE English. The English are the people that put the Anglo into everything Anglo hyphenated.

The English are the descendants of the Northern European peoples who came together to create England, both geographically and spiritually. The modern day English are the descendants of those of earlier generations of English who did not yield, one way or another, to the pressure placed upon them to leave England. Thus the English are aware they are by inherited nature incredibly stubborn and tenacious, that they have an ability to endure the unendurable almost second to none. Given the standards of living and the freedoms enjoyed by Anglo-Saxons abroad, some might judge this decision not to leave as an indication of group insanity. The English are aware they are heavily submerged in and subjugated to that which is known as British. It is entirely due to the past efforts of the English and the English alone that the words English and England still have meaning today. The English know they are the us in "them and us".

The modern day English are those people who believe they are primarily, principally, substantially, significantly, or dominantly descendant from the Northern European peoples living in England (meaning herein excluding Cornwall) prior to 1066 and all other peoples who have been absorbed into the English peoples such that they are no longer distinguishable from the English and neither claim to be nor are recognised by the English as belonging to another ethnic group. Any person, for example, claiming Norman ancestry does not satisfy this definition. The English are THE indigenous people of England, the country they created and gave their name to. The English know that although it is not so true today, the ancient English from whom they are descendant were by and large blonde and blue-eyed.

The English are the people who claim native indigenous title to all the lands of England. They claim common ownership of all the intellectual property and other rights of a proprietary nature in the name English, ethnically and nationally speaking. They claim unabashed even though the current British Government has provocatively declared to the world, by word and deed, that there is no such thing as the English and no such thing as England.

The English know that the British Empire lives on and that England was its first colony. The English know that long after the British Empire and State and all its colonies, including those in the UK, have passed away into history there will be an England and an English, as they understand each to mean. The English harbour a knowledge that they intend both themselves and England to make it to the third millennium, and they are not deflected in this intent by the obstacles the

British Empire and State puts in their path. The English suspect that if they do not make it to the third millennium, no one else is going to either.

The English think that in the pecking order of priorities it is the survival of the English that comes first then the survival of England. The English have come to this understanding by way of explanation as to why so many of their numbers have left England. The English are aware that the British Empire and State through a policy of stick and carrot persuaded many millions of their kind to leave England *voluntarily*. The English are aware that as a matter of deliberate policy of cleansing troublesome natives, the British Empire and State between 1776 and c1868 removed from England not less than 750,000 of their number to Australia; in addition to the vast numbers previously dispatched involuntarily to America. The English are aware that in 1807 the British Empire and State outlawed the transportation of African slavery, a vile trade principally undertaken by the financial empires of the Norman dominated British aristocracy and by foreign British monarchs, for among other reasons, to free the slave ships to undertake an exponential growth in this forcible removal of the English.

Thus the English share with the Jews the accolade of being the only groups the British Empire and State has ever sought to deport from England. It was just the shear numbers of the English and the lack of alternative cheap labour that made their total removal impossible. The English know from this experience that the British Empire and State, if it suits its interests, has the ability to efficiently remove persons from England. The English know that if the British Empire and State chooses not to undertake any such efficient removals it is because it suits the interests of the British Empire and State not to do so. The English believe that in a fair world the descendants of those directly and indirectly forcibly removed from their English communities would be granted that which rightfully is theirs - British State issued passports, the right to reside in England, and the right to vote in UK and European elections. The English know that ethnic cleansing of natives does not cease to be ethnic cleansing just because it apparently took place in accordance with the rules of law. The English have the intellectual capacity to understand, even if the British do not, that rule in accordance with the rules of law is not the same as the rule of law. To the English, the descendants of the fair, if a law is not fair dealing it's not law but oppression. The English know that they have a Diaspora that dwarfs their numbers.

The English are tempted to ring up their Diaspora to ask if they are aware of any indigenous group living in the Diaspora's environs who do not have to share with the Diaspora everything that group owns, who have a birth rate that is not in free fall, who live under their own rules, who live under their own culture, who are self governing, who control the education of their young, who are optimistic about the future, who do not under compulsion have to mix at all times cheek by jowl with the Diaspora, who are prospering financially for their own benefit, and whose ancient rare and vulnerable communities are not being ethnically resettled for the sin of homogeneity. If they do, now would be a good time for the Diaspora to let the English know. The English would hope that if they made the enquiry, they would not thereby cause parts of their Diaspora any embarrassment.

What the English would really like to say to their Diaspora is, "May Day, May Day, calling the Anglo-Saxon Diaspora on all frequencies, May Day, May Day". Yet, it is the English way to accept that no matter how bad things get, it could be worse. The English know that rather than grumble they are much more likely to ask the Diaspora, "What's the weather like over there?" Acceptance is the path to depression and defeat. Denial and Dunkirk go hand in hand. In truth, the English suspect that when the Diaspora hears the voices of the English, and the emphasis is on the word *when*, (for the Diaspora tends to mistake the voice of the British for the voice of the English), the Diaspora hears nothing more and nothing less than a homing beacon.

The English know that if one were to put a cross section of persons residing as British Subjects/Citizens in conurbation England in a room and say the phrases: - "Homing beacon"; "Night sky"; "Are you receiving Squadron Leader; over?"; "Squadron Leader, are you still receiving, over?"; "Peter can you hear us, over?"; "Peter are you there, over?";...... "Roger that Peter, will tell the chaps you have gone for a "Burtons"; over and out", a fraction of those in the room would choke. The English know that those who choke would be "one of us".

The English know the racism of the British towards the English inherent in the suggestion that the English, especially their so-called underclass, have no respect for learning. The English know that the British point to phrases such as - "Too clever for his own good", "Too clever by half", "A little bit of learning is a dangerous thing", "Dumb Blonde" - as evidence that this *no respect* attitude exists. Only the English know the horrors being conveyed in those phrases. Only English hearts stop when they learn of the Englishman who got up before the Admiral of the British fleet in the late 1700s and said in effect, "Sir you are sailing towards the rocks off the Isles of Sicily". Only the English flinch, knowing it was infinitely worse, when they learn he was hung instantly from the yardarm for getting above his station. Only the English weep for the callous loss of life of the men pressed into the service of the British Empire and State against their will, when they hear that the entire fleet sank having struck the rocks off the Isles of Sicily within a matter of days.

Only the English know the account of their continuing struggle to access education, for the right to have control over their education, to have knowledge of their choosing, to have knowledge of benefit to them, to retain their own cultural knowledge and the oppression faced at the hands of the British Empire and State. Only the English know why their ancestors treated Newton, one of theirs, almost as if he was the re-incarnation of the symbolism of Beowulf, in the funeral they gave him. Only the English understand why the British State systematically set out in the late nineteenth century to totally destroy independent education for the really ethnic English, the poor. Only the English know the racism in the British Empire and State's decision to lump them indistinguishably into the category "White British". It excuses the British from having to face up to the horror of the *keep your place or we will keep it for you* prison society inflicted via legal and social terror by the British Empire and State on the English; the legacy and unhealed scars of which are still felt by the English and their young today.

Only the English know that there is no such thing as an English aristocracy, only a Norman/British clique calling themselves The Blue Blood Aristocracy and their hangers on. The English know it is they who are the ethnic group called The Common. Only the English know how the Anglo-Saxons learnt that it is self evident that all men are created equal. The English know their aristocracy was wiped out in the genocide that took place in the decades following 1066. The English know that in those years the Normans systematically ethnically cleansed many parts of England; that in one summer alone, the Normans slaughtered by sword and famine about 130,000 English men, women and children living between York and Durham; one-tenth of the entire English population. It is said in some quarters that not less than 1/3rd of the entire English population perished in those genocidal years. Only the English know why there are no memorials to their victims of genocide, not even in York. It is not because the English do not want to remember.

Only the English know how insulting it is for the British to ignore centuries of English history and name William the Bastard, the Low Life, the Mass Murderer, as the first king of England and of the English. Only the English know how many monarchs imposed on them since 1066 have actually been English. The English have not failed to notice that to date the British Empire and State has not financed nor permitted any DNA research to take place on any Norman remains, when it has done so on Anglo-Saxon and on other ancestral ethnic remains. The English know how seismic the result would be if DNA research showed, as well it might, that the Normans were not fellow Northmen; contrary to what the British Empire and State's history and education industries would have people believe. The English know that when someone says to them, "My ancestors came over with William the Conqueror", they get the urge to ring up their Diaspora and say, "You know what they say about time dissipating hate, its not true, the urge to slit throats remains even after a thousand years. You might want to take that on advisement."

The English remember the acts of ethnic cleansing and genocide, which have been inflicted upon them sporadically over the millennium past. Only the English know the horror of the gender genocide, genital mutilation and sexual exploitation summed up in the phrase "the fairer sex". The English understand the message in the Book of David that controlling elites use war to ethnically cleanse in the choice of whom is sent to the front. The English know that the Grim Reaper came in the form of a British shilling. The English have not failed to notice that there is a link between British wars, the need of the British for pressed or conscripted men and when the British Empire and State embraces enthusiastically the concept of England and Englishmen.

The English imagine that they would like to say to a section of the Diaspora, "We know what it meant when you kept the faith, when you did unto others as you would be done by, when you did less than had been done to you. We understand the starting point and knowledge limitations. We understand why you turned a year and a day after arrival to an instant on arrival. We understand even if nobody else does why attempts to end the principle could lead you to kill. The English are aware that their Diaspora knows it was not only a Southern Tree that bore a strange fruit, the Weeping Trees at the crossroads did so as well - abundantly for nigh on nine hundred years. Fruit was harvested even from the young at rates sometimes in excess of 4,500 a year; fruit as early as six."

The English know there are folks they should ring up and say, "You know how everybody undertakes anthropological studies to get an understanding of the past and where they came from, would you like to be the first people to undertake an anthropological study to assess were you are going, what your choices could lead to? Would you like to get an understanding of the parameters of the *Been there, had it done, got the tee shirt* attitude of the people you are destined to keep the company of unto eternity?" The English know that they would like to say to some folks; "In keeping with the dimensional expansion of the Theory of Everything - String Theory - have you ever considered the possibility that the reason there were so many mammas was that there existed people who had been through social systems so inhumanly distorted, so dysfunctional, so randomly traumatic, so dominated by non-breeding men, and for so long, that they needed to relearn the skills of mothering and are too proud to admit it."

The English know that they would like to invite their Diaspora to attend a seminar weekend entitled:- "Male irrationality has reason: - fear, the historical dialectic", with the caveat that "only men with strong dispositions should attend; preference given to men with community leadership potential/responsibilities." The English know that they would like to invite their Diaspora similarly to attend a contemporaneous study weekend entitled; "The right to choose: - choice restrictions, the historical dialectic". "All women welcome."

The English suspect that when they first heard the term WASP their reactions were very varied. The English can imagine the adventurous types would have sent out their young to seek out the illusive creature *the BASP*, with the instruction to observe and report. Another section would have had the urge to call on the relevant part of the Diaspora to account for themselves, seeking assurances from them that all those who call themselves Anglo-Saxon understand that to be an Anglo-Saxon one has to keep the honour code of the core. The English could imagine that a bright spark at the back, having got their collective undivided attention, opened a dictionary 90 years in the making, looked up the word ASP and declared in the circumstances WASP was preferable. The English know that within the Manor of the holy settlement lying on the River Don, English parents are teaching their young the principles of algebraic equality:- WASP < = working class = ((Anglo + Saxon) = nonconformist/low church protestant). The English know they that do are telling no lies.

The English believe that it is they that hold the high moral ground guidance for their Diaspora. Thus the English believe that, should it come to pass and there be no more English in England, their Diaspora would reoccupy England, in the sure and certain knowledge that no matter what they did, they simply could not cause any collateral damage. The English suspect that if there were no more English in England the world would encourage the Diaspora to reoccupy England. The English suspect that the world thinks the place for English people is in England. It's why the English never left England. The English suspect that changing one's name to Anglo-Saxon is not fooling the world.

The English suspect that they should on behalf of the Diaspora apologise to any non Anglo-Saxons outside England who find themselves as a result of their Diaspora's influence, stuck with worshipping a historically incorrect depiction of

Jesus. The English know that their Diaspora were themselves only complying with the core's instincts. The English know it's Woden, the God of War, transmuted into the God of Peace. The English are not sure why folks just do not solve this problem by getting their paintbrushes out. The English have a love of decorating makeovers, especially the instant kind. Nothing is sacrosanct from this urge, not even churches. The English have not been backward in coming forward to demonstrate their love for sledgehammer instant redecorating. The English know they harbour a desire to redecorate the British Houses of Parliament by the total demolition first method. The English know what the outcome would be if it came to a choice for them between having a historically correct Jesus lording it all over them or openly worshiping the God of War.

The English know from personal experience that Orwell was thinking of the British Empire and State (including the BBC) when he wrote: "Who controls the past controls the future, who controls the present controls the past."

The English are aware of why it is they are not allowed their own history from 1066. Embarrassing things might happen, like having to change the ethnically offensive title The Peasants' Revolt of 1391 to The Anglo-Saxon/English Uprising of 1391. The English truly know that the phrases *ethnic social mobility* and *the medieval age* are mutually incompatible and that the exception does not make the rule. So great is the stranglehold of the British on the perception of the English that the expression, The Peasants' Revolt, abounds everywhere. Yet that said, few English would not agree that the phrase *The Slaves' Revolt in Jamaica of 1831* is ethnically offensive. The correct title has got to be at least *The African-Caribbean Uprising*.

The English know why they are not allowed to have a version of their history prior to 1066 other than that approved by the British Empire and State through its academic institutions. The story of Canute, for example, might get rewritten to tell the truth, as the English know it. Canute's inability to turn the tide did not prove that Canute was mortal, but rather it proved he was the wrong kind of mortal to be a true English king. Canute, by getting his feet wet, confirmed to the English onlookers what they already knew, Canute was not one of them. Real Englishmen can decipher the movements of earth and can calculate the impact of timing. The English know that the tide will turn on an Englishman's command; all he needs are a pocket watch and tide-table. Both are of English invention. The English know with a little knowledge that the tide does turn.

This English trait for timing and patience is the basis of so-called English tolerance. To the English tolerance can mean simply complying with the sergeant major's growled command, internalised in each and every one of them: - "Wait for it". This internalised command means to the English literally what it meant to their sergeant majors: - "get in sync and then with impeccable timing act as one". Acting as one means to the English common effort not same effort. Finding an outlet for this innate desire to act as one, as a group, was the drive behind English invented team sports. The inherent power in the English acting as one is also the reason for the willingness of the British in the past to acquiesce to English concepts of individual freedoms/liberties/rights but not to English concepts of communal freedoms/liberties/rights. The English as one, in common, as a group, are terrifying to the British. Few English could ever forget the sight of the British Minister, Jack Straw, metaphorically wetting his underpants in fear when he admitted that he was afraid of the English becoming self-aware. Nor will many English forget the moment when John Prescott, a British Minister, admitted that he is so Anglophobic that he could only deal with it by denying that the English exist. His denial is ultimately pointless and powerless. The English do not have to be self-aware or have the recognition of the British to be a community; they awake every morning as a community. The proof of the truth of this statement is to be seen in the story of Canute; it is a matter of timing, patience, knowledge and perception.

The English see the silver lining in every cloud. For them, the silver lining is the opportunity created by events to move forward their common dream even if the dream's journey is multi-directional, multi dimensional and multi-parallel.

The English are fully aware that they are a people who have for a millennium dreamt unabated of the restoration of English liberty, of English self-rule, of English self determination under England's sky. Their achievements along the way are well documented. The English know that in the pursuit of their dream the English have made gifts to humanity of which they can justifiably be proud; gifts ranging from football to the concept of the rule of law. The English know that their desire and determination for the realisation of their dream accepts no restraint. The English are aware that they are a people who at the behest of the British have killed and been killed in unimaginable numbers. Such is the reality of the millennium past that the English know it is only the British who speak of the loss of sovereignty. The English are more prone to say "Sovereignty, what sovereignty, when did we, the English people, know sovereignty?"

The English know the British monarchy is bound to them by an unwritten treaty known as an employment contract. The English know it is they who are the employer and the monarch the employee. It is the British who believe it is the other way round. The English know that the first clause implied into every employment contract is: - "The Employee shall not attempt to deceive the Employer and fail." The English are aware that the outcome of a breach of clause 1 could be as serious as, instant dismissal, or dismissal with notice, or dismissal by reason of redundancy. The English know that the employer must give an employee an opportunity to attend a so-called disciplinary hearing so that the employee may have an opportunity to dispel the employer's perception of deception. The English sense that the rule of law would not look kindly upon those who do not give a long standing well regarded employee with an apparently unblemished previous record a fair hearing. The English also know, however, that the employer is entitled to hold a hearing in any place the employer acting reasonably shall determine and that the choice of venues open to an employer can include the Coroner's Court.

The English know what it is like to struggle for over 900 years for a political voice in that foreign created state now called the British State, and for nearly 400 years to openly engage in a bitter struggle for the right to vote for all of the English in that State's representative institutions. The English know what it feels like to have obtained the right to vote for all only to find that the British Empire and

State within three decades has deliberately introduced a policy of electorally cleansing the English. Only the English know how deeply ethnically offensive it is to hear the British proudly declare that the UK has a long historical tradition of democracy and freedom. In a truly free society the English would be able to openly ask "exactly when" and obtain the honest answer "for the many, never - for the Common, all in all, never - for the English, never". The English know Orwell was really describing the attitude adopted by the British, when forced by the English to accept the concept of equal worth, when he wrote, "All animals are equal, but some animals are more equal than others."

The English dream of the day when for the first time in over 900 years they, as a matter of law, enjoy equality with those who have long been able to openly celebrate their ethnicity and enjoy ethnic rights. They dream of enjoying the simple pleasure of being able to turn on the equivalent of the radio to hear at last "Goooood Mornnnning Diaspora, this is the voice of the Free English broadcasting live on the Anglo Network from somewhere deep in England. We start the day for you with a couple of tracks to get you in the mood. The first track is entitled *White Riot I Wanna Riot* by that great English band "The Clash". This is then followed by The Clash's version of that immortal song by the European-American, Sonny Curtis, *I Fought the Law and the Law Won*.

The English know they are one of the few ethnic groups to have survived the Roman Empire, its collapse and re-instatement by other means. The English know the British Empire and State is in terminal decline but that the English are not. It is only because some among the English see the collapse of the British State as their misfortune that the English are perceived as depressed, impotent, worried and defeatist - they shouldn't be. For the English are innately aware they are not an artificial creation like the British. The English know they are naturally a nation – a community bound together by a shared history, ancestry, and way-of-life. The English know that freedom made them English and tyranny made them British. Inconveniently for some, the English can still remember how few of their ancestors where able to say yea or nay to The Act of Union - virtually Sweet FA. For the core of the ethnic English, the British Empire and State has never had any legal legitimacy. The English know they have already survived Armageddon, the end of the world. Compared with that, dealing with the inevitable breakdown of the British Empire and State is a walk in the park which brings with it the novel prospect of looking forward not back.

The English along with others have noticed that some in England are becoming irritated with the efforts of the British Empire and State to stay alive by transplant operations and to control the future beyond its grave by seeking to alter the beneficiaries under its will or intestacy. Figures banded about in Commission for Racial Equality (CRE) circles guess those openly irritated to number not less than 40% of the population of England. The English know it's only a matter of time before some bright spark tries to break down ethnically just who is irritated. The break down could show, as well it might, that the irritated are none other than the majority of the English people and that those who are not irritated are mainly non English persons. One can see in such circumstances why the British State and Empire would want to hang on to the classification "White British" and deny the existence of the English for as long as possible.

Unfortunately for the British, the English now know why the British Parliament used the word *ethnic* to describe a distinct group entitled to add on communal and individual rights: - the maintaining of the British Empire and State's status quo. The British Parliament had nothing to gain by being open about the effects of its legislation. Ethnic was a word that entered the language of the English in the 14th Century to refer to a person who was not Christian, probably a foreigner. Ethnic until the intervention of the Race Relations Act of 1976 meant to the English literally "not one of us" in the equation "them and us".

The English could not see how the race legislation granted them communal rights, for to be an ethnic is to be "not one of us". If there was anything that could demonstrate the cultural insensitively of the British Empire and State to the English it was the choice of this word by the British Parliament. For nearly three decades, and despite a clear indication otherwise, given on behalf of the English Law Lords, the English have believed they were not an ethnic group. Not one of the institutions created by the British Parliament has in all that time sought to dispel the English of their false belief. The English now know otherwise and the future is but an English writ away, for it is not for a British Minister to say whether the English exist or not. It is for the English Courts. As an ethnic group the English have more communal rights than they have ever known since 1066. For a people who created the concept of common as in common effort, common bond, common wealth, common land, common purpose, common law, etc these communal rights have been a long time in the waiting.

The English are very aware that there is no other ethnic group in England that has suffered human rights abuses in England at the hands of the British Empire, State and others on a par with that suffered by the English. The English know there is no other ethnic group in England that has suffered in England genocide and ethnic cleansing at the hands of the British Empire, State and others, that comes close to what they have endured. The English know there is no other ethnic group in England that has suffered a reign of terror in England at the hands of the British Empire and State on a par with that suffered by the English. The English know that no other ethnic group has suffered in England land theft sanctioned by the British Empire and State on a scale as that suffered by the English. It is plain to the English that no other ethnic group in England has a well of suffering deep enough to understand why compensating someone for a misused word is an affront to the English, when the English remain uncompensated for so much more.

The English know that no other ethnic group in England has suffered by virtue of being an ethnic group in England as much as the English have. The English know the British Empire and State would not dare to give to the English funding on a scale and in proportion to their numbers that it gives to other ethnic groups to further their ethnic grievances. The British Empire and State knows that if it did it would have to meet the English on the floor of the Courts of England where it would be forced to admit the truth before the world. The truth that none in England have suffered at its hands and that of others in England as the English have and none have had their grievance so uncompensated as the English.

The English appreciate it was they who proved the truth in the phrase just because "one lost the battle does not mean one will lose the war". 'The English know that they have fought their best, more successful and most far-reaching battles by acting in common, often from the comfort of their own living rooms. For example, though it took the English almost 300 years of persistent refusal to change their ways, the language of the English started to become again the dominant language of England when in 1362 it became useable once more in legal proceedings. The first book in their own language read by the English at large was entitled *The Little Gest of Robin Hood*. The legend was set down in book form upon the invention of the printing press and the book was bought in such numbers in common by the English it became THE English medieval bestseller.

That book's story is so powerful it remains known today and is more widely known than any of the stories of Shakespeare. It was a story created and transmitted by the English independently of and in defiance of any Norman state institution. The story did not need monarchical patronage to be heard, for the story is a people's story. The legend of Robin Hood has given the English such a common voice, such a common knowledge, that the English remain unperturbed by Hollywood's and the BBC's denial of the Northern European ancestry of the English in their re-enactments of the legend and presentation of English history. The English suspect it is only a matter of time before *the* film version of the legend is made; the one which has the same lasting impact on the English and their Diaspora as the book did. The one stamped A-S Authentic™ as a certificate of quality. The English know when it is so made, every other film will be an also-ran and soon forgotten.

The English are aware that the ancestral English believed "Seek and you shall find, knock and the door shall be opened unto you". The English know it was by seeking in common that gave power to their lines, it was by seeking in common that gave strength to their shields, it was by seeking in common that their ground did not yield, it was by seeking in common that their freedom was bought. Such is the legacy of Alfred, the father of the English Nation. The English are aware that their ancestors made themselves into the English through common effort, found a common voice through a common language and after the end of the world they made and found the common in themselves again, under the shadow of oppression, through the things they sought in common. The English innately comprehend that it was the seeking in common that gave them birth and that it is the seeking in common that gives them perpetual life.

The English know that when their right keeps the company of their left and their left keeps the company of their right, the English are seeking in common. The English know that when their left and their right seek in common, the left and the right will work in common. The English know that it is only when the left hand and the right hand work in common that a treasure is made; a work of art is born. The English know such is the door that shall be opened, such is the morrow of England, such is the future of the English and their allies, and such is the common dream of the English.

Meanwhile, in a dusty back room in one of the Inns of Court, a pupil barrister is drafting an application to the High Court of England for a Writ of Habeas Corpus, (a writ directed to someone who has custody of a person, ordering him or her to bring that person before the court issuing the writ and to justify why the person is detained in custody). The Applicant: - The English Peoples, one and all. The Respondent: - The British Empire and State.

And the Lord spoke unto Moses,
Go unto Pharaoh, and say unto him,
Thus saith the Lord,

Let My People GO...

The Battle of Maldon
Extract – lines 301-319

There was fierce fighting: firm stood
the warriors in the battle.   War-men fell,
worn down by their wounds   dropped lifeless.
Oswald and Eadwold   all the time
- brothers to the end -   urged on their fellows,
told their kinsmen   these words
that in this time of need   they must stand firm
summon their strength   be fierce in the fight.

Byrhtwold spoke,   he raised his shield;
he was an older warrior;   he brandished ash-spear
and full of courage   addressed his comrades.
Minds must be the firmer,   hearts the bolder,
courage the greater,   as our strength dwindles.
Here lies our lord,   cut down,
good man on the ground.   May he grieve forever
who from this war-work   would consider withdrawing.
I am old in age,   but I will not leave,
instead by my lord,
by so beloved a man,   will I finally lie.

Spa Witness

Roy Kerridge

Many a traveller pauses in rapt admiration as the town of Cheltenham Spa comes into view on the hilly road from Cirencester. Cheltenham's motto is "poor, proud and pretty". The descent into town reveals treasure upon treasure of Regency architecture. As far as this story is concerned, our journey ends at a great white house in a crescent near the silver birch studded lawns of Pittville Park.

By the side of this house, among drainpipes and fire escapes, steps lead down to a narrow area and to a small brown door with flower tubs outside. At one time, this had been the outside door to the kitchen, but now that the big house had been divided into flats, it opened onto the home of Mrs. Vaughan and her six-year-old granddaughter, Emily.

Mrs.Vaughan, a widow in her sixties, was a stout white haired lady of vague yet anxious appearance, faintly bohemian, yet with a slightly vapid expression in her blue eyes. Her late husband, the Colonel, had been an Arabist, a friend of Glubb Pasha, with leanings to Islam. Many of the attractive decorations had been brought from the Near East, and Mrs.Vaughan often played records of Turkish or Arabian music, to which Emily danced.

Little dark-haired Emily, a happy, skipping, pink-cheeked child of vivacious beauty, was the mainstay of her grandmother's life and the cause of her anxious expression. For Emily suffered from asthma, and had to use an inhaler from time to time. Dancing and ballet meant a great deal to Emily, and the girl grew angry with herself, in quite a grown-up way, if a coughing or gasping fit came upon her during a dance. When Emily had been smaller, Mrs. Vaughan had sat up with her for many a weary night, as she tossed and turned, holding her grandmother's hand. Each year, however, the spectre of asthma seemed to recede.

Emily felt very safe in bed with her grandmother at night, accompanied by her two friends, Bear and Duck, both reassuringly fluffy. Sometimes, in the daytime, she would write them little notes, with hearts and xxxxxs. "Duck I love you" and "Bear you are fery (furry)" were two of her more recent efforts. She attended a small local private school, and had grown fond of note-writing as soon as she had learned her letters. Much praised as the brightest child in the school, Emily was comically well spoken and precocious. There was one important fact she did not know. She thought that her grandmother was her mother, and called her Mummy. One day this deception would have to end, another worry for Mrs. Vaughan.

Emily, to her serene delight, had two Aunties. One was Aunty Dolly, a tough, ironic little woman who came in for two days a week to clean the flat. Somehow, the name "Aunty" had been applied to the cleaning lady and stuck. The other was Aunty Rose, a flamboyant Aunty who wore silk robes, had once been an actress and now lived at Bath with jolly Uncle Ahmad and their little girl Cousin Zebba. But Aunty Rose was really Emily's mother, and four year old Zebba was her half-sister.

Mrs. Vaughan had been widowed in middle age, and the Colonel had not had the pleasure of seeing his daughter Rose leave the Ladies College and go into Rep. One day, Rose had returned home, left the infant Emily with her mother and rejoined her Company. As Rose grew irritable whenever Emily's father was enquired after, Mrs. Vaughan dropped the subject. "Every child needs a father" may have become a popular saying, but nobody had told Emily, who seemed perfectly happy without one. Aunty Rose visited her at least once a month, and Zebba and Emily became best of friends. Though slightly darker, Zebba looked and spoke like a smaller, jollier version of Emily.

Upon meeting Ahmad, a prosperous businessman brought up in Pakistan and Swindon, Rose had left the stage with many misgivings and regrets and settled down as a very independent and far-from typical Moslem housewife. Colonel Vaughan, a disciple of Burton, had never dreamed of converting to Islam, but admired what he thought of as the Islamic way of life, a manly way, with tent, gun and a hawk named Memed. His daughter, however, converted with great glee, and seemed to have found almost perfect happiness with roley-poley pacific Ahmad, a very different branch, or fruit, of Islam.

Since the freethinking Colonel died, Religion had come to dominate the Vaughan household. For many years now, Mrs.Vaughan had been a member of the Jehovah's Witnesses. Being a Jehovah's Witness was the second most important thing in her life, Emily being the first. Easily persuaded by a door-to-door Witness to attend a meeting, Mrs. Vaughan found all the answers to life in the Kingdom Hall and the Watchtower Magazine. The magazine formed a Holy Writ by instalments, and much of the time at Kingdom Hall was spent in study of its wisdom, with question and answer sessions but no arguments. ("We are not a Democracy, we are a Theocracy, under the direct rule of Jehovah.")

Both the Aunties, Dolly and Rose, made light of Kingdom Hall and Kingdom Come, but Emily almost from birth was a fervent adherent. It was so cosy, just her and Mummy knowing the Truth, in loving togetherness. She was sorry, in a respectful way, for the teachers and other children at school, who seldom spoke of God by His right name, Jehovah. Occasionally she would put them right, but on the whole she preferred to keep her beliefs for just her and Mummy, and of course the kind Brothers and Sisters of Kingdom Hall. Good-natured, simple and child-like, the faded-looking Brothers and Sisters made a great fuss of Emily, who wouldn't stay in her seat during a service, but flitted around the Hall handing out little love messages she had written for her favourite grown-ups.

Living in an enclosed world, that of the Truth, gave Emily confidence, happiness and a feeling that the world was a safe and easily-explainable place, under the control of Jehovah and Mummy. Her precocious air of perfect ease among grown-ups strange and familiar, to whom she would self-importantly announce:- "I am now about to do a special dance", owed not a little to the exclusiveness of Witness life. Her world felt as safe and ordered as that of a peasant child in a land where one religion is believed by everybody. At the same time, she felt that she enjoyed a privilege not given to everyone. Much as she admired her Mummy, she could grow anxious at her Mummy's daring and adventurous way of making pleasantries with shopkeepers and others who had probably never heard of Jehovah's Witnesses.

If her Mummy, while out shopping, stopped to speak to a grown-up in the street, Emily would loudly whisper, glancing back at the departing adult, "Is she in the Truth?"

Last and probably least of the Vaughan household in Cheltenham was the cat Stoat. Mrs. Vaughan had found Stoat as a lost starving kitten, and brought him home, to Emily's joy. The cat, a scraggy, scrawny, stretched-out-thin-and-wizened animal, half-blind, and with an uncertain temper, was shaped rather like its namesake, inexpertly stuffed. Mrs. Vaughan was convinced that the cat was half-stoat by birth, and solemnly told visitors that the fawn-coloured animal was a cross between a stoat and a moggy.

Only Aunty Dolly believed this, and indeed felt it only too likely, as she and "that creature" glared at one another.

So, on a fine day in spring, let us accompany Mrs. Vaughan and Emily to the Kingdom Hall. They hold hands as they toddle along, Emily hopping and skipping and shaking her grandmother's arm like a fish on a line.

The Hall is a large bleak place, and to an outsider, the service too would seem bleak and never-ending. There are no musical instruments, the few hymns are plain and tuneless, and the Bible, re-written to Witness standards, has lost a great deal of its poetry. Everyone studies their Watchtower literature as if it is school homework, while Brother Richardson asks questions about it, pointing eagerly at those who hold their hands up and brightly calling out "Right!" or "Wrong!" Over an hour is spent in this fashion.

Emily and her grandmother frowningly pursue their papers, occasionally looking around the congregation to see who's there and what they're doing. Look, five year old Brian has fallen into a tantrum (something to do with losing a crayon) and his Mum has had to carry him into the soundproof room as if he were a baby. So notes Emily, while Mrs. Vaughan is more interested in the gloomy expression of young Brother So-and-So, who has been forbidden to speak and has been sent to Coventry for a crime known only to himself, his newly-married wife and the minister. Probably fornication, the only allowable reason for divorce among members.

"Just look at this picture of a monster, in the magazine," whispered Emily. "Look, it's a giant lamb with a dragon face and a frog jumping out of its mouth!"

"It must be one of the sinful nations of the earth," her grandmother replied. "Yes, look, it's Anglo-America and the frog symbolises Babbling. That's because Americans are always babbling, like film stars and Billy Graham. Admiring people like that is creature worship, you know! It's terrible to believe in nations – it can lead to patriotism!"

"What's that, Mummy?"

"It's too hard to explain now. Turn over the page and read quietly to yourself *The Story of Jute*. It's very interesting, all about string."

"Hello, my name is Mr. Jute," Emily read effortlessly. She could read better than some of the adult Brethren, who stumbled over their Bibles and had to be helped by the minister.

Regular breathing soon showed Emily that her Mummy had fallen asleep. She gave her a poke, and found her place in the Bible. However, Mrs.Vaughan soon succumbed to slumber once more, and Emily left her seat and walked up and down the aisle greeting people cheerfully. She was the pet of the place. Her greeting of young Brian, returned from the crying room, left something to be desired.

"You should stay in the Truth. Jesus said we must hit people, specially cry babies."

Her tone of polite yet strict censure was copied from that of the minister, who often spoke more in sorrow than anger over the evils of celebrating Christmas and birthdays and of claiming that Jesus died on a cross and not on a stake. However, she made a merely playful punch in the direction of Brian's head, and then skipped back to her seat.

Today there would be a special treat. In place of Holy Communion, when wine and bread were passed around from hand to hand and then returned untasted to the rostrum, there would be an after-service Practice Meeting.

"I especially urge all those with children to stay behind for the Practice," said the minister. "Children must learn everything about the Truth while there is time. As we know, in the New World that Jehovah has promised to make for us here below, children will only continue to be born for a short while. Eventually there will be no more children, so we must do our best for the ones we have. Our New World is even now being prepared for us by Jehovah. It was begun in nineteen fourteen, completed in a spiritual sense ten years later, and will finally arrive ready made as the Old World ends very soon, in nineteen seventy five. We may have only two years in which to bring the people of Cheltenham to the Truth. That is why Practice is very important, and everyone on the stage must leave as soon as they hear the bell."

With great glee and gusto, family parties mounted the stage, some acting the parts of reluctant householders, others those of door-to-door Witnessing Witnesses. The idea of Practice, the amateur dramatics of Kingdom Hall, was to train the Witnesses to convince total strangers of the Truth. This was to be done by dint of fascinating conversation, full of flawless logic, culminating in the householder's invitation to come in for a cup of tea and a Bible study. In this fictitious version of Witnessing, the householder would usually agree to seek the Truth without much delay.

Children at Kingdom Hall greatly enjoyed these plays, which may have compensated them for the loss of Christmas. Apart from snivelling Brian, the Witness children seemed unusually confident, well-mannered and innocent, compared with their school-friends outside the Truth. Each Practice lasted for ten minutes, with a rapid "all change" whenever Brother Richardson rang the bell. Anyone who wished to take part could do so, and all dialogue was invented on the spot. Mrs. Vaughan and Emily remained as spectators, as their friends came and went, all over-acting noisily.

In one sketch, a man answering the door reacted to the question, "Have you ever thought about the End of the World?" by rushing out roaring and seizing the chief Witness by the collar.

"My son died because he believed you lot, he refused a blood transfusion and now he's an angel flying round and round in the air!"

"Calm yourself, my friend," came the suave reply. "Your son is not flying, he has prepared himself a place in the New World. Would you like to meet him there? You can do so if you read the Bible, but the Bible cannot be understood without help. We offer you that help."

"Really? Come in!"

Ring! "Next, please!"

A swift rearrangement of chairs and a screen transformed the street and doorstep scene to that of a front room in a Divided Household.

"Whenever I want my dinner you go out Witnessing to the Truth, and I'm starving!" a bad-tempered husband complained.

Divided households and methods of humouring unsaved husbands were issues of great importance for many Witnesses. It never happened the other way round, either in these plays or in life – no Witness husband ever confronted a Truthless wife. Mrs. Vaughan watched this sketch with interest. If the Colonel were still alive, she well knew, he would probably have reacted to a Witness knock on the door with a blast from a Lee Enfield rifle. Only after his death had Mrs. Vaughan stumbled on the Truth.

"My God, woman!" the husband in the play raved.

"You speak of God, dear, but do you know His proper name? It is Jehovah. Please do not use His name in vain."

"How can I use His name in vain when according to you I don't even know what it is! Jehovah, eh?"

At the sound of the holy name, a religious light dawned in the husband's eyes, but was quickly extinguished by a ring of the bell and the all-about-turn of the next sketch.

Tired but happy, the Witnesses eventually emerged into the fresh air and set off for their various homes. Next morning, many of them would be out, a cloud of Witnesses, descending on the streets of Cheltenham in groups of five or six, all clutching black briefcases.

Before going home that day, Emily and her Mummy went for a walk as usual in Pittville Park with bread for the ducks. They walked up the hill to the mansion-like Pittville Pump House, peeped through the French windows, then descended to the place where a semi-circle of stone bridge met its reflection in a perfect letter 'o'. A mallard swam through the reflection, scattering it in ripples. Emily sighed and thought of Duck and Bear at home.

"Isn't it lovely?" said Mummy. "Just think, the New World will be even better than this."

Emily had something else to look forward to. Aunty Rose, Uncle Ahmad and Zebba would soon be coming over for a day.

"Taken at Sebastapol." This proud emblem, engraved with large iron-inset lettering, impressed all who saw it on the huge stone pedestal in Imperial Square at the heart of Cheltenham. Uncle Ahmad, Aunty Rose's husband, was puzzled.

"*What* has been taken at Sebastapol?" he asked.

"The cannon," Mrs. Vaughan replied.

"What cannon? There *is* no cannon."

"Of course not. It was taken away in the war for scrap and got lost," Mrs. Vaughan explained.

Ahmad still looked a bit befogged, but Aunty Rose gave a peal of laughter.

"Daddy always used to say it should have read *Retaken at Cheltenham*," she said.

Meanwhile, Emily and Zebba played chasing games around the pedestal. They looked rather like twins, as Zebba was large for her age, and combined Eastern girlish bounciness with West Country pink cheeks and sparkling eyes. With many zig zags the family crossed the park-like Square to the railings where a worldly friend of Mrs. Vaughan exhibited her watercolour pictures along with many others, in the Art Society show.

"Why, Mrs. Chandler, I haven't seen you since so-called Christmas," the diehard Witness greeted her friend.

Emily and Zebba's day out ended in the white-tabled teashop across the road from the fountain. There, the children played at hiding under the table and the grown-ups drank cappuccino and leafed through glossy magazines.

Their conversation would have struck an eavesdropping outsider as odd, for both the women spoke ardently at cross purposes about their respective religions, Jehovah's Witnessing and Mohammedism. Aunty Rose spoke vehemently about the English and the Hindus, enemies of Islam, while Uncle Ahmad smiled indulgently and kept an eye on the children. If Aunty Rose had originally converted to Islam in order to please her husband, then she had long ago left him behind in the fervency stakes. He was only a token Moslem, far too fat to bend to Mecca and far too good-natured to be a fanatic. Whereas Aunty Rose was forever on the lookout for slights to Islam from the Eternal Infidel.

"Look at that!" she cried, brandishing an article about Historic Turkey. "It says here that Crusaders from England killed Moslem Turks in the Middle Ages! That's imperialism! What right had British Crusaders to carry on like that?"

"Oh dear," murmured Mrs. Vaughan. "Perhaps they were angry at the way Turks treat women. Look, it says that English girls must be careful when hitch-hiking."

"That can't be what annoyed the Crusaders! Those girls only get into trouble in Moslem countries because they're so ignorant that they wear short skirts."

"That's like us, we don't encourage short skirts at Kingdom Hall. But then we are allowed *into* Kingdom Hall, while I doubt if women can go into mosques alongside the men. Your father always used to say ..."

"Never mind what Daddy said! Of *course* women are allowed into mosques, only not the part where the service is going on."

"Look, Emily!" Mrs. Vaughan said, peering under the table to show her granddaughter a picture of two lion cubs. Emily and Zebba both admired cats and their relatives for their spitfire fury. Sometimes Emily provoked her cat Stoat on purpose and got scratched.

"They'll all be there," Mrs. Vaughan continued dreamily, staring into the middle distance with a spiritual expression.

"Who'll be where?" asked her daughter testily.

"Lions and tigers and their cubs. Just look at this week's *Watchtower*. There is a very good picture on Page Seven of Jehovah's Kingdom on earth somewhere near what looks like the Rocky Mountains. Couples of every race, a Coloured couple, a White couple and a Chinese couple are all having picnics while their children are playing with tamed lions and tigers. When Jehovah reigns on earth, the lions and tigers will be tame and a little child shall lead them. Won't it be wonderful? Emily and Zebba will *love* it, I'm sure. That's the true meaning of Safari Parks. Jehovah has arranged for the lions and tigers to be here in England already, so He can make them gentle when His Kingdom is established."

A few chocolate éclairs later, the family boarded a bus, alighted at the ornate Victorian pillar box with the pinnacle on top, and made their way back to the flat. Aunty Dolly, the cleaning lady, had already let herself in and was glaring at the cat. Quite one of the family, she switched on the television and sat watching a noisy game show while the others talked.

Emily and Zebba whispered something to Mrs. Vaughan, who clapped her hands and announced, "The Arab dance!"

With great assurance, Emily, now dressed in a floating flimsy Dance of the Seven Veils attire, ran into the middle of the room and began a mannered dance learned at school. Zebba helped out with spirited hops.

To Aunty Dolly's fury, Ahmad leaned over and turned down the volume on the television. Looking more pickled-in-vinegar than ever, the angry woman pointedly ignored the children and tried in vain to listen to the show.

The dance ended, and everyone applauded except Aunty Dolly, who remarked, "I wonder what he's saying on telly now?"

Zebba demonstrated an Eastern dance, and Ahmad turned off the television altogether. To Aunty Dolly, this smacked of blasphemy. She stared at the silver dot on the screen as if willing it not to vanish, but vanish it did. Inwardly, Aunty

Dolly vowed vengeance on Uncle Ahmad. Outwardly, she turned on the vacuum cleaner, which ended the dance and gave Emily a slight asthma attack.

She would show them. They all knew that she, Aunty Dolly, had nearly been a famous dancer and might yet become a famous writer. She had already thought of the title of her autobiography, "Cloakroom Lady", and now only needed an enterprising publisher to write it for her. Gathering up her things, she made ready to leave, pausing at the door to deliver a lengthy speech.

"That's a lovely dance the liddle girls 'as done, but as I've often said, I could 'ave been a dancer." (Aunty Dolly dropped her h's with great emphasis, opening her mouth wide each time.) "It all began when I was only four, I used to dress up and kick so strong I once put my foot right through the mirror. When the Tiller Girls came yer to Cheldnam, I nearly joined 'em only the manager got familiar. So I went to the theatre and asked if they 'ad a job and the man says 'aye' and so I became what I was for twenty years, a Cloakroom Lady.

"That way, I met all the stars and all the best Society. One day the Duchess of Gloucester came in. She looked at me just as I'm looking at you. 'Yer's your coat, your Grace,' I said. Do you know, she spoke to me just like I'm speaking to you. 'Thank you,' she said."

"Close the door after you, Aunty Dolly, there's a draught," put in Uncle Ahmad helpfully.

Slam!

" Bye bye, Aunty Dolly!" called Emily.

On a hot summer evening, not long after her humiliation at the television-turning-off hands of Uncle Ahmad, Aunty Dolly could be seen emerging purposefully from the dark snug of a small pub that smelled strongly of sweet sugary beer. Having spent several hours cleaning over at the posh side of town, she was now making her way home along a narrow but busy shopping street that led towards her council estate.

Popularly thought of as an old people's town, Cheltenham is actually the reverse, and the pavements thronged with teenagers. Even the skinheads in their shaved heads and big boots moved absent mindedly aside to allow Aunty Dolly and other tough old birds of the treaclebeer streets to pass.

Supermarkets had not then come into vogue, and Aunty Dolly turned briskly past Victorian red brick shops, ironmongers, sticky bun shops and record shops where the young gathered to gaze at posters in the windows – "All the Young Dudes" and "Diamond Dogs".

At the entrance to Phoenix Passage, she stopped to greet a friend, then gave a cry of amazement.

"What's the matter?" asked her shopping-laden neighbour.

"I know that man – it's that darky!" came the reply.

The friend followed Aunty Dolly's gaze towards a car driven slowly through the traffic by a middle-aged brown-skinned man. Beside the man, leaning on his shoulder, was a young blonde with long hair. If that was Uncle Ahmad, then that certainly was *not* Aunty Rose!

"Oh no, I don't think that's him!" Aunty Dolly said, after a pause, in a voice of deep disappointment. A second glance had shown her that the man was a stranger. It wasn't fair! She nearly had Uncle Ahmad where she wanted him – in trouble.

By the time Aunty Dolly reached her door, she had had second thoughts. Suppose that *had* been Uncle Ahmad! It might just as well have been. Both men were brown. Both wore suits. If the false Uncle Ahmad carried on with blondes, what might the *real* Uncle Ahmad do? Before long, Aunty Dolly felt convinced of Uncle Ahmad's guilt.

"Fornication! Just what Jehovah doesn't like," mused Mrs. Vaughan when she'd heard the 'news'. Something of a gossip herself, she could not long conceal her thoughts from her daughter. Discord followed.

In less than a year's time, Ahmad and Rose found themselves in the throes of an acrimonious divorce. Zebba sided with her father, who claimed custody of the child. He wanted to take her back to his mother's house in Pakistan, and she wanted to go.

Aunty Rose's belief in Islam vanished so completely that she could scarcely remember anything about it.

"I hope we get Judge So-and-So, as I've heard he's really colour-prejudiced!" Rose exclaimed with passionate vindictiveness.

This remark shocked Mrs. Vaughan, who had a Quaker-like sympathy for all coloured people. She believed that they all had been slaves before they got independence.

The Judge did not live up to his reputation, and Mrs. Vaughan, Emily and Rose were never more to see Uncle Ahmad and his devoted Zebba.

For Emily and Mrs. Vaughan, nothing could be the same. Somehow, during the divorce, Emily had discovered that her *Mummy* was really her Gran and her *Aunty* was really her Mummy. An acute attack of asthma followed. Emily recovered her health, but not her love and respect for her grandmother.

"You're not my real mother! Why should I listen to you?" she would taunt.

Duck and Bear were forgotten, but Emily and Stoat became allies. Aunty Dolly no longer came to see them, but sometimes cheerfully greeted them in town. Aunty Rose was now Mummy, and occasionally called to take her out.

At the age of eight, Emily started a poem called *The Darkness of My Heart*, but could not finish it. Her grandmother's influence waning, Emily felt her real mother's scepticism. Her safe world seemed like a wall full of cracks, about to fall, like Jericho. With her own hands, she was pulling at the wall that so long had protected her, the wall that had kept her safe from harm in Fairyland. She had begun to doubt the Truth.

Multiculturalism: Is it a viable and acceptable concept?
An Analysis and Examination of the Concept of Multiculturalism

The Revd. John G. Lovejoy

Introduction

Recently - I had occasion to visit Newcastle-upon-Tyne, and leaving the Central Station took the bus to the East End along the Shields Road. An elderly man sat down next to me, and we struck up a conversation, as happens rather easily in this city. On hearing I was arriving from London, the man exclaimed, "Fram London! Aa heor it's a madhoose doon- theor; they're trying to git us aal ti accept this *multi-culturalism*, but we div'nt want it, man!" You will probably get the general drift of this. The man alighted before more could be said but his remarks are not untypical of the puzzlement and suspicion with which the concept of *multiculturalism* is viewed in the area. So we must look at *multiculturalism*, but first of all we must remind ourselves what we mean by *a culture*.

A The Basic Terms – *Culture* and *Nation* – Patchwork Quilt Theory

We can suppose that for innumerable ages mankind has lived in societies, and that each of them developed a way-of-life that differed from the others, so that there would have been a great diversity of cultures the world over. Such diversity was required in part by the equally remarkable contrasts of terrain and climate, but only in part, for Man could develop quite different cultures in a very similar setting, while he also had a cultural tenacity which enabled him to transfer, albeit with modifications, a culture to a region of the world in which it did not evolve. For this global cultural diversity I like to use the analogy of the *Patchwork Quilt*, but there is another useful analogy, that of the wild botanical strains which underlie our modern cereal crops, suggesting the global diversity of human cultures might be far more important than most people realise. Now a culture, in this full anthropological sense, is the way of life of a particular people, or nation; that is, a group of human beings who have belonged together for a long period of time and who assume that they will continue to do so, sharing their cultural traits as a sort of common coinage. It takes very many cultural traits to make up any particular human culture, even in the archaic 'hunter-gatherer' societies of the Middle Stone Age, but they can be divided roughly into two sorts - the physical and easily observable traits on one hand, such as cooking methods and weapons, and on the other hand the mental and conceptual traits which together form the underlying meaning-pattern of the society in question. This latter has to be examined, by looking at the language and other interactions of persons in order to find their semantic content.

Physically you may see a form of dancing, but the meaning of this activity will differ widely according to whether you look at an Australian Aboriginal Corroboree or, alternatively, at an English Old-Tyme dancing class. It is the mental-conceptual basis of a human culture which is more durable, and thus in many ways more important. Australian Aborigines, again, are clearly unable to live in the way their ancestors did, but they can still allow their ancestral culture to inform their minds and to underpin their still distinct societies as well as making sure that this shared communal pattern of thinking and values be handed on to succeeding generations. Now a human culture does not exist in a vacuum. There has to be a particular grouping of people such as will share and live their culture together, as well as transmit it to successive generations. Such a grouping of people is usually called a 'nation', but we also have 'ethnic group' and 'a people' (prefixed by the article). There is a problem here in that the word 'nation' is often used loosely, especially with the intended meaning of 'all citizens of a particular State', but this is very far from the original and still correct sense. Here, the word 'nation' will be used for a grouping of people who share a common culture and communal identity, who have a sense of common origin, and who are able to transmit this shared identity and culture from generation to generation. Usually a nation will have a particular territory as its homeland. The modern term 'ethnic group' has essentially the same meaning as 'nation', but is used especially frequently in a situation where there are fragments of a nation, perhaps far from their original homeland. For example, it would be natural to speak of 'the Slovenian Nation' in Slovenia, but should there be a substantial number of them in Britain with a well organised communal structure, then they would be referred to as 'the Slovenian ethnic group/community'. In all likelihood they would have British nationality in the sense of State citizenship. At this point someone might well object to the very notion of the Patchwork Quilt. It might be objected that the world would be a much more peaceful and safer place without all these potentially conflicting cultures and identities. A value judgment has to be made, and the view put forward here is that a multiplicity of cultures and national identities on Earth is fundamentally a good thing, even with the attendant risks of conflict or misunderstanding which the human race as a whole has always had to deal with.

The reasons for this view are adduced briefly as follows:-

a Hitherto, before the development of modern communications and marketing, it has always been impossible to envisage the unification of the world with a global culture and identity. Arguably, it might now be possible but is it realistic to think that there could be global agreement that such an aim was desirable? If not, the process would have to proceed by forcible means, and this would be abhorrent.

b Different cultures have different insights and strengths, and who knows when they might be more widely needed? It is readily conceded that one culture may profitably borrow from another on occasion, but this is possible only if there are other cultures in existence.

c Sometimes a particular culture will evolve a trait which most human beings would regard as dangerous, unjust, cruel, inhuman, degrading, or abhorrent in one way or another. Again, this is not readily to be seen unless there are other human societies such as will provide a contrast and counterbalance.

d It is not at all certain that conflict is more likely between widely differing cultures. Very often the bitterest conflicts are between two peoples who share almost everything in common, culturally, but who differ mainly in that they have quite distinct senses of communal identity, and have a conflict of interests. In such a situation it is likely that they share a territory or have contiguous territories. Northern Ireland is a classic example of this, and it should be emphasised that difference of religion is not the key issue here, but rather the inherited sense of belonging to two quite different ethnic communities.

e If, in some futuristic setting, human beings in general were to be induced to adopt just one culture and one communal identity, such a situation would be inherently unstable, and new lines of fissure would develop, perhaps based in the first instance on differing tastes in consumer products. In the end, the contrived and artificial world society would break up and reform under warlords and rival political leaders, scrambling for territory.

f A great virtue of the Patchwork Quilt model, which has been the *de facto* situation for the human race up till now, is that it gives us all the challenge and the task of reaching out to the other, to the different, while at the same time having one's own culture and nation as a basis from which to realise this. In this task there have been terrible failures in the past, but also remarkable successes, and the failures do not at all invalidate this proposition, that awareness and respect for other cultures and identities should beneficially balance and complement appreciation and enjoyment of one's own. Moreover, such awareness of the other, that which is different, ought usually to enable us to perceive our own culture and to reinforce our own sense of nationhood with a clarity and depth which would not otherwise be possible. Where this does not happen there is something terribly wrong, as we shall see.

B Difficulties – Factors which disrupt the Patchwork Quilt model

The analogy used, the Patchwork Quilt, might suggest a near-perfect state of harmony in diversity, but it is clear that the reality is all too often far from this. In the past, empires have arisen where a particular state, representing a vigorous and populous nation, which might well run the risk of outstripping its resources, begins to bring neighbouring peoples into subjection and to conform them to its own culture in many respects, as well as to exploit their resources. Thus were the Assyrians in their time, though some empires were more benign than this example. But there are more immediate problems. The modern State demands our attention, for while in some cases, and ideally, it may represent the interests of a particular nation, at the same time it makes possible a quite different model of communal identity based not on shared nationhood inherited from time immemorial but rather on legally expressed citizenship recognised by the modern State government. Under modern conditions most people would agree that the State is a necessity, but here are some possible complications, apart from the risk of emergent empires as already mentioned:

a The State tends to usurp the functions of a nation, as it takes over the institutions of government, generates symbols of citizenship, evolves machinery for enacting legislation, controls the economy and monetary system, becomes responsible for external relations and foreign policy, and polices the nation itself. By controlling the educational curricula the State can warp or weaken even the national awareness of identity. *National* identity is often seen as a competitor to *State* identity (citizenship) and is *discouraged*.

b The State is not always co-extensive with the nation. Clearly, some modern States have frontiers which run through the middle of a traditional national territory, as happens in post-colonial Africa and in the extreme case a nation may find itself without any State willing to accept its very existence, as in the case of the Kurdish People. Conversely, many modern States comprise a number of nations, or fragments of nations, and while in some cases one particular nation may act as a core, providing the dominant culture and language, in other instances the State may be the one unifying arbiter between many ethnic communities.

c The State may be too big. The obvious instance of this being the U.S.S.R., which comprised very many ethnic communities and whole nations, but in which centralised control became very wasteful of resources, and necessarily oppressive even had there not been an ideology which favoured ruthlessness.

d A particular development in recent centuries has been the formation of what are here labelled *Settler-States*, where a large, sparsely-populated land came to be discovered by migrants from other parts of the world. In most cases, the first incoming settlers to these lands were predominantly of one nationality, and they formed the core identity, culture, and language of a colony, or group of colonies, which later gained independence and became a state. The USA is the prime example of the Settler-State. In all such States there was an indigenous nation which was overwhelmed and submerged in the process. The quest for industrial and economic growth created the *need* for a larger population, with the result that immigrants were sought from places other than the mother state. Hence, the populations became ethnically mixed and the need became greater to merge them into a new inclusive civic identity which owed loyalty not to the nation but to the state and its symbols, e.g. flag and constitution.

In this way, the State took on a much greater role than usual in defining, or even fabricating, a sense of communal identity and common citizenship. Even so, ethnic communities cling to a sense of common origin, as they have done in the USA, Canada and Australia, but the meaning given to the word *nation* is often transferred, with reference to Federal or Commonwealth citizenship as an artificial nationhood, supplanting all ancestral ones. The Patchwork Quilt model for human diversity has, however, been further disturbed by the proliferation of modern applied technology, systems of global communication and travel, the trend to globalisation of trading systems with the emergence of the E.U. and other trading blocs, trans-state corporations, and the appearance of many vast conurbations of unprecedented proportions. In short, we have to take into account all that is meant by *modern civilisation*, as we loosely call it, in whatever current form it has attained. One could write a separate book on the effects of these developments on any individual human society or nation, but what, in outline are the main ways in which modernity has impinged on nations and ethnic communities? It is not only archaic tribal peoples that have suffered a massive disruption of their earlier patterns of living, though on them the effect has been devastating and often wholly destructive.

a With vastly increased facilities of travel, young people are often lost to their home region, perhaps to the cities, to other regions or to another part of the world, when English students attend an American university.

b With successive new forms of rapid global communication, the sharing of thinking by individuals is less likely to be with others of their own nation or community and more likely to be with others, wherever they might live globally, who share these individuals' particular interests and tastes. This cannot do anything to reinforce any individual national culture.

c The globalisation of marketing has already led to an internationalisation of fashion and consumer goods, to the extent that, among young people in the conurbations, loyalty to a particular fashion concept may be as strong as loyalty to a football team, and just about as divisive. Such loyalties may already have submerged any sense of national or ethnic culture and origin.

d The international scale of trade and corporate commercial structures has entailed a corresponding globalisation of the market in human skills, so that it becomes progressively less likely that an individual will ply his skills within the confines of his own nation and culture. Apart from the obvious danger of cultural clash for the individual and his/her family, there is the added danger that some nations may become impoverished of skills, as in the case of the 'brain-drain' as it is often called. Further, when young single persons live and work in another part of the world, it is hardly a surprise when they find a partner - marital or otherwise - in the society where they work. In this way, a nation may be drained of a substantial proportion of its young people, and the children of such couples have the not-too-easy task of making sense of two cultures and identities, and perhaps of choosing between them.

e Quite apart from any transnational or global implications of technological advance, there are very many ways in which the modern way of life, based so much on applied technology in ever increasing ways, has led to a fragmentation, degradation, and loss of transmission of particular national and ethnic cultures. Elsewhere this has been labelled *deculturalisation*,[1] and it shows itself to be an erosion of the mental patterning which until very recent times would persist in a nation through countless generations, despite periodic disaster and reverses of fortunes. This is not the place to describe deculturalisation in detail but in any large city one can observe very large numbers of people - not all of them very young - who either do not know how to live as human beings or else do not know who they really are. In the latter case, typically, they will appear to have affected some substitute identity, borrowed from another part of the world or suggested by international marketing. It is to be noted that in certain parts of the world, such cultural erosion is consciously resisted and becomes a political issue. South Korea is such an example.

f There are no doubt many who would argue that we should all make a virtue out of necessity and simply tell ourselves that the modern civilisation, however we understand it, is here to stay and that the human race as a whole had better get used to the fact. Against such a view we must recall that when and wherever Modern Man first appeared on earth, it must have been a very long time ago indeed, and that for most of those vast reaches of time (by any human reckoning) men lived in late Palaeolithic or Mesolithic conditions. I seem to belong to the generation which made the leap from naked fires, manipulated with bellows, tongs, pokers, shovels and the like, to the electronically controlled systems which we see about us now. In short there is no good reason to think that Man is equipped for living in our modern conditions and conurbations. What I observe around me would seem to bear out this view. It is one thing to generate the modern way of life; it is another thing to have to live with it. Another objection to the view anticipated above is that whatever the modern civilisation is, it is not stable. The generation of applied technology and of commercial frameworks for its efficient mass-marketing seems to proceed not merely without abate but rather with an accelerating tempo. This fact is reinforced by the application of technological change to all means of mass communication and information sharing. Yet such advances - if such they be - seem to be matched by a parallel decay of those elements in human society which have always been thought to underpin human cultures and civilisations.

Human beings in the so-called *advanced* societies are experiencing unparalleled confusion in what can collectively be called sources of spirituality, and I have long noted a marked decay in the usage of the English language - the language which has become the international language. Other *bedrock* features of human society which seem widely to be threatened are: - the normal patterning of human family and kinship; the stability of the way of life in the rural areas - exactly where the roots of culture and society usually lie; the clear expression of inherited regional identities, which is a feature of any culture; and the unwillingness to include, without question, a grounding in the beginnings and origins of one's culture in

---

[1] *The Deculturalisation of the English People*, J. Lovejoy, Athelney, 2000.

the curricula for instruction of the young. We could go on, but what is said here must now continue in an even, more condensed manner. The foregoing discussion is intended to be a background to the view, here expressed, that the Patchwork Quilt model of global human cultural diversity is not the only one which was generally valid in traditional times, but continues to be so. This whole argument serves as a prelude to the critique of *multiculturalism* as conceived in England, and this is what must now be addressed.

C England – the situation for the English nation and the policy of the state

Currently, there are many reasons for supposing that the Westminster Government is at best indifferent, and at worst hostile, to any continuing English culture and awareness of English national identity. Reasons for this view are listed:-

a *The change in meaning of the term 'Great Britain' since my own boyhood.*

When I was very young, *Great Britain* was taken to mean a Union of Scotland and England, with which Wales was included, and it was understood that the three nations continued to exist within the one political framework. Thus, our nationhood, or ethnic identity, was that of England, Scotland and Wales, respectively, while our State Citizenship was collectively *British*, and we thus referred to ourselves as *British Subjects*. Now, however, the political-legal machinery of the State is being used by the Westminster Government to displace the historical ethnic/national identities – this especially applies to English identity. British Citizenship is being used to embrace everyone, of whatever origin, whom the Government is willing to include, and to exclude all others. The word *nation* is now used by many politicians and others to mean the State and its citizens. As might be expected, it is a practice adopted from the USA.

b *The massive scale of immigration into England during the past fifty years.*

It is understandable and acceptable that there should be immigration at a certain level, especially as the nations of Britain have in the past taken in various groups of *refugees* - in the traditional sense of that word. It follows that there should be no difficulty in accepting the existence among us of ethnic minorities of whom some, such as the Greek community, have existed here for a very long time. However, it is clear that the sheer scale of immigration, since the late fifties, has been on a massive and unprecedented scale, such that in some urban areas the English themselves have become an ethnic minority or non-existent. It is impossible to contradict this. It is necessary only to venture into the main streets of many a suburban area to test this observation. Those of my own age are acutely aware that this situation is of very recent origin, for when we were very young there was no visible indication that ethnic minorities existed, with very few minor and local exceptions. This massive immigration seems to me to have been encouraged by successive Westminster Governments for economic reasons, and the indigenous nations of Britain were not consulted.

c *The United Kingdom is deemed by the State to be a USA style Settler-State.*

It is impossible to avoid the conclusion that H.M. Government no longer views Britain as the homeland of the English, Scots and Welsh nations, but rather as a Settler-State into which all are to be welcomed as long as they fit into the economy, as the Government from time to time defines it, and the constructed ideology of loyalty to the concept of U.K. (British) State Citizenship. English people, it has come to seem, are to be classified merely as *White Britons*.

d *There is a proliferation of propaganda at all levels of public discourse, in the broadcast media and in the press, suggesting that any attempt to develop an English ethnic voice is to be regarded as 'extreme right wing', 'potentially violent', 'without historical basis' and also morally beyond the pale.*

One example of this is The Future of Multi-Ethnic Britain, (The Parekh Report) published 2000 by The Runnymede Trust. Another example, seen recently in Newcastle upon Tyne, features a poster displaying the colours of the *Toon* soccer strip, Black and White. As I understand it, these colours symbolise the coal and the snow which have always been so prominent on Tyneside. However, the poster seizes the chance to suggest that the correct symbolism is that the soccer team is to be regarded as multi-ethnic, drawing on up to sixteen different nations. The double standard implicit here has escaped the formulators of the poster. The ethnic minority players belong to *nations*. Geordies, it seems, are to forget that they are members of a nation and belong to a very distinct region of a particular country, and to forget that they were once represented in football by their own men. Black and White. Hmm. Snow tends to melt, doesn't it?

e *State institutions seem impervious to any view other than Multiculturalism.*

I have personally contacted Government ministers about the implications of multiculturalism, writing through the local MP, but the replies have always suggested that my views about the English people are obsolete, and that the economic advantages of embracing multiculturalism are incalculable. The Church is remarkably silent on the issue, except to echo the Government view. As a Christian myself, active in the Church of England for many years before transferring recently to the Orthodox Church, I have tried to point out to Church leaders that the English people are being threatened with the collapse of their identity and culture but the prophetic awareness that I looked for seems to be missing. However, I have found that the Orthodox Church does have an understanding of the issues involved, but they are currently a minority body in Britain, and without the influence that the Church of England should have, or the Roman Catholics.

f *The Education System fails to reinforce and to transmit an awareness of English culture and identity.*

I am not a teacher or educationalist, but I meet those who are, and I meet children and young people. I see no evidence that English children are receiving an introduction to their own culture or to the stories about the origins of the English nation such as would enable a clear sense of communal identity: rather, I get the impression that history is being distorted and falsified in such a way as to put the English in a consistently bad light or to suggest that they never had any clear, significant existence as a distinct people. This impression is all the stronger when one remembers that education in such matters is not just a matter for schools, but also takes place through the broadcast media, or through Local Authority libraries and exhibitions.

Such distortions include the following:-

(i) *Concentrating on the history of the land rather than on the people – the nation – that lives on it.*

One hears such things as, 'This is a land which has always welcomed new peoples from elsewhere.' Nonsense. A *land*, as such, neither welcomes nor shuns anyone. As for the English people, they have not always welcomed new peoples from elsewhere, as anyone with a rudimentary knowledge of history would know.

(ii) *'There have been waves and waves of immigrants all through the centuries.'*

This is simply not true. Waves and waves of closely related Germanic tribesmen in the fifth and sixth centuries, yes, and collectively they came to be called *English*. The Danish and Norse presence was also considerable (not welcomed but resisted), though being far fewer in number they were assimilated. Yes there have been Huguenot, Irish, and Jewish settlers but nothing approaching the scale of the massive immigrations that came after the Second World War, which were with the encouragement of the British government.

(iii) *Making history begin at the Norman Conquest, or with the Tudors, or with the Industrial Revolution.*

It is vitally important to begin history with the known Beginnings of a nation, for that is what lays the foundation of a communal identity which the children need so much. Accumulated history can be simply too much, so it is better to be selective about succeeding centuries, and to concentrate on times of crisis and change in the nation's history. The principal reason for the British state selecting 1066 as the start of history is that it marks the beginning of the British state and British monarchy.

(iv) *'The English were a bad White people, who had an empire.'*

Every nation should take responsibility for its mistakes, though it is open to question to what extent the *British* Empire was a mistake, and to what extent ordinary English people were its victims or had much say in the matter. They provided the cannon fodder. But if you wish a nation to take responsibility for any particular events in their history, you first have to allow that they continue to exist. Demoralised *White* children cannot take responsibility for anything in the past – they have been stripped of their national identity and been allocated a racial identity. Moreover, I have had the impression that history, for some children, seems to consist primarily in learning about the exact layout of eighteenth century slave ships. What about the conditions of the new urban working classes in newly industrialised England and Scotland?

No. The primary task of an education system is that of reinforcing the communal culture and identity of the children of a particular nation - in this case the English and then, on that basis, to prepare them for the adult world into which they are growing up. First things first.

D What is *multiculturalism* in the minds of those who promote the concept?

There seem to be two main models of multiculturalism, and I will summarise them separately: -

1. Britain as a mosaic of many ethnic communities, with the over-arching state in total control.

In this concept, there is an intention to reproduce the *Patchwork Quilt* notion on a small scale, within the individual State as well as on the global scale. The State evolves its own ideology/political doctrine, which justifies its existence and reflects the ethos, values, and interests of its governing elite. In doing this it may perhaps draw on the political culture and traditions of one of the ethnic communities in particular, but not being strictly bound to do so, and conversely aiming to appear equidistant from the particular interests and beliefs of any of the ethnic communities in practice. The State is generally stated to embrace *Western Liberal Values*, and these are supposed to be shared by all the political parties so that these latter, having no clear matters of fundamental principle to argue about, concentrate largely on the relative efficiency or otherwise of the party currently in office, and on the worthiness of the office holders.

What is wrong with this model, as applied to Britain and to England especially?

(i) The English, if anything at all, would be only one among many of the 'mosaic' pieces. At worst, they would be known as *White British* with no clear ethnic identity, and thus despised and vilified, not being regarded as one of the 'mosaic' bits. There are many 'ethnic minorities', but no recognised 'ethnic majority'.

(ii) A 'mosaic' of different societies is not itself a society: it is rather a State-controlled political construct. In such circumstances, the risk of inter-ethnic friction cannot be eliminated. In Croydon, Surrey, for instance, inter-ethnic tension usually involves the non-English communities. Slough, Peterborough, Oldham and Bradford are only four of the other centres that have seen inter-communal clashes.

(iii) The English are in a weak position, in relation to the others, for many reasons:-

*   On this 'mosaic' model they are not recognised as the core, indigenous community.

*   The English progressively lose control of the State in any residual sense, as their communal voting power is diminished.

*   The English lack a milieu, a viable ambience, for the needed reconstruction of our damaged culture and its transmission among our own young people. Effectively, that is, we are unable to have the space to be ourselves. The English lack a communal voice. Any attempt to break the silence comes to be labelled 'racist'. (Words like 'racist', 'communist', 'protestant', and so on usually have no clear objective meaning for the speaker, but are serving mainly to convey such attitudes as hatred, scorn, contempt and intimidation.). Even the very act of using the word *English* in a communal, ethnic sense, can elicit this sort of reaction. In modern England you can be

Irish, it would seem, but not English. State ethnic monitoring forms include the option *Irish* but not *English*.

- And a very important point indeed: unlike all the other ethnic communities, the English have no ethnic/cultural base elsewhere in the world. The significance of this cannot be stressed enough. Most ethnic communities in England are very heavily reinforced by the continued existence of the main community within their ancestral homeland, as well as by the parallel religious/spiritual centre that applies in each respective case.

(iv) It is a fallacy to suppose that English culture and identity can or should be reinforced by Australia and Canada, who are busy forging their own patterns. As for the USA, this vast federation is the source of much that is actively dissolving what remains of Englishness, especially among our young people.

As the English are, after all, an ancient North European people, it could be said that the cultures of Germany, Scandinavia, Greece and Russia may continue to reinforce our own, especially in the classical arts, but in the main we stand by ourselves. As for religion and spirituality, it would be best were we to start with what we once had, way back in the first millennium. There are those who are qualified to help us in that quest.

The Irish are a special case. In the first millennium their culture and ours were curiously intertwined, but after the Norman Conquest they came slowly to be subjected to the British state, both politically and economically. Many English people are in part of Irish descent, and many Irish people are derived from an English origin. The problem of the Loyalist community in Northern Ireland is, partly, that they have a crisis of identity. History can be distorted, falsified, ignored and forgotten. It behoves all Irishmen, and Englishmen, too, to go behind the events of the sixteenth and seventeenth centuries (without forgetting them), and to remember the more balanced relationship that we had in the first millennium before the advent of the expansionist Norman/British state. It is there that we shall find things to unite rather than to divide us. In the meantime, there is a strong Irish minority in England, while other Irish people have through choice or habit been assimilated into the English community. And there are elements in early Irish culture that do have a bearing on a full understanding of early English culture, especially in its early Christian phase.

(v) In a 'mosaic' State it is not clear where the ultimate loyalties of the ethnic communities lie, and some communities, and even families and individuals, may find themselves torn. Even as I write these words, at the end of October, 2001, I read of young *Britons* from British-Asian Muslim communities who have chosen to go to Afghanistan to fight alongside the Taliban. Given the strong tendency of young males to look for a cause for which they can fight, as we see also in Northern Ireland, this bodes ill. Such a situation makes us all ask afresh, What exactly is Britain? What does it mean to be a *Briton*? What qualities, traits, institutions and traditions are *British*? Is it not true that, in the last analysis, Britain is an artificial state, a political entity that has no greater, or less, significance than the original Treaty of Union of 1707, in which England - with Wales - and Scotland became part of the same state?

(vi) Moreover, in a State such as this there is no clear value-system from which the State can draw in order to underpin its policies, to follow them through in the teeth of opposition, and to explain them publicly. You cannot get ethics out of a hat, and simply to speak of *Western Values* only clouds the issue, without making anything plain.

Is the State to look for an uneasy and contrived consensus among the leaders of the 'mosaic' of ethnic communities? Would the British government try to listen to the English, and if so, who could speak for us in our currently disorganised and demoralised condition? If the English, who famously 'haven't spoken yet', are to be listened to, will the other communities be told to fall into line and to remember that they are, after all, minority ethnic communities? It is readily agreed that there are some core values which seem to reoccur throughout the human race as a whole, and that the United Nations seems to embody that general drift, but it is also true that ethnic and ethical cleavages often coincide. A particular nation is needed to act as a reservoir for a particular ethical system, which must be integral to that nation's culture as a whole. The English and other indigenous historical peoples of Britain are needed in order to keep a check on the right development of the instruments of central government. The government itself should not set out to be the source of values and beliefs, but rather, in its legislation, to be their corporate and effective expression. Nor can the government please all the ethnic groups.

2.   Britain as a *Western Society*, with a state embracing secular Western values, but where individuals define themselves as they wish, adopting cultural traits on a *pick-and-mix* basis.

In this concept, the much-vaunted cultural diversity has been driven to an even more extreme level, to the level of the nuclear family and the individual. All individuals, from cradle onwards, are encouraged to have maximum exposure to other cultures and religions. The result, where this path is followed to any extent, is said to be *vibrant*, a code word if ever there were one. Such a model starts to fail as soon as we start to think about it. Why?

(i)   First, some highly-coherent ethnic groups from other parts of the world would be exempt from this exposure because they would be greatly resistant to extreme individualism of beliefs, values and identity. The English would not be allowed exemption, and any pretensions of Englishness would be labelled as 'racially coded'.

(ii)   On the *pick-and-mix* model the English would not be recognised at all, or their culture, and there would be further attempts to recycle the very word *English* with the meaning 'All who lawfully live in England'. This would be a merely territorial meaning, not national, and would mean no more than *Southern British*.

(iii) In line with this it will be said that England is a territory that has always welcomed new peoples. It is worthwhile to point out the fallacies behind this remark, which is often repeated: -

- Territories do not welcome anyone. It is peoples who welcome or refuse to do so.
- We do not know what happened in Prehistoric Britain, before England existed, and are not bound by that.
- When the English and related tribes arrived in the British Isles in successive migrations, they were illiterate Iron Age peoples, and it is generally accepted that migrations that occurred in that cultural phase should not be criticised by

later standards. Are the Longobards criticised for entering Italy, or the Slavs for entering Central Europe and the Balkans?

- Similarly with the Scandinavian invasions of England, which were disastrous at the time. However, the English most certainly did not welcome the Northmen.

- Nor did the English welcome the Normans, who took advantage of the dynastic weakness of the English at the time, and of the English preoccupation with the concurrent aggressive intentions of the Norwegians.

- Later incomers come rather under the heading of accepted refugees, and the modern English can be rather proud of our record of accepting people fleeing from persecution. Such peoples, however, were almost always people who were closely related to the English, such as the Huguenots, and who could be easily assimilated. Assimilation was indeed their intention. When I was at school in the late 'forties and early 'fifties, I cannot say that I came across more than about four names that were of French derivation. The Huguenot influx cannot have been anything near as great as has been claimed by some. Since they were assimilated, it does not matter, anyway.

(iv) More importantly, the individualistic *pick-and-mix* model is anthropologically nonsense. Individual human beings need a whole society and a culture to grow up in, and because of our human limitations we can only successfully make one culture our own. Simply, culture is not an individualistic thing, and it needs a particular nation to embody and continue it. Human culture must never be debased to the level of an individual *lifestyle*.

(v)   An individualistic *pick-and-mix* society will in practice result in confused, unhappy individuals all trying to live out some aspect of the *American Dream*, while having a dilettante approach to world religions, philosophies, the arts, alternative therapies and lifestyles, the 'New Age' movement and so forth. Worse still, without a clear communal cultural base, many will become anti-social, criminal, mentally ill, highly dependent on the Social Services, and suffer from various addictions. Drug-taking is *not* an aspect of English culture.

(vi) Such an unstable society will collapse if subject to attack from without or from within.

(vii) An atomised society of this sort is a passive target for international marketing. It seems to me that modern marketing goes so far as to manipulate the minds of people in such a way as to make them want the products.

In practice, multiculturalism seems to fall somewhere between the models (1) and (2) on a sliding scale.

E The reasons why multiculturalism is being urged upon the English people.

It must be admitted that it is not wholly clear to me what the explanation is for the incessant and relentless promotion of multiculturalism by all those agencies that are best placed to mould public opinion. However, we have sufficient information to start the discussion.

The concept of multiculturalism seems to fit in with the preoccupation of the central government's over-arching ideal of the global free-market economy and with its regional manifestation in the EU. Regarding the latter, of course, there is much disagreement about the political aspects of the developing EU, but there is wide consensus in governing circles about its commercial and economic machinery.

The fact is that the *Patchwork Quilt* analogy of human cultural diversity fits ill with modern global economic theory, and the existence of markedly differing human cultures, in the full anthropological sense of that word *culture*, is a hindrance to the globalisation of markets and of consumer tastes. Governments would far rather that culture, like religion, were made, as it were, a matter for consenting adults in private and relegated simply to personal taste. It must be emphasised strongly that it is normal for a nation's economy to be wholly integral to that nation's culture, and forming one aspect of it. It follows that all particular human cultures are threatened in some degree or another by predominant pressures to replace local, culturally-based economies by one global one with its corollary of an unrestricted market in raw materials, finished goods, information, and personnel - skilled or otherwise. Could it be that this anthropological fact is what underlies the evident bitterness and anger that erupted so dramatically on 11th September 2001? This anger seems to be directed against anything that can be labelled as *The West*, and England is clearly seen as being as much part of the *The West* as the USA, for the English are no longer seen as a distinct Northern people with its own ancient culture, origin and identity.

It seems, then, that multiculturalism is being promoted as a necessary part of the process of globalisation in economics and commerce.

A factor which reinforces what has just been said is that the British government is increasingly taking the USA as a model because it is a *Settler-State* with no predominant ethnic culture. Ethnic identities are to be tolerated as long as they are subordinate to an inclusive *American* civic identity and do not interfere with the working of the free-market economy. Perhaps they are perceived as being part of a necessary *social glue* which holds together the fabric of society.

There remains a problem, though, for the USA's Federal government and for its counterpart in Westminster. To what extent can they count on the loyalty of persons who are British or US citizens, yet retain a far more deeply rooted attachment to a nation which is based in some other part of the world? It is ironical. The government would like English people simply to see themselves as *Britons*, yet *Britons* from English cities have gone to fight alongside the Taliban! A modern Settler-State has shallow roots. The English are needed.

Another reason for the promotion of multiculturalism must be looked for in the widespread feeling of shame and guilt that many individuals seem to bear because of the way the British Empire has been portrayed by the media, on which quite savage and scornful denunciations have been noted. Some writers and parts of the press have also had a hand in this, as well as those responsible for the presentation of history in schools.

I am prepared to listen to criticisms of the British Empire, including any assertion that the whole enterprise was a mistaken venture, but this must be done in a balanced way. It should be remembered that ordinary people from England, Scotland and Wales had to suffer dreadfully and to be the cannon fodder so as to extend and to maintain the Empire. Meanwhile, those who stayed in Britain often fared even worse, and one should read what Friedrich Engels wrote about the condition of the English working classes just at the time when the Empire was reaching the pinnacle of its power. Nor, at that time, was there universal male suffrage, and democratic processes were subservient to the *class* system.

None of this stops shame and guilt being loaded on all ordinary English people who happen to have a T.V. set or sit in a history lesson. It can be assumed, then, that this process has also affected many individuals who are active in our political life, and who hold office in H.M. Government.

The *cringing* attitude on the part of some English people, who would no doubt prefer to be called *Whites*, is very marked, and I have observed it on many occasions. It is having a very destructive effect on young English people. I will not elaborate on this; one only has to look in the streets.

Another, and parallel, observation is the likely effect of English cultural disintegration – deculturalisation - on English people among the governing class. If the main contention is right, that English culture has been severely damaged and is not being transmitted as it needs to be, then those English people who govern us can hardly be immune from the effects of this phenomenon.

Those who hold high office tend to be clever individuals, with a range of strong personal qualities and great confidence. All these characteristics, however, are wholly compatible with a very weak grasp of one's communal and ancestral culture. It is evident that many able persons of English descent are only dimly aware of their communal history, and in school have been brought up on a diet of *British* and *World* history. Out of school they were heavily influenced by *Western pop-culture*, which promotes multiculturalism and an urban identity. In addition to this, they have been subject to the pressures of the modern way of life, which demands that we specialise from an early age. Thus the Renaissance ideal of a wide and varied education is long gone. It would therefore be unsurprising to find that most English government officials have a very poor grounding in their nation's culture, and are prone to promote the British and Western identities that have been foisted on them.

Of course, a nation's culture should be transmitted in hundreds of ways, communally, and not simply at school, but that is not happening for the English.

If what has been said here has any substance, it would be expected that there should be warning voices, but these are all too few, and an effective voice, warning against the mistaken concept of multiculturalism has not been forthcoming from those quarters where it might have been expected. In particular, the Church of England has seemed reluctant to criticise multiculturalism, and in some places, notably in South London (The Anglican Diocese of Southwark) multiculturalism has been actively promoted. I have corresponded with Anglican Church leaders, but without positive result. It would be possible to contact the Roman Catholic hierarchy, but I have preferred to leave that to those who are members of the Roman Catholic Church. Others might be well placed to write to highly respected persons in intellectual circles, and I hope that some of us will do that.

It can be said that there is an ascendancy of multiculturalism in England, and that the ideology and its advocates are dominant in central and local government, in the media, and in intellectual circles.

Once a concept has taken root in society in such a widely diffused way it tends to become self-perpetuating, and can only be effectively challenged with organised, determined and persistent effort, and with good intellectual grounding. In the absence of such, we should expect multiculturalism to hold the field indefinitely.

Other important but ultimately questionable concepts which have taken root in this way have been 17th century Puritanism; the 19th century belief in Progress based on the supposedly ever-advancing frontiers of science and on the consequent proliferation of assumedly beneficial advances in applied technology; and the 20th century Cold War notion that we were to see ourselves as *The West*, while the Russians were to be regarded as remote, untrustworthy *bears*, with whom we were doomed to be locked in perpetual antagonism. As for the 18th century, it could be said to have fostered the notion that the Black and south Asian races were somehow inferior and in need of improvement while not being exploited, and this notion of relative superiority/inferiority could be seen to have survived till the present, albeit in an inverted way. For multiculturalism seems to carry the implication that the English People are, in some sense, inferior and incomplete, and that only by an admixture of cultures from other parts of the world may we become complete.

Lastly, on this question, we should not discount naked commercial greed as a powerful motivation behind multiculturalism. Those who manufacturer and market consumer goods want a passive and pliable market in which the *tastes* of the targeted population are easy to manipulate. Global corporations therefore want consumers who have been *liberated* from communal identity and culture. These consumers are conditioned to think themselves *daring individualists* who are free from convention but they are in fact conforming to a herd mentality. They are subject to fashionable tastes and the dictum; you are what you conspicuously consume. The startling conformism of many young people, with a brand-loyalty to designer labels rivalling the erstwhile political loyalties of earlier times in its passionate commitment, is enough to give us pause for thought. Multiculturalism is overtly promoted by, amongst others, the *United Colors of Benetton*. In other words, it doesn't matter who you are or what you believe, as long as you wear the right gear, and eat and drink the right stuff. The casualties of this process are visible in our streets. Only too often I see (in 2002) young English girls who are grotesquely over-weight, and who wear black tights, a denim jacket, the shirt hanging out, and with hair in rat's tails. Down-at-heel trainers enhance this effect.

F What should be our reaction to multiculturalism, and what can we do?

(1)   Some Principles to Bear in Mind.

First and foremost we have to insist absolutely and unequivocally on our communal and personal identity as the English, a nation in the full and original sense, which means an ethnic group. We have to learn to exist as an ethnic community even in our historical homeland because we now share this land with fragments of other nations. But we must never forget that there are many English people whose home is not now in England, and who may not have a British passport. In other words, we must show that we have the same sense of national identity, irrespective of who we are among or where we are, as is exemplified by the Greeks, a nation from whom we could profitably learn and receive encouragement.

(i)   It will help to forestall criticism and suspicion if we make it clear that we accept the adage, recently heard at a London meeting of Steadfast, that in order to love one's own nation it is not at all necessary to hate any other. If we are English, and such a claim is to have any substance at all, it must be absolutely clear that we define who and what we are in a way that arises from our own origins and from what has been received by us from our own forebears and antecedents. We must never fall into the error of seeming to define ourselves negatively, simply as rejecting someone else's identity and culture. What we are not is far less important than what we are.

It is true that we no longer have the luxury of sole occupation of our ancestral homeland, but it is equally true that whether we and our distinctive culture are to survive or not depends entirely on ourselves. If we do not work to wake our compatriots up and fire them with enthusiasm for the task of reconstructing our damaged culture and communal awareness, then nothing can save us, and we should not then blame anyone else. Conversely, even if we were to find ourselves as merely a minority, numerically, in our own country, that would not stop us from being a vigorous and whole ethnic community, capable of withstanding all adverse pressures and of redeveloping our own culture in all its varied aspects. It is what is rooted in our minds and hearts that counts.

(ii)   The main reason why we are insisting on our communal and ethnic identity as English is that we are Human, and have the same needs as human beings everywhere. We need to say 'we' as well as 'I', to have a Nation to belong to, and a place which we can call a homeland. It follows that any struggle that the English have in the process of reasserting their communal existence as a nation can be seen as a much wider struggle on the part of particular peoples and their respective cultures anywhere in the world. Our own difficulties may have the effect of making us more aware of parallel cases of peoples whose identity and culture are in danger of being obliterated for reasons not unconnected with modern global economics.

(iii)   There is no room for complacency. There does appear to be a concerted and ongoing policy of erasing English identity - seemingly for economic convenience and in line with fashionable political theory imported from elsewhere.

This sort of policy, which in another context I have heard to be labelled *ethnocide*, is not to be withstood with guns and bullets, but with our minds and our thinking. Concepts and well-grounded assertions are to be our ammunition!

If the English were to be attacked physically, and an attempt made to obliterate us physically by some hostile State or alien nation, then an armed response would be entirely understandable, but our actual circumstances are such that the battleground is not a physical one, but is rather the hearts and minds of our compatriots, who must be awakened from lethargy, ignorance and complacency. The English must not allow themselves to be defined out of existence. For it is that, rather than mass slaughter, which awaits us if we do nothing. I have mentioned the Greeks, but the continued existence of the Australian Aborigines can also serve as an encouraging example.

(2)   What should be done in particular: England in relation to the British state.

(i) We English should insist that in England we live not in a *multicultural society*, but in a multi-ethnic state, within which the English should be accorded respect as the indigenous ethnic community and nation, effectively from time immemorial, alongside the Scots and the Welsh. British, then, is not a national identity but a political construct, and the UK, both in its constitution and in its laws, should defer to the original nations within which lie the roots of its own validity and authenticity.

(ii) We English should explain that we believe in a global human plurality, a world order which respects the diversity of nations and cultures, while acknowledging the need of each to a homeland as a normal situation. This must include the English themselves.

(3)   Resistance to falsification and disinformation concerning the English.

(i) The English should disallow any falsification of English history and origins, especially in widely public forms such as education curricula and the broadcast media. Books, such as the infamous Parekh Report (2000), must simply be countered with true arguments.

(ii) It should be insisted, as a matter of truth, that the Black and South Asian ethnic communities in England are of very recent arrival, and that in the early 'fifties of the last century they were a rarity in England. This was so even in London. I personally know this, for in my mid 'teens I had the habit of cycling all over London at the weekend, and I would have been fascinated and astonished to see Black and South Asian people. I did not. This is important, for attempts to rewrite even recent history are not conducive to good inter-communal relations. My very vivid memories of the three schools that I went to in South London, during the war and in the immediate post-war years, reinforce what I have already pointed out. On this point, however, it becomes apparent that the testimony of those old enough to remember the period just mentioned is of paramount importance, as it provides first-hand witness and evidence which cannot be gainsaid.

(4) Redress of grievances in respect of pressure from other cultures and peoples.

(i) While few of us would want to refuse entry to refugees in the traditional sense of those individuals and immediate families who are fleeing from inhumane imprisonment, torture, mass slaughter, political executions, and the like, it should also be insisted, as a general principle, that refugees must never be allowed to call into question the continued existence of the host nation, its culture, or its institutions. The indigenous people merit respect corporately, as a nation in their homeland, but also individually, in inter-personal dealings and relationships. England must not be an exception.

Similar remarks apply concerning the large number of foreign and Commonwealth students who study in England. It is quite wrong for disaffected, footloose young males from this or that perhaps oppressive regime to attempt to treat young English women as *two-legged visas*. Nor would any young English women want to behave in such a way were they to have a full grounding in their own culture and the experience of growing up in it.

Further to this point, it should be explained to those who are properly admitted to England and to Britain as a whole that this is not a settler-state like the USA but the homeland of a particular set of peoples of ancient origin, as is the Republic of Ireland, a similar and neighbouring example.

(ii) The English should urge that economic migrants are not necessary. The economy of a state should be wholly integral to the culture and way of life of the nation, or nations, that the state serves, and should also adjust itself to the nation's demography. Let us be clear about this: it is better that we undergo occasional phases of adjustment and hardship than that we should lose our identity.

The English birthrate is very much below replacement level and this is almost certainly because of the demoralised condition of the English population at the present time, both in the rural areas and in the conurbations and towns. Deculturalisation, which is what the English are suffering from, should be expected to lead to a loss of the communal and personal will to reproduce, just as the culture itself is not being transmitted. Whether or not the ethnic minorities are suffering from a falling birthrate, it is far from clear that they would find large-scale and continuing immigration to their liking.

How did the indigenous peoples of Britain generate the population needed to man the original Industrial Revolution? This at a time when the frontiers of Empire had to be manned, and the rate of infant mortality was high.

(iii) The model that is being proposed here, the *Multi-Ethnic State*, is to be understood very differently from the *Multicultural Society* model which has just been critically examined. A return to something like the original 1707 Union is called for, but with a more balanced relationship between England, Scotland and Wales, and with an extension, too, as fragments of some other nations now share British Nationality as the *minority ethnic communities*.

In this situation the English must insist that in any definitive matters, such as would touch on state and constitution, or on English cultural forms, no changes be made or recognised in law except by agreement of the English alone, through instruments of communal representation such as would have to be set in place. Parallel arrangements would have to be made for the Scots and the Welsh, and both for them and for the English it would necessarily have to be ethnic representation, and not merely territorial representation, on the sort of matters here envisaged. In other words, the indigenous nations of Britain need the means to express their own will in matters which touch on the nature of the State, their own continued existence, and their own culture.

These reserved, definitive matters would be restricted, and on most matters which affect the lives of ordinary people, of whatever ethnic community, we should surely vote together. But here, in Britain, we are the indigenous peoples, effectively. And Britain is not a *settler-state*.

(iv) The English People should start to resist and to reject alien cultural forms. There is a healthy level at which some cultural interchange may occur, but this level has been vastly exceeded for many decades now. We have to challenge our people to work on regenerating their own culture, but the central government should also help by making it difficult to import culturally sensitive material. The Government cannot be expected to act unless it can be sure of sufficient political support, and it is here that there might be a considerable convergence of interests between the English and some of the minority ethnic groups. Many of these latter must be at least as alarmed as us, at the massive impact of urban American culture in England. It may at first sight seem insensitive to complain of Americanisation in the aftermath of the events of 11th September, 2001, but surely this is not so. The USA does indeed need allies and friends, but the latter will prove to be more useful and effective if they are not simply extensions of the same cultural system, but continue to retain a cultural base of their own, and a wholly independent voice. I have never thought of myself as a *Westerner*, but that does not make me anti-American.

At the very least, we can begin to develop our own cultural forms in respect of food, clothing, popular music, films, novels, drama, dancing, and many other things which impinge on our everyday lives, such as educational theory and the study material used by the Social Services. We should begin to question those *jumbo-jet persons* who ply the Atlantic to attend seminars and then return to tell us how they do it in *The States*. Let's stop wearing baseball caps! And do we really need American Line Dancing when there are so many forms of English folk dance to rediscover?

What has just been said of American culture might also be extended to Afro-Caribbean culture, which has also become oppressive in some areas.

(v) Having just written so much in a style which is probably the literary equivalent of woodworm-infested Edwardian furniture, I make the next point with some embarrassment!

We, the English, must begin to defend and to promote our own standard usage of our own language - a language which is coming under pressure from all sides. A language used like English, under modern conditions, needs a very clear and well-defined standard form, along with a continuing respect for the regional dialects of ancient origin. Moreover, there should be a popular awareness of whatever was the classical form of the language in question.

None of these conditions is being met in the case of English, and at the same time the language, albeit increasingly in the American form, has become an international language. At the same time, theorists are heard on the radio who publicly expound that there is no such thing as Standard English, and that the language is doomed to undergo extensive and ongoing mutation under the pressure of derived forms of English from elsewhere, finally to break up into mutually incomprehensible dialects. So we are told.

It is true that English in England is currently under pressure from many of the non-British patterns of the language, and these include American, various African forms, Afro-Caribbean, Continental European (self-taught), South Asian forms, and lastly, though not least, debased English from the most socially disturbed areas of the English conurbations, as promulgated on the T.V.

But we do not have to accept any of this. Indeed, a language does evolve slowly with its own internal dynamic, but we should not, and need not, allow our language to be debased and to collapse as a result of the highly artificial conditions that have arisen in recent decades. Rather, we should insist on having a clear standard form based on what was current in the immediate post-war years, before the debasing and disintegrating influences really got under way, and we should show a renewed interest in our ancient regional dialects, as well as being aware of Old English (Anglo-Saxon), which is most certainly our classical tongue.

To some, the very notion of a carefully defined standard may seem artificial, and so it is, in a sense. But it must be remembered that modern languages, and English especially, are not being used in a natural way, and are being placed under pressures which are quite unprecedented, and far from the conditions under which language existed in archaic and traditional times.

It is usual for a modern language to have a standard form, which is developed from a central or politically prominent dialect, and Italian would serve as a good example of this. In other countries, such as France, Russia, Norway, Greece and Italy, the language is regarded as something precious, something to care about. They are right, for one's language is a very intimate and vital part of one's humanity and of one's own communal culture. If we care about being English, we must insist on protecting our own form of the language, whatever forms other peoples may or may not wish to develop for themselves.

Rediscovery of the English language as ours, and as something to cherish, will enable us to develop poetry and drama, the novel, and other artistic modes, thus using English to express our common way of life. It is not without reason that many of the most attractive works in Modern English have emanated from Ireland, Wales, and Scotland, and the reason for this is surely the relatively strong social cohesion and the persistence of the feeling that they have an identity and culture which they want to express. Moreover, they have not been ashamed to use English as a medium for their literary talents.

(5)   Particular Forms of Action, for which the English Might Press.

(i)   In line with what some of the minority ethnic communities already have, the English should require communal facilities, such as English cultural centres, and these would serve as places where English culture and communal life would be regenerated, reinforced and transmitted. These would be especially useful in multi-ethnic areas, and in some suburbs where the English are clearly a minority themselves.

The guidelines for running such places would have to be worked out, and the experience of another friendly ethnic community, such as the Greeks, would be invaluable.

(ii)   We English must reach agreement among ourselves as to our communal norms regarding relationships and family life, in the broadest sense. No one can deny that there has been a breakdown of earlier norms and this has put the English at a disadvantage when compared with some of the ethnic minority groups who benefit greatly by their retained social cohesion and patterning.

Perhaps we should initiate studies which draw upon indigenous and traditional Christian wisdom and insights, in this delicate matter. The present situation is communally and personally self-destructive.

(iii) We should insist that our children receive grounding in the beginnings and origins of our own nation, in education. This should also be matched by a corresponding commitment in local government adult education.

Schools, however, cannot bear the whole burden of educating English children in their own culture, and this must also take place in the home, in the cultural centres (mentioned above), within the churches which English people may frequent, and in as many aspects of everyday life as possible.

(iv) We should urge that the rural communities and their economies be stabilised, and that the maintenance of an English culture be encouraged in these areas.

This is already a matter for public debate, but the English themselves do well to remember how the rural population has dwindled over many decades, and we ought also to reflect that traditionally, the roots of any given human culture lay in the rural areas. The increasing popularity of organic farming may well give a boost to the rural economy.

Although it is a difficult point of economics, which cannot be discussed in detail here, the English might try to press for a reinstatement of some of the older heavy industries which we had till not very long ago. Shipbuilding springs to mind, and perhaps textile production based on linen rather than on cotton.

The principle which is very much in my mind is the anthropological point, that as far as possible, a nation's economy should be integral to that nation's culture, and forming an aspect of it.

(v) The English should press for a review of the law, and of particular legislation and administration, so as to ensure recognition of the English as a nation and ethnic community in the full and particular sense that has been outlined in these pages.

This is necessary, because our legal system as a whole took shape slowly over many centuries, during which time the existence of the English People was never called into question. Only very recently has the continued existence of the English been called into question, and attempts been made to redefine the very meaning of the word *English*. One example of the damage that has already been done is the omission of English identity from the last two National Censuses. In consequence of that, questionnaires issued by local government departments all over the country adopted the same list, and English people were in consequence encouraged to register as *White* (a racial identity), as if they had no clear ethnic identity, culture or origin.

But why are ordinary people so supine? Why did not ordinary people rise up in protest, and why did not ordinary local government employees at least query what was happening? Would a Greek census omit the Greeks, or a Turkish census omit the Turks? In England now, it would seem, you can be Irish but not English.

(6)   A refusal to allow double standards, such as would operate against the English.

(i) The remark at the end of the last paragraph is an instance of the double standards that we commonly encounter. The English must insist that the same respect be given to our communal and ethnic identity as is accorded to other ethnic communities, but with the proviso that we should have certain *reserved rights,* as before explained, in matters pertaining to certain culturally or constitutionally definitive matters.

The provision of English cultural centres should be sought, along the lines of those provided for many of the ethnic minority communities, and if they are *disallowed*, it should be seen as a case of double standards.

So, too, the ethnic staff associations, like the Black police officers' association. Would an English police officers' association be permitted?

This is not the place to deal with the issue in detail, save to say that double standards, to the detriment of the English, have been very diffuse and widespread, so that vigilance is necessary. Vigilance lest there should be, locally, such things as positive discrimination in employment in favour of ethnic minority personnel; asymmetrical reporting of crimes, reporting them as *racially motivated* only when perpetrated by *Whites*; relegation of English people to obscurity in posters, press photographs, local government exhibitions and the like; the absence of an English voice in the broadcast media; and many more. Be vigilant.

G Some concluding remarks

The concept of multiculturalism has been rejected as being a muddled and humanly-destructive pattern of thinking, and as one which is being promoted for rather base motives to do with modern economic theory, modern marketing and administrative convenience.

I have noted that multiculturalism, if followed to its conclusion, leaves the state as a self-defining arbiter of communal identity and culture, with no effective control from below and thus with no indisputable source of fixed values and core beliefs.

The term *British* simply comes to mean those whom the state defines as its citizens.

The classification *non-British* would cover all those whom the government did not so choose to admit, while the rules for making the distinctions would rest largely with the Home Office.

Instead of multiculturalism I have put forward the concept of a multi-ethnic state, in which the English would be fully recognised as the core population, having our own origins, culture and identity, with England as our ancestral homeland in a unique sense, fully recognised under the law.

Immense damage has already been done to the English culture, and it is urgent that we reach the hearts and minds of our own people.

We must also look for friends where we can, and unlikely individuals may support our cause. I can testify to the understanding of the British Greeks: their example of communal networking is phenomenal, and we could learn from it.

We need to develop an effective communal voice: other ethnic communities in England usually have this, in the form of newspapers, radio stations and cultural centres.

We must remove the sense of shame and guilt associated with being English: it has no good basis at all, but is being induced by the broadcast media and in some educational curricula.

We need to be active all over England, and also wherever in the world English people are to be found.

At all costs, resist the false *territorial* definition of being English. English is an ethnic designation, and most certainly does not refer to the sum total of legally recognised inhabitants of England. The famous Duke of Wellington showed how nonsensical the territorial definition was. His statue stands proudly just outside Dublin to this day. When he was reminded that he had been born in Ireland, the good Duke replied, "You can be born in a stable, but that does not make you a horse!"

On the same general point, we could adduce the example of the Armenian community, whose homeland is now a fraction of its original size, mountainous and terribly impoverished. But the Armenian nation continues, and they retain their culture and identity in all the lands and cities where they find themselves.

One thing the English now lack, is a strong, unifying religion such as peoples like the Greeks, the Armenians, the Lithuanians and some others undeniably have, and which, in each respective case, has helped the nation in question to weather all sorts of adversity.

I hope there can be a constructive dialogue within the English community on this issue, and in particular, between representatives of those who adhere to the old heathen religion in a recovered form, and those who belong to the historically well-rooted rites of Christianity. They may be opposed, but not, if I understand things correctly, diametrically opposed. Also, I think that Christians would do well to look to how their faith was expressed in the first millennium, especially at the time when the faith reached England.

In practice, let us try to awaken the awareness of contemporary churches on this matter of the English and *multiculturalism*, for many of us are Christian, and should thus be able to get a hearing within our own faith-community (to use the modern jargon!). I have tried to do this, but it is not easy.

H A tail-piece

Just after World War II, a black-and-white film appeared called *Passport to Pimlico*. In this film, which was indeed set in the area near London Victoria known as Pimlico, we see an excavation for an unexploded bomb unexpectedly reveal an ancient document, subsequently to be examined by an archivist (Margaret Rutherford), who declares that it unmistakably proves that the whole area belongs, not to the British Realm, but to a certain continental Duchy, or some such.

Word gets around, and the post-war inhabitants, hungry for some excitement, gain enthusiasm for the new situation, and start erecting barriers and so forth. Eventually, the central government gets worried, and a minister from the Home Office arrives, and tries to persuade the people to desist from any hasty action. Then, a voice from this very English crowd is heard to shout, "We've got a right to be foreign: we're English!" It is a woman's voice.

Certainly, everyone in the crowd scenes looks English, and the period portrayed was the same as when I myself used to cycle alone all over London as a schoolboy. It was just how I remembered it.

But there could hardly be a better way of pointing out the essential difference between ethnic identity, on the one hand, and state citizenship, on the other.

It is as a distinct nation, a people with our own ethnic identity, that we insist on being recognised, and voice our determination to continue as such. Far from embracing multiculturalism, we have the task of recovering our own culture from the degradation into which it has been allowed to fall.

In this, we will succeed.

English Roses
T.P. Bragg

Middle-aged women with studs in their noses
Tattoos round their arms, down their legs one supposes
Their children stroll past a man as he poses
This kid is his kid while the baby one's Rose's.

Pork chop and ciggies the whole house it dozes
Sunday night telly with Macca not Moses
Johnny is thrown out when the Public House closes
She wipes off mascara as he nips back to Rose's.

Folksongs: Neglected Roots

Veronica Henderson

When I sit down to play the cello I begin by improvising around some Scottish tunes, some of them by heart and some of them from a collection that I have brought with me. Playing them brings me straight back to my Scottish childhood, to the places the songs describe, to our history as taught in a Scottish classroom, our customs and landscape. Some of the language has fallen out of use, some I might have used as a child. I am back at my grandparents' knees, back with my classmates, tramping along a track in the Highlands or standing up to sing alone at a special occasion, with all the memories that attend such events.

A Scottish song can have an almost liturgical effect: it can bring people to a place in their hearts that links them to their community and their past. In my life it brings me a form of continuity and this can reach across centuries and across continents to the people of Scottish descent who have left our shores.

My first memories of learning the cello are of picking out these tunes by ear, before I had really learnt anything properly. There must have already been a foundation there, laid down at nursery and early primary school, on which I could build, and it seems to me to have been a very intuitive way of learning. Now, as a teacher in England, I find it very difficult to tap into the equivalent resource among English people despite the efforts of compilers of beginner-level cello music to use their traditional tunes in the early stages of learning.

The work of the great song-collectors of the late 19th and early 20th centuries, Grainger, C. Sharp and Vaughan Williams, does not seem to have reached the grass roots' consciousness to anything like the extent of the Scottish folksong tradition, aided by Burns and Scott. With some effort *Keys of Canterbury*, *The Vicar of Bray* and *Down among the Dead Men* are remembered, although *Greensleeves* is more easily recognised, the harbinger of the ice-cream van! I am unable to assume that my new pupils will have heard these songs often enough to recall them usefully for learning an instrument. I believe that the neglect of this tradition is a loss: of knowledge of their past, their music and their community, and to some extent of knowledge of themselves.

The Internationalists
Robert Henderson

Men who do not understand
What is beyond
The satisfaction of plodding reason
And mundane wants and needs;
Men who do not see
That a land is more than
Rocks and rivers, trees
And fields or the
Atom called a man,
But a myth of oneness
Which a people has,
Where rich and poor
Live half separated lives
Yet still believe
Themselves a part
Of something greater
Than a vulgar mass of
Coldly counted men.

Hidden England
Richard Todd

English folk music, unlike its *Celtic* counterparts, has remained largely ignored by the mainstream media in recent years. One could be forgiven for thinking that it exists only on the borders of our culture, a dated, backward and insular pastime last practised in the 70s, now only useful for nursery rhymes, and country folk festivals where it is performed by drunk overweight men with bells on their ankles. This image, though not altogether unjustified, has been peddled by the media to such an extent that many English people laugh or feel awkward and embarrassed by it. At a recent folk festival, dozens of people happy to watch a display of Irish dancing lasting almost an hour vanished as soon as the Morris groups came on stage. At the opening of the Scottish Parliament, broadcaster and radio presenter Sheena Wellington performed the song *A Man's a Man*, which is a *Scottish* song celebrating independence, national identity and unity - a symbol of their new found freedom. Any effort to do the same in England would be met with widespread derision and ridicule, and calls for a more inclusive, multicultural event, more in keeping with the 21st century.

A recent publication, *World Music − The Rough Guide*, described the current image of English folk music as "ridiculed and kicked around by a mainstream popular culture seemingly sympathetic to every hybrid known to music-kind except its own traditions". Look in any music store and you will find folk sections titled Scottish, Irish or Welsh but not *English*, English being filed under 'other' general folk music, despite the wealth of our recorded material. Recent collections from record labels such as Topic under *'Voice of the people'*, *'English Originals'* or *'Hidden English'* (perhaps the most apt title) have gone some way to redressing the balance. English music is also being promoted in magazines and journals like *Folk Roots,* which accords it the same status as other *world music.*

Despite the poor popular image, a close look reveals a thriving and independent culture as rich, diverse and varied as any − and comparable with any. England has hundreds of folk festivals, large and small, regularly held throughout the country, the most popular being in Cambridge during the last week of July. Most large towns have their own folk club to showcase both local and visiting talent; pubs throughout the country have folk nights. Morris dancing - perhaps the most ridiculed of all our folk culture - remains extremely popular throughout England. The traditional image of white clothing and bells belonging largely to the Cotswold Morris from Oxfordshire but each region has its own distinct clothing and music. Likewise long sword, horn, and clog dancing each have their own regional variations. The diversity of English music ranges from Northumbrian and Border song and pipe music with its distinctive traditions to the unaccompanied singing style of East Anglia. The different types of song are just as varied - carols, rhymes, sea shanties, and hornpipes. There are also political songs and songs of protest.

The Collectors

Cecil Sharp House was established in Camden, London in 1930 as a centre for the preservation of folk song and dance. It is the *keeper* of our tradition, regularly holding cultural and folk events, and it houses The Vaughan Williams memorial library, which is a much ignored national treasure containing many books, not just on music but general folklore, and is a resource for modern musicians.

But in order to understand and have an appreciation of some of the characteristics and nature of our folk music we must also understand some of the history and see it as *narrative* that *we are part of* and *responsible* for. Not *past* but *present*. Broken and enigmatic as it is, this narrative is important in telling us why our forebears made music, and it reveals the social, political, cultural and social pressures they experienced from early times.

English folk music probably evolved in much the same way as other traditions. Most folk song started as an oral tradition, a shared experience passed down through generations of family and community. It reflected the concerns of the day, such as war, class, law, religion, love, betrayal, and murder... . Most songs have come from labouring people and their communities. The poorest or lowest on the social ladder used songs appropriate to their occupation to help them through the day. A song would help them while away a strenuous or repetitive chore, such as ploughing, or help them wind down after a long day, perhaps with musical accompaniment, which was relatively new in some areas. But by no means would these songs have been just the property of country workers, nor were they necessarily rural. With the advent of the industrial revolution and the movement of population from countryside to towns, folk traditions adapted to urban and industrial trades such as mining and shipbuilding.

Probably the most thorough research into the history of English folk song was carried out by A.L. Lloyd, who traced its evolution from the 14th to the 20th century. Lloyd suggested that 'true' folk music evolved its protesting nature at around the time of the Peasants' Revolt and the Black Death. Feudalism and class resentment inspired folk songs which provided a means of expressing the widespread discontent felt by the lower classes - a type of Robin Hood mentality. Before this we have little recorded material of its time, which is due perhaps to its oral nature and widespread illiteracy among the lower classes. The nobility probably thought that folk music was not worth recording. Maud Karpeles quotes Trevelyan, who believed that the subjugation of ethnic English culture under Norman rule gave it its distinct characteristics:

> One outcome of the Norman Conquest was the making of the English language. As a result of Hastings, the Anglo-Saxon tongue...was exiled from hall and bower, from court and cloister, and was despised as a peasant's jargon... it ceased almost...to be a written language.
>
> The learned and the pedantic lost all interest in its forms, for the clergy talked Latin and the gentry talked French. Now when a language is seldom written and is and is not an object of scholars, it quickly adopts itself in the mouths of the plain people to the need and uses of life... During the three

centuries when our native language was a peasant's dialect.... it acquired the grace, suppleness and adaptability which are among its chief merits.

The same might be said with equal truth of our folk music. It is comparatively recently that it was written down and came to the notice of musicians and scholars. Before that there was a long period stretching into antiquity when it lived by oral transmissions and in the 'memory of man', adapting itself as did language to the needs and uses of life. [1]

Roots

No music survives from the early Anglos-Saxon period, so we must look to the poetry and literature of the time as an indication of the subjects about which they sang. There are many gaps in our early history but Old English poems, charms, and riddles give clues to the values of the people and their aspirations. Literature such as *Bald's Leechbook*, the *Exeter Book*, and *Bede's History of the English Church and People* reveal a past in continental Europe and the migration of a people who brought their heathen culture and attitudes with them. We find the best clues in the oral tradition of the early Anglo-Saxon scop - a professional songster who held an important place in society as the living 'folk memory' of the community. He was bestowed with the responsibility of passing on the history, legends and stories that were part of the collective memory. The scop in the Anglo-Saxon poem *Deor* describes his position in the community and how he fell out of favour with his Lord and was replaced by another. He starts by briefly describing four legends, including that of Weland the Master Smith who suffered at the hands of King Nithhad. The Weland legend, which is also mentioned in the Anglo-Saxon poem *Waldere* and in *Beowulf*, was known throughout Western Europe, and is possibly a forerunner to the smith of the folk song 'Brown Adam'.

Many of us are familiar with the song *Scarborough Fair* made popular in the sixties by American songwriters Simon and Garfunkel, with a reworking of the traditional English folk ballad by the musician Martin Carthy. Few realise that its roots are in an ancient Norse song, *The Elfin Knight*. The song is derived from a riddle (a popular device in Western Europe) in which a woman hearing a Knight's horn from her bedroom wishes that he were in her company. When the knight appears to her, he demands that she make him a shirt 'without seam or needlework'. It was an impossible task and the maid's reply would determine her fate. She in turn asks him to plough an acre of land 'between the salt water and salt sea' and plough it with a lamb's horn, an equally impossible task; and so it goes on, each making demands of the other. The words were passed down in the oral tradition and were first printed in the mid-seventeenth century under the title *Lady Isabel and the Elf-Knight*. Over time it spawned many variations, its meaning changed and it evolved into traditional favourites known today throughout England as *The Cambric Shirt - Sing Ivy - Acre of Land - Widecombe Fair*.

---

1 *An Introduction to English Folk Song*, Maud Karpeles, Oxford University Press, 1987
Maud quotes from Trevelyan's *History of England* p131-2

In the same vein the folk-song *John Barleycorn*, known widely throughout England and Scotland, uses the analogy of a man being beaten to death time and again for the sowing and reaping of barley. This could be seen as a relatively recent song, the Scottish poet Robert Burns having re-written a famous version, which is a celebration of the importance of barley as part of rural life. This accords with English tradition in which songs celebrate the harvest of barley and its role as an ingredient in the making of alcoholic drinks. Or, it could be seen to suggest a more ancient pre-Christian belief:

> They ploughed him in the earth so deep,
> With clods upon his head,
> Then these three men they did conclude,
> John Barleycorn was dead.[2]

Though the roots of these songs cannot be proved, since the origins were in an oral form, we can see that they have evolved in written form.

Many of the surviving medieval English songs were found by chance from fragments used in the bindings of more recent books or used as flyleaves. Perhaps the lack of care for them at the time indicates why so little of them exist. The best known piece of secular medieval English song is a canon recognisably similar to the tune we know as *three blind mice*, which was probably written by a Monk at Reading Abbey around 1240. If we look at the manuscript we see another aspect of our folk music – the secular and the sacred side-by-side; the Anglo-Saxon *folk* script celebrating the coming in of summer, underscored by the sacred Latin hymn. It is unclear whether the Latin Easter hymn came first and then the secular English song was written over it or not.[3]

> Sumer is icumen in,
> lhude sing, cuccu
> Groweth sed and bloweth med
> and springth the wude nu
> Sung, cuccu.

The practice of borrowing folk tunes for religious purposes has never ceased. The English hymnal contains many folk melodies that have been adapted for religious themes. A song such as *Shepherds arise* being an example. Before the church organ took hold in England, music was made by church bands and singers - a 'church folk band'.

So, English folk music evolved through its early period to the beginnings of the *broadsides*, which carried the tradition on until the early 18th century in a form of street literature containing songs, stories and news. These were written by hand until the invention of the printing press. The broadsides became

---

2 *Sing a song of England: a social history of traditional song*, Reginald Nettel, Phoenix House Ltd, London 1954

3 With the introduction of Christianity, the Church set about Christianising those heathen festivals, customs and (probably) songs that were too popular to ban or replace.

extremely popular and widened the movement of localised folk song as a result of being sold by travellers and merchants moving from town to town. In this way they were brought to a wider audience and played a part in blurring regional variations and differences.

Reclaiming our folk culture

In recent years there has been a move by some to assign English folk songs and music a Scottish, Irish or Welsh origin, usually carried out by people hiding behind a political or personal prejudice – *'the English are unable to create anything of their own so it must have been stolen or borrowed from elsewhere'*. This argument can only be perpetuated because the origins of most songs are vague, coming from an oral tradition without the need of being written or printed. A song that moves from one country to another is likely to pick up mannerisms of the local style. So, for example, a song with Scottish mannerisms might not have its origins in Scotland but may have simply *passed through*. Song families such as the 'Dives and Lazarus' are widely known throughout the British Isles (each nation claiming ownership of it) and have produced countless offspring. Each of the *siblings* have words to suit the needs of the host culture.

Each of the countries of the UK has given and taken songs but only the English are accused of *borrowing*, as if they have little or nothing of their own. The fact that the other three nations rarely, if ever, admit to borrowing English songs indicates the shallowness of their accusations. It is absurd, given our rich cultural heritage, to suggest that we are unable to put our emotions and experiences into song or create our own original melodies.

There are few border controls on music, and that is especially so in the modern world where nearly all societies are open to influences from across the globe. The cross fertilisation of cultures that comes from the movement of people means that cultural lines become blurred. The polka, for instance, (a folk dance originating from the Czech and Slovak republics) has become popular throughout Britain and Europe, somehow fitting at ease with our music and dance – but a polka will always be a polka, its name and sound establishing its foreign roots in the mind and ear of performer and audience. The adaptation of the polka was a success story but some attempts to merge different styles have produced disastrous results, a good example of this being the attempt to blend reggae with rural English music.

We should not be shy of promoting English folk song and dance, and defending it from those who demean it. The influence of a once strong folk tradition has reached many parts of the world, sometimes taken by English migrants, at other times gaining influence because others saw something worth copying. For example, the hornpipe (widely believed to have originated in England) became part of Irish, American, and Canadian folk music, and modern rock in general. Yet many people wrongly believe the influence to be of *Celtic* origin.

Is there anything specifically English about our folk music?

Efforts in the past to define a national folk music have mostly failed. Consider the diversity of English folk music and then try to define it in technical terms. Any attempt to form a consensus on the characteristics of a national music are fraught with many difficulties – e.g. *what makes English music English*? In his book *English Folk- Song: Some Conclusions*,[4] Cecil Sharp mapped out the things that he felt characterised English folk song, which included the various modes and scales commonly used, along with time signatures, tone and so on.

Time and further scrutiny has found that these *distinctive traits* are shared with other cultures but often sound very different when played elsewhere. In general, a folk song will sound Irish when played by Irish in Ireland, Scottish when played by Scots in Scotland, and English when played by English in England. The music of all these countries belongs to a wider Western European tradition that shares many similarities. The music of the British Isles is a branch of that tradition.

Despite the similarities, there are certain common characteristics that help shape and set apart the sound of English folk music. The most telling distinction is the phrasing. English folk music by its nature is economical in its use of expression and ornamentation such as slides, bends and vibrato - dare I say freer of sentimentality. In some ways it reflects what the English language should be - to the point, tight and honest. English folk music is perhaps more simplistic than other traditions in its phrasing and rhythm, which leaves space for improvisation - room to breathe. Eastern European music often has complex rhythms which are unsuited to the English style of dance. For example, Morris dancing requires a less complex, rhythmic tradition, and this is reflected in the music that has grown up around it.

The Dorian and Mixolydian modes are common in English folk songs, whereas the Pentatonic scale was quite rare in rural English music but abounded in Scotland and Ireland. It seems that the modern *major scale* established itself in England earlier than on the continent, perhaps this was due to the European Church stemming its growth by calling it the *Modus Lascivus* or "wanton mode". Nevertheless, it was used widely in England. A.L. Lloyd writes of England in the thirteenth century:

> ... and it may well be that its appearance [the modern major scale] is one
> of the first signs of national character in our music and that early budding
> of artistic nationalism, connected with a growth of English self-
> confidence consequent on the emancipation and increasing power of a
> new social element in feudal life, an individualistic, enterprising
> merchant class . . . [5]

---

[4] Cecil J. Sharp *English Folk-Song: Some Conclusions.* London: Simpkin; Novello; Taunton: Barnicott & Pearce, 1907.
[5] *Folk Songs in England*, A.L. Lloyd, International Publishers, New York 1967.

Our music has also been shaped by the use and range of the instruments and voices used by musicians – for example, the limited range of the Northumbrian pipes dictating a style of its own. An unaccompanied song that stretches to an octave and a half would imply an outside influence, the melodies usually lying within comfortable reach of the voice. Stock phrases form the framework upon which a traditional singer weaves his song. Opening phrases common in England are, 'As I walked out one morning', 'Oh come all ye' (as in 'The Sweet Primroses') or 'Twas down in yonder . . .'

Anyone looking for a definable *Englishness* in our folk music, must surely seek it in the sheer simplicity of the earthy, gravelly, unaccompanied voice of Harry Cox. The son of a Norfolk herring fisherman, he was probably best known for the inspiration he gave to the folk revivalists of the 1960s, whose songs drew on recordings that folk collectors had made of him. His singing links us with pre-industrial England and its culture. From an early age Harry listened to songs in local pubs, and learnt other songs from family and friends he met at social gatherings. His father passed down songs learnt from his trade as a fisherman, and in this way Harry Cox built up a huge collection of songs. His straightforward style of using only subtle ornamentation can be said to embody the unaccompanied English singing style – it is *distinctly* English, belonging to a long tradition of East Anglian singing.

It is accurate to say that today, few people continue these traditions in the true sense - the traditional activities of labour such as harvesting no longer exist, being replaced instead by mechanised methods; the need for the collective experience has gone. Whereas singing would have once been used to help relax people after a long day at work, it has been replaced by passive and solitary activities such as watching television, or listening to music on a hi-fi. Although other parts of the developed world have followed this path, it was perhaps in England that *community* was hit hardest by the Industrial Revolution. The upheaval of that time goes some way to explaining why our folk traditions have suffered so much. Rural life underwent many changes and there was much migration from the countryside to the rapidly expanding towns. The lives of many were uprooted as they moved to unfamiliar surroundings, and in doing so the shared communal experience being lost. They left behind the sense of place, identity, and belonging that gave the songs an enduring meaning. It shattered the sense of continuity that keeps traditions alive.

Revivals

English folk music has had two main revivals, the first being led by music and dance collectors such as Cecil Sharp. They were generally middle-class, educated professionals who were eager to collect and display an English music. They did it in response to the overbearing European music and culture of the time, travelling as far as the Appalachian mountains in the USA to collect songs from descendants of English settlers. Collected folk music often influenced classical composers like Vaughan Williams, freeing them from some of the constraints of regimented composition. Mainly for political reasons, collectors of this era have been widely criticised for their approach to the *lower classes* and the way they gentrified folk music, trying to keep it in a glass box, thus making it unpopular to the very people it belonged to and who would have kept the tradition alive.

Though there is some truth in this, the collectors were only reflecting the attitudes and thinking of the time. They should be admired and appreciated for the sheer scale of the material they collected and made available for future generations to draw on.

The second revival by contrast in the early 1960s was inspired by left-wing politics, drawing upon the reworking of materials collected by the likes of Sharp but set to a socially conscious, protest theme.

Once again, English folk music is undergoing something of a revival, this time with an even younger generation. As before, enthusiasts are drawing on traditional English songs, the most successful of the performers staying faithful to the originals, and proving that traditional themes such as love, betrayal and murder never go out of fashion. Surprisingly, this movement seems driven not by a political force but a cultural one. Many are discovering this music for the first time, perhaps feeling drawn to it in response to a sense of rootlessness imposed on them by media and cultural elites that scorn *parochial music*. Despite the negative perceptions from above, many are attracted to folk music in their quest for a localised and meaningful sense of identity and belonging. The growing rejection of economic globalism and ideological universalism is encouraging more and more young people to question an elite contempt and disdain for our English folk culture. Such freethinking is causing them to reassess the acquired prejudices that stop them from enjoying a richness that is rightfully theirs. All forms of our folk culture must be restored to the nation's consciousness.

A Taste of True England - with the Copper family
Mak Norman

Although my musical taste has always been inclusive of most styles, one purchase of a Spinners album back in the seventies was the closest I ever got to folk music. Discovering The Copper Family 10 years ago changed that.

The Copper Family are from Rottingdean, in East Sussex and consist of Bob Copper (now in his eighties) his son John, daughter Jill and her husband Jon.

The first time I saw them perform, I was left feeling that I had just caught up with some old friends. I have since collected their work on CD and more recently purchased a beautifully presented songbook. Now it's common for my 3 year old daughter and I to break into a rendition of *Charming Molly* as we stroll down our lane to the village store.

Last summer the Copper Family performed at a local village hall. Unexpectedly, there was a TV crew there, but that was nothing new to the people on stage. The BBC were broadcasting The Copper Family as far back as 1950 when Bob Copper and his father Jim were the first non-professionals to sing on-air and unaccompanied.

In a most humble fashion the Copper Family allow the songs to take centre stage. Bob Copper can remember his grandfather (who was nicknamed *Brasser* Copper) singing the songs that you can hear the family perform today. In turn, James *Brasser* Copper could remember *his* grandfather George Copper singing the self same songs. George Copper was born in Rottingdean in 1794. As far as we know there is no other example of such an unbroken family singing tradition in the whole of Europe.

Their music takes us back to a time when songs had far more importance and function than many of us can imagine. A time without TV and radio, when people made their own entertainment and sang of the changing seasons, their loves and their working lives.

> *These were the men that in their younger days had ploughed the fields with teams of oxen, sowed their seed-corn by hand from seedlips slung across their shoulders, precisely the same as had the Saxons on the self-same lands a thousand years before.*
>
> Bob Copper

Despite the hard graft, the workers of the land gathered around the hearth fire in the tap room or at home and they sang. And the songs would start at the drop of a hat.

Bob recalls how as a boy he would be in the kitchen with his mother and father. His grandfather sitting in his favourite chair. The clock would be ticking a slow tic...toc...tic...toc, when out of the silence Brasser would say, "Best 'ave a song, and't us?"

133

A Taste of True England – with the Copper family

Musically the Copper family provide a protected haven for Englishness. The songs themselves are a celebratory account of the social and working history of English country people, who alone retain the true identity of our folk.

Like thousands of others both here and abroad, I found a true connection on first discovering The Copper Family. That evening in Wivelsfield Village Hall in East Sussex made me grateful for a vital experience, but sad that this opportunity was like glimpsing a rare bird.

The modern environment with its urban onslaught deprives us of so many simple yet essential experiences that were once normal in rural life. The truth is, we need the likes of The Copper Family to allow us the privilege of connecting with our history with its lost images and values. Their songs are supported in a live performance by some funny yarns, a tankard or two of ale and warm Sussex accents. The latter being equivalent to an endangered species as London-speak is noticeably wiping out the Home Counties accents and dialects.

During that evening performance in Wivelsfield I noticed some young people distancing themselves at the bar, while the seated audience (mostly aged 40 and over) sat engrossed. I made my mind up that at some point I would go up to them and say 'One day, you will be able to tell your children that you saw the great Bob Copper'. Fortunately, my embarrassment was saved as before I made my move the three young men were invited to the stage. They were Bob Copper's grandsons. In fact all of his grandchildren had sworn their commitment to carrying on their family's singing tradition. Their decision was made with no family pressure. The grandchildren had secretly rehearsed and sang for Bob on Christmas Day.

I sat feeling quite overwhelmed particularly when one of the boys sang a duet with Bob. It was a song which dear ol' Bob had sung with his grandfather. And so in that simple village hall a profound cycle of English heritage continued into another generation, which I celebrated with a pint in my hand and a tear in my eye. And I was not the only one.

In recent years the Copper Family has performed in the United States where audiences have been known to queue just to touch Bob's arm, such is the unique importance of the Copper Family.

For more information log on to www.thecopperfamily.com

Afterword

On 25 March 2004, just a few weeks after I wrote the above article. Bob Copper was invested with an MBE from The Prince of Wales. The following Sunday a party was held for Bob, but by the evening he was taken ill. He died peacefully in hospital the next day.

On Saturday 17 April Bob's ashes were carried on a decorated farm cart through the village of Rottingdean with a procession of over 300 people, including friends and admirers from the USA.

A remarkable memorial service was conducted in Rottingdean Church. Thirteen speakers (including one who read a letter from Prince Charles) said everything that could have been said. They spoke of his love for his family, his wisdom and knowledge of country life. They spoke of Bob the artist, the poet and storyteller.

Bob was a gifted raconteur and an author of several publications on Sussex. In his eighties he visited 23 states while performing in the USA. He learnt the English concertina in his seventies and forever made people laugh. It is said that he never seemed in a rush, yet somehow found time for so many people. Those who met Bob were quickly hooked by his charm and warmth.

Bob with his beautiful Sussex tinted chuckle will of course be missed, but his work and his family will carry him into the future. As for myself, I will hang tightly on to the moment I once shook Bobs hand and simply said 'thank you'.

Bob Copper has been an inspiration to me. I am proud to say that I have now performed solo in front of 200 people at my village music festival. As a tribute to Bob I sang four songs from The Copper Family repertoire.

What a pleasure and what an honour.

Grandfathers

T.P. Bragg

Tell me
Could you
When faced with my grandfathers
Veterans
Of the First World War
Victorian men

Could you - hand on heart now
When faced with my grandfathers
Veterans
Men I knew only second-hand

Soldier, fireman
Blacksmith, husband
Father, grandfather
Old man, dead

Could you - you and you

News reporter
Commissioner, policeman
Spy, writer
Government man
And quota filler

Could you - hand on heart now
Tell them
Tell me
That England is a better place now
For replacing them?

What will be will be
What will be will be - Que sera sera
What will be will be
What will be - c'est la vie

Or would you
Rather they, rather I never existed?
Hand on heart now
Rather they, rather I never existed?
Hand on heart now

Lyrics from *Fields of England*, TP Bragg's latest album

England - In Search of an Anthem

Mak Norman

It's in moments like the Rugby World Cup final, when you really want to get your tongue around some stirring words and sing aloud for your country and its folk. But the English have a serious problem in this department.

The national anthem we are expected to sing is in fact the anthem of the British state; it is dedicated to The Queen (Head of State), not the land and its people. *Rule Britannia* is also a British song but it is not as irksome as the rugby supporter's anthem, which briefly seeped onto the football terraces - *Swing Low Sweet Chariot*.

So let's pretend we are back in Sydney for the 2003 rugby final against Australia. You're with 60,000 other England supporters and the England team is minutes from victory. The tension is almost intolerable. What shall we sing as a battle cry?

We all launch into "Swing Low Sweet Chariot".

Am I missing something here, because I can't find even a tenuous link between our land, our ethnicity and this song?

How strange it is to see pictures of English fans singing with so much adrenalin-fuelled emotion- their faces all squidged up, blasting out words that have no real meaning for England or the English; like so many loud cannons firing duck down. And I'll wager the fans don't know why they sing the song either.

Swing Low Sweet Chariot is a spiritual song born from the experiences of enslaved African-Americans. The song is about life seen through the eyes of an individual who has no rights and no voice. The one hope is that faith in the Hebrew God Yahweh will see the slave reborn and free in the Promised Land. It all stems from the story of Moses leading his chosen people out of Egypt and out of slavery.

> I looked over Jordan and what did I see,
> Comin' for to carry me home!
> A band of angels comin' after me,
> Comin' for to carry me home!

Our Welsh neighbours exude vigour and *attitude* when they rally their teams with *Men of Harlech*.

> Heroes, soldiers, rally
> On the foe we'll sally
> We will chase the hostile race
> From stream and hill and valley
> Conquest's banner proudly bearing
> We'll exult in their despairing
> Victory the shout declaring
> Cambria live for aye!

The Scots have *Flower of Scotland*, which has rousing words (which reflect the anti-Englishness that underlies Scottish nationalism).

> O Flower of Scotland,
> When will we see your like again
> That fought and died for
> Your wee bit hill and glen.
> And stood against him,
> Proud Edward's army,
> And sent him homeward
> Tae think again.

So what songs do we have that talk to and for the English people? *Land of Hope and Glory* is stirring enough but it does not mention England. The tune we need may spring from a modern day Elgar. Or the vital spark may be hidden in a folk song or Morris tune as recognised by Ralph Vaughan Williams and other classical composers who researched and utilised English folk melodies.

For now, the English have nothing to express their collective folk soul in the way that *Flower of Scotland* does for the Scots. Rather than celebrating our Englishness in song we are instead forever looking over Jordan, building Jerusalem on England's green and pleasant land or wishing our British Queen glory while she rules over us.

Another peculiarity is the use of tunes like the theme to the film *The Great Escape*. It can be heard at England football internationals – played by a brass section. The tune is customised by a section of immense subtlety where the crowd shout *Eng–Lond* over the *boom - boom* of a bass drum. Well, yes its fun, but how is a melody titled *The Great Escape* supposed to inspire a team to victory? It's as negative as the West Ham club song (I'm forever blowing bubbles), where fans admit in verse that just like the dreams of a Hammers supporter, bubbles will fade and die. No wonder West Ham United flounder. They need a better song!

I am sure that if England's international sporting teams heard a stadium filled with the might of lyrics akin to the Welsh National Anthem they would be more inspired. So, in order to encourage debate, I offer an unofficial English version of the Welsh national anthem.

> The land of my fathers, the land of my choice,
> The land in which poets and minstrels rejoice;
> The land whose stern warriors were true to the core,
> While bleeding for freedom of yore.

Anyway, nearly forty years on since England's last world cup victory we have at last got the right flag flying at international events. I only wish that the flag was known as The Flag of England and not The Flag of St George.

wæs hæl England!

The Third Fable

T.P. Bragg

Jack stood in front of the grave. The wording was simple and the dates defined his mother's span on earth. But they spoke nothing of a difficult birth and her long suffering into death. Then again, who were the dates for? The church was now situated in a non-Christian part of the city. Few people would visit the churchyard and there were no longer services held at the church. Jack came to the grave solely to speak to his mother's memory.

'You would be proud of me,' he began, 'I've taken in a Newcomer. A gentleman in his late twenties. Seems pleasant enough though his English isn't easy to understand. Keeps himself to himself. I wasn't forced to take him – I know I have the house to myself these days – but I wanted to volunteer. I wanted to do something for them. I know you'd be proud of me. That helps me to be a good citizen.'

Jack spent moments in quiet thought. The stone of the church appeared black against the dark afternoon. Rain threatened to burst from the low, rolling clouds. The city was dark and over-crowded. Rooks chattered and cackled as they rose from the top of the church tower. All around him were untended graves. People who had fallen silently into the earth. Fallen into the ground their ancestors had cleared and set aside for burial and a long wait for the soul's journey back to God. In the city surrounding, they did not believe in this fashion.

Driving back through the city Jack witnessed the depressingly endless terraces of modern houses appearing as bleak as anything Dickensian. He found it hard to be a part of that teeming place. The veiled women made him feel alien and un-connected. The gangs of boys in robes and caps made him feel threatened and uneasy. Yet he had been willing to take in a Newcomer. There were so many. So many who wanted to come to his homeland and share its relative peace. The world was tearing itself apart. The Middle East was like a volcanic fracture in the earth's crust. Hot lava of hate was spewing forth. Jews were escaping to America. In Pakistan, Afghanistan and the Islamic countries surrounding Russia, teems of migrants were heading for the West and for Britain in particular. Russian soldiers were fighting on many fronts and Indian troops were battling with Pakistani forces in the hills and mountains of Kashmir. In South America a dozen Republics, with CIA aid, were fighting Revolutionaries. In Europe, Christian people were rubbing raw against the new wave of Islam. But in England, the people withdrew without offering resistance or violence. And the old ways and old thoughts slowly disappeared.

As Jack mused upon this he noticed a part of the city he had known so very well as a child. Or rather he didn't notice it. Where the familiar park and bandstand had been was now built over. Was there a mosque there too? He craned his neck about. As a child he had loved to play in that park. It had given him breath in an asthmatic city. Given him a way out...a chance to observe a different life apart from people, people, people. The part of the city he drove through was where he had lived until his early teens. Where they had been a family. Distant times, distant memories. And now physically obliterated. But people needed homes - didn't they?

Gradually the city thinned out. Pylons became apparent and wires shone against black skies. The countryside seemed at first dirty and unnatural but eventually, like a snake sliding from its skin, he drove into farmland. His house lay on the edge of a village that was almost in spitting distance of the new estates being built as satellites to the city. But it was still a village and his house – his mother's house – was large. Four bedrooms and a study. He was a lucky man. Enough people told him. Enough people stressed this fact. But it wasn't their pressure that led to his application for a Newcomer. No. That was human decency – and in the memory of his mother.

It did come as a shock when Abdullah told him that he had invited his family to join them. At first Jack was angry. Angry that, as owner of the house, it should have been him to invite anyone else. And he surely would have been happy to invite Abdullah's relatives if they were fleeing war and persecution. Though Jack never discovered if this was the case he nevertheless and begrudgingly assented to more Newcomers. At the end of the month Abdullah's young bride, her mother and Abdullah's two sisters (the un-married ones) duly arrived. Jack gave some thought to the sleeping arrangements. Naturally, Abdullah and his bride would have a room of their own. The mother would also have her own room. The sisters would share a bedroom. Jack was happy that he had his own room and his study. His study was of great importance to him. This was where he kept his dolls' houses. He would make them in the garage – his car long abandoned to the drive and the elements. Once finished he would carry them carefully to the study. From the study he would add finishing touches and consult books on historical details. These dolls' houses were not simply walls enclosing furniture, no; they were loving re-creations of houses from the past. And he would sometimes fill the houses with dolls dressed in period costume – tenderly and painstakingly made by his steady hands.

It was both sad and joyful when he had to sell one of these houses. Little girls and their parents or adult girls with twinkles in their eyes would come to his house and up to the study either simply to view his creations or buy them. The pleasure they gave almost made up for their loss.

Abdullah's bride was very young. If she had not been a Newcomer she would not have been allowed to stay married to Abdullah. Jack thought she might have been twelve or thirteen years old. But the marriage was re-blessed at the mosque and the Religious Authorities rubber-stamped all paperwork. The Newcomers were welcomed into the Islamic Community. Jack and the young bride seemed to have an instant attraction. The bride's mother and Jack seemed soon to develop a growing hostility. Abdullah was his usual carefree self now attended to by so many women. His sisters were covered from head to toe and Jack had no idea of their beauty or otherwise. The mother had a scarf thrown about her head but Jack was able to create some idea of her looks.

Jack hadn't a great deal of money. His house was in poor repair. Selling a dolls' house helped. And now, with so many extra mouths to feed he needed to sell more. In the garage, while Abdullah's bride, mother-in-law and sisters cooked and cleaned in his house, Jack busily cut templates for the walls and roof of his next building. Tudor and Georgian style were the most popular and a lady had ordered the former for her little girl's tenth birthday. As ever, Jack would make the house as historically accurate as he could – though "candles" and "lanterns" would be illuminated by electrical power.

On a cold, windy Thursday morning Jack drove out to the city to buy Halal meat and certain spices for Abdullah and his family. Jack was not especially used to the food the mother-in-law and Abdullah's sisters cooked. In fact his stomach troubled him more often than not. Having parked his car, Jack walked into one of the city's many Islamic enclaves. Many non-Islamic people would come – by day – into one of these lively and exotic quarters. There was much bustling and jostling – much colour and noise. Part of Jack enjoyed being immersed in such a different culture and yet part of him remembered a simpler time – a time that might have been grey and uniform but was very familiar and reassuring to him.

Before leaving the city - as always – Jack visited the grave of his mother. To reach the church and its yard, Jack had to walk down an alleyway winding through the backs of Victorian terraced houses. In front of the church a low stonewall encased its graves. Wrought iron gates squeaked open as he made his way into the churchyard. On the wall some youths with round white caps and loose-fitting clothes kept an eye on him. 'Praise be to Allah,' they called. Jack turned and nodded.

At his mother's graveside he began to speak, 'Mother, I hope you can be proud of me. I have now opened my house to a whole family of Newcomers. This has called for some re-adjustment in my way of living, and some hardship. Not as great a hardship as for the Newcomers – but I'm being forced to build more dolls' houses. I am doing my best mother, doing my best for my country and my fellow human beings. What more can I do? Everything I have done I have done of my own free will. Nobody from the government has had to order me to do this or that. And the Newcomers eat and behave in the manner they are accustomed to. No Religious Authorities have had to admonish me. I hope and trust you are proud mother. I'm afraid your garden is not as well tended and your room has had to be used. I gave some of your clothes to the Newcomers also. Not under-garments, mother.' The wind blew around the blackened gravestones and seemed to shake the very foundations of the church. The city squeezed against the church and its burial ground. The brown-eyed boys watched him from their distance – cool-faced and impassive.

At the weekend Abdullah had a serious talk with Jack. It was decided that a room had to be given over for prayer – Abdullah and his family needed somewhere quiet and reserved for this. Jack made many suggestions where this prayer room might be. Could the mother-in-law move in with Abdullah's sisters? No. Could they transform the garden shed? Jack would make it warm and comfortable – No. That would insult their God. Perhaps Abdullah's and his young wife's room could be sub-divided – it would certainly be big enough? No. There might be children in the near future (Abdullah stated stony faced). Then where? Wasn't it obvious? Why, the study. The study was the perfect room for them to hold their prayers. The study? But that was where Jack stored his dolls' houses and supplied the finishing touches and kept his books, drawings and computer equipment. Dolls' houses to take preference over prayer? Was he insulting them? Was he insulting their God? Jack would think about this...

Jack was worried. He needed to speak again with his mother. On Friday afternoon he decided to take a break from building the Tudor dolls' house and visit his mother's grave. But before he left the house Abdullah's young bride swished her robes along the hallway and pulled at Jack's coat. Jack turned, surprised, and smiled at her beautiful features. The young bride could not speak English but she pressed something into Jack's hand and then quickly swished herself away. Jack did not immediately open his grip – but as he walked to his car he opened his fist and gazed at the bride's offering. There he saw the most beautifully sewn doll's dress. Small, perfectly to scale and marvellously detailed. Jack quickly spread the dress and jacket out and stroking the costume, smoothed it. It was a traditional costume – probably Pakistani – maybe Turkmenistani. Honestly, Jack did not know. Jack did not know where the young bride came from – Abdullah would only say that he came from Pakistan. But his young bride had fairer features – as if European blood still faintly infused her.

'Hello mother,' Jack said at the graveside. He was quite alone. In the distance he could hear the Muezzin calling the faithful to prayer. Had things been different once? They must have. And he also had vague memories of a different time. His mother certainly knew a different country to the one he lived in, but then the past was another country – wasn't it? 'Let me show you this first,' Jack said, holding the doll's costume towards the headstone. 'The young bride I described to you, she made it for me – or rather for one of my dolls. But I am troubled mother. It seems the house isn't as large as I thought. The study is needed as a prayer room. And I know I must be a good man – follow in your footsteps (though I haven't the Christian faith that you had) and give them this room. Everything is changing so much, mother. More so than after you died and I was left alone in the house. It seemed so spacious then. So devoid of life. Now it is full. Where can I store my books and equipment? Where can I put the finished dolls' houses? I suppose I shall have to utilise a corner of the garage – clear away some of your old furniture. Perhaps I could fit out the shed and supply electricity to it. We shall see. At least you can be proud of me mother – for doing the right thing.'

With a heavy heart Jack cleared out the garden shed (which was large enough and had windows) and wired up electricity to it. He installed an electric heater and swept the floor. On a bright and cold Sunday morning whilst he was cleaning the shed's windows, Abdullah's young wife came to him. With a worried expression she let herself in. She carried a bundle in her arms. 'For you,' she said. These were the first words of English she had spoken. 'Thank you,' Jack smiled. 'Curtains. Just what I need. It will make the shed cosier to work in. Thank you.'

'For you,' the young bride said again with a smile almost upon her face. As quickly as she came, so she disappeared.

Jack smiled to himself and began eyeing the window, working out which kind of rails he would need to put up to hang the fine curtains. And very fine they were too.

Eventually Jack had the shed looking as well as it might. It was clean, with electrical supply and a naked bulb dangling from the roof. A padlock was fitted to the door and all the equipment that had been in his study was crammed into the shed space. At least it meant a shorter walk from the garage to consult books, drawings or relevant websites. Yes there was something to be gained. And also he found being in the shed quieter and more relaxing. In the house the mother-in-law squealed her orders and the sisters jabbered to each other. Only Abdullah and his young bride were almost silent.

Five times a day the house would pray in the study. Though it was no longer a study. It had been decked out in as fine a manner as any mosque or temple. It glittered and shone with Eastern opulence. Jack wondered where the fine clothes and ornaments came from. All he knew was that his savings dwindled and his output of dolls' houses increased. And for the first time ever the quality of his workmanship was held up to question. Jack was distraught. He was working too hard and too fast and forgetting the enjoyment of building his splendid houses.

By his mother's grave he watched as the sun drifted below the black smudged houses and billowing factory stacks. The air was cold; he shivered. Lights snapped on from nearby houses and the heady perfume of oriental dishes pervaded the air. Two boys stood near the wall of the churchyard and kept their eyes upon him.

'I am tired mother,' said Jack. 'My workmanship is suffering. At night there are rows in the house between Abdullah and his mother-in-law or between the sisters and the mother-in-law. And I feel uncomfortable at prayer times. I think that I should pray with them. But I can't help remembering that we were … are … Christians. Or at least that you were mother. What should I do? I am doing everything I can. It seems not enough. I have an ulcer now mother. The food is too rich for me – you remember the way my stomach has always been. Ever since I was a child. I remember how you cared for me. There is no one now to care for me. It's almost as if I am disappearing. Fading away. And now my greatest gift – my craftsmanship – is being questioned. Is it my eyes? My temperament? Or is it simply that I am rushing things?

'I will have to go now mother. Go back to my house. Our house. But it doesn't feel mine any more. It doesn't feel like home. But I have done the right thing haven't I? I have done the Christian thing. I have heard a knock and I have opened my door. I have given shelter to the needy. That's all that can be expected of me isn't it?'

On his way from the graveside Jack passed close to where the boys were standing. One said something to him. But he didn't understand the boy's tongue. The wrought iron gate clanged behind him and Jack was made suddenly aware of how quiet everything had become. So strangely quiet. Was the city at prayer? Everything seemed distant and unreal.

On Sunday morning Jack drove out into the wild countryside wedged between the two great metropolises. On a hill, with the grass bending in wavelets to a strengthening breeze, he cast his gaze towards his home city. Factory chimneys pumped out sulphurous smoke on the horizon. Not for a hundred years or more had so much smoke been discharged into the air. Already the stacks were black. The outline of the city smeared itself between distant moorland and a cold blue sky. Not much could be grown on the countryside about, only hardy cattle and sheep grazed in dotted lumps on far-flung fields. Many were destined for a slow death – their life ebbing with the rhythmic pump of scarlet blood. Unluckier ones were housed in great long huts close to the cities. City/urban countryside/long-huts/villages/countryside – and then the encroaching city once more. And yet he was all alone on the top of that hill which rose from the moorland.

He walked the whole day. Wanted to stay away from his house. Wanted to be alone again with his thoughts. Wanted to escape the Political and Religious Authorities. Wanted to rid himself of the overbearing stench of people. To be free. But he would have to return. Have to see that everything was all right. Replace things that had been used or hidden. Keep the peace – if they listened to him. What a strange life it had become. Clouds banked low on the horizon and the light seeped below the line of hills distant. The wind rouged his face and blew his hair across his forehead. It was time to drive home.

Pulling up on the drive he sat for a moment and looked at his house. Outwardly little had changed – apart from the gaily-coloured curtains. But he had an uneasy feeling creep over him. When he placed his key in the lock it didn't turn. He tried many times but it didn't quite fit. Prodding the doorbell ferociously he waited for someone to come. Slowly, laconically, Abdullah came to the door. What was happening - why wouldn't his key work? Not to worry. No worry. There had been some problems and Abdullah had had to change the lock. No there were no spare keys, unfortunately, the lock had been reconditioned. He would get Jack a copy. Calm down. What was the problem? There was always somebody in the house. And even today they had relatives staying in the house. That was okay wasn't it? Today they were beginning their preparations for a great feast. The relatives were musicians. There would be lots of music and fine food. Jack was lucky to have found such tenants for his house. Yes, of course, they did not pay rent – but please don't embarrass them...

Inside the house everything seemed to have changed. Cloths were draped down walls and furniture was missing. Jack rushed up to his room. There were drums and stringed instruments on his bed. A perfumed smoke filled the air. He rushed downstairs. The living room looked as if it were a shrine. The sisters giggled when they saw him. One was using his mother's sewing machine; another was re-arranging the room's décor. Through the bay window he saw a van parked outside. Had he not seen it when he pulled onto the drive? He blinked his eyes to moisten them. In the kitchen everywhere was stacked with food. The mother-in-law was cooking. Steam and smoke wafted through the air. Where had the food come from? And there was another woman with the mother-in-law. But nobody spoke to him. It was as if he were invisible. And yet he lacked the courage to say anything, to shout, to strike, to wipe the table clean as Jesus had wiped clean the tables of the moneylenders. Where had this thought come from? A distant memory from school? From Sunday-school? From church? He was aghast. Turning from the kitchen he walked past the living room and the giggling sisters and up to his bedroom again. There he gathered personal belongings.

Was it Friday? He didn't know. It was November. He sat in his shed and huddled round the electric heater. Drums banged in the distance and melodies weaved intricate patterns on closely tuned strings. There was wailing. And he was alone. His shed was cramped. A camp bed was folded up and left close to the door. He had a stove and a cooker. Later he would get water from the outside tap. And from there he would urinate in a bush and look up at the windows of his house filled with colour and life. Filled with strangers who he had welcomed in.

The night grew colder. There came a knock on the door of the shed. As Jack opened the door he saw Abdullah's young bride. She smiled at him. It was the first time. And she gave him a tray full of sumptuous food. 'Thank you,' she said quietly.

'Thank you,' Jack answered. There followed an embarrassed pause. Then the young bride added, 'Not right.' And again, 'Not right.' Jack watched her. She was a child. Beautiful. Lost. Alien. He went to take her hand – he wanted to touch her. But she backed away. And ran from the door. Jack sat down in his chair. He ate the food. Only then realising how long it had been since he had eaten. As he mopped up the last juices on his plate with the un-leavened bread he was suddenly plunged into blackness. Complete and utter blackness.

In that utter void, that twinkling deathly dark he assembled his bed – feeling his way as a blind man. Pulling blankets over him he listened out at the voices and music. Squeezing his eyes tight he tried to concentrate on sleep. He was no longer angry – but resigned. And melancholic. And it was as if he were lying in the grave. Entombed by the passing of days and nights and weeks and months. He belonged to a different world.

In the morning he couldn't bear to go to his house. He slipped away without being seen. While he was gone a lady and gentleman picked up a Georgian styled dolls' house. Abdullah took the money on Jack's behalf. Near the church in the city, Jack parked his car as usual. But when he got to the wrought-iron gates, having walked through the filthy alleyway, he found the gates locked. A sign in Arabic said something. He tried to push the gates open. They would not open. Then he went to climb the wall. But as he touched its stone he first heard and then saw the gang of boys racing towards him. 'Out, out,' they shouted. Jack remained fixed for a moment than turned about and ran for his life. He reached his car with aching lungs. As he sat in it he caught the shouts of the boys echoing through the alleyway. As in a film, his car at first refused to start, but just as the boys tore from the alley's entrance the engine spluttered into life. Quickly he drove away, watching the white-clad boys disappear. Through the narrow streets he drove past icy stares and defiant eyes.

On the hilltop in the middle of the moors with the sprawling cities surrounding the horizon, Jack sat. 'I'm sorry mother,' he said softly, 'I have failed you. I have failed everyone and everything.' Then Jack sprang up, as if with renewed vigour and set out towards a distant spire. Perhaps there was greenness beyond that. Perhaps there was somewhere else to go where he could seek refuge. Seek asylum. Be at peace and safe. He strode out, fixing the distant steeple in his eyesight. Sometimes the vision would be lost – but he remained resolute. Walked and walked – the soles of his feet aching. But the most remarkable thing happened to him as he walked across the moors and hills. He began to feel the slightest sense of faith being awakened. Not that Jack was a religious man. But he realised what a fool he had been. How weak he had been. And with every step he took, strength returned to his body and soul. That was the lesson he learnt. And he spoke with his mother about times past and about the future. The conversation rolled from his tongue like the hills rolled beneath his feet. And as he talked he found himself looking into the distance with the sun rising - not into a headstone and blackened earth. And he could feel the presence of many souls around him.

Onwards he strode.

Are you English?
Robert Sulley

"What do you mean when you say you are English?" This is a question often asked today in our so-called multicultural society. Many do not seem to be able to answer because although they instinctively feel and know they are English, they are unable to express that identity in words.

To be able to answer the question, which it seems is only asked of the English, it is necessary to have some idea of what is a nation. A nation is the most extended of families. It is a group of people who share a communal history, ancestry, culture, and identity. The key to preserving a nation is to pass from one generation to the next knowledge of national origins and history. Like other nations, we English need to pass to our children knowledge of what our ancestors achieved, and the challenges they overcame, as a community. Such things have shaped how we think of ourselves and how we view the world. If you have no knowledge of the successes and failures of past generations and how your communal way-of-life has evolved, you will be severely handicapped in understanding the present and shaping the future of your nation. You risk repeating the failures of the past and having a lack of understanding as to what holds a nation together and allows it to flourish. Such ignorance will lead to the decline and collapse of English society. To lose your country and culture is to experience total degradation.

Since the Second World War, many different peoples with greatly differing cultures have settled in England. Most immigrants have come for economic reasons, and to enjoy the benefits of our education, health, and other services. Very few came with the intention of embracing our way-of-life and cultural norms. The vast majority brought their cultures and traditions with them and maintained them. Some, with the active encouragement and help of liberals, have insisted that the English people change their laws and way-of-life to accommodate the differing needs and values of immigrants. Part of this accommodation involves the creation of a British history and the notion that we are all equally British. Clearly there is no room in this for the English and the idea that England is their homeland. No wonder that the English, and particularly the young, are unable to articulate their sense of Englishness.

Things have changed greatly in the past 1,000 years. At the battles of Stamford Bridge and Senlac Hill,[1] in 1066, Englishmen led by King Harold II fought and died to defend their homeland and way-of-life. What followed that fateful day, on the 14th October 1066, was the beginnings of the cruel and bloody suppression of the English people and their culture. The English lost the ability to govern themselves and were instead ruled by a foreign governing elite which brought upon the English centuries of hardship and suffering. Norman-French became the language of the state, and the courts. English men and women could no

---

[1] The Battle of Senlac Hill is commonly known as the Battle of Hastings.

longer represent themselves in court but had to hire the services of a lawyer who could speak Norman-French. A once prosperous country was plundered and made poor by the taxes raised to build a repressive state and finance centuries of warfare in Britain and on the Continent. Yet the English survived the turmoil, and in 1413 English again became the official language of England.

To lose a great battle and suffer the degradation and loss of freedom that inevitably follows is bad enough, but to voluntarily give away your right to be governed by your own kinfolk, and to encourage your children to forsake their cultural inheritance is madness. No generation, however worthless and indolent, has the right to disregard the hard work and sacrifices made by our ancestors to defend our land and make it a pleasant place to live. Our communal achievements are equal to those of any other nation, yet our children are taught next to nothing about them and are instead encouraged to learn about the cultures and histories of other nations. To suggest that English children should learn something of their birthright is treated as quaint and unreasonable by the very people who are eager to help and encourage foreigners to retain their communal identity.

We have, thankfully, enjoyed many years of peace in England, and few people have found themselves in situations that truly test their character. The downside of this is that recent generations have not, for the most part, been put in situations where they are confronted with profound thoughts about their life and the nature of the society in which they live. In other words, they have not had to think hard about what is important in life and what is worth fighting for. Without this experience, and a heightened sense of communal identity, it is difficult for them to understand the sense of community and love of country that enabled our kinfolk to endure hardship and sacrifice throughout our history. In an age when politicians justify their acts and policies in economic terms, many have yet to appreciate that communal and cultural wellbeing (quality of life) is at least as important as economic wellbeing. Man cannot live by bread alone.

It is pleasing to see so many young people enthusiastically supporting England's sports teams and wearing England shirts. The sight of their team playing evokes in them a sense of pride and communal identity; they feel good about themselves and their fellows. That this can happen after the many years of liberal propaganda to which children are exposed, demonstrates the tenacious nature of national identity. Although this is encouraging, it has yet to be seen if their will to defend their birthright has been sapped by the education system and broadcasting media. Supporting a football team does not require the sheer valour and sacrifice that many have witnessed in war situations. I am not advocating our nation should be in a constant state of war, but merely drawing attention to what constitutes true sacrifice and love of one's culture and kinfolk.

It has been said that the youth of ancient Sparta were told by their elders, "If you love this land and want to keep it, you may have to fight for it and even die for it". How many English men and women would today respond favourably to such a statement and the communal sentiments embedded in it? How many think there is any cause worth fighting for?

We live in an age where our political masters have powers of propaganda far greater than politicians of past generations. I am thinking of radio and especially television, which in addition to being an entertainment medium, is increasingly used as a tool for propaganda and social control. It is regrettable that politicians do not use that power to address problems that can no longer be ignored. The worst of these problems is that our planet is overpopulated, increasingly polluted, and has a shortage of natural resources, but politicians still advocate economic and population growth. The UK government advocates immigration and population growth because more people means more economic activity (GDP[2]), which gives rise to the empty boast that, "We have the world's fourth largest economy". They clearly have no appreciation of the fact that GDP is not a measure of quality of life. Worse still, they apparently see no limit to either population or economic growth.

Probably the most important natural resource is fresh water, which is in increasingly short supply. This problem is likely to lead to conflict between states because it seems beyond the intellect of politicians and scientists to find solutions. One could continue speculating on possible disasters, from the effects of super volcanic eruption or a large asteroid crashing into the earth, both could destroy mankind. But consider the continual effects of global warming and the real catastrophic effect on England. Many people think that the idea of England becoming warmer by a few degrees would be quite acceptable. The real effect would in fact create such conditions that our winters would become much colder with heavy falls of snow and subsequent icing. Our society could be brought to a standstill, resulting in many deaths and great hardship. Global warming could even switch off the Gulf Stream, which enables England to enjoy temperate conditions. Most scientists are now convinced that global warming is in part due to mankind's misuse and abuse of the earth's eco system. If we continue to adopt an expanding economy and population with finite resources, then massive problems await us. If we encourage the rest of the world to do likewise, the result will be catastrophic. The obsession with growth is an integral part of the liberal global economy. It runs hand-in-hand with the aim of a unified world population under a liberal world government.

I have travelled to foreign parts in my lifetime and I am thinking of America especially, which is supposed to be an example of a multicultural society and a model we should follow. From what I have seen, US towns and cities are sectioned into different cultural and racial areas, where the US citizens within each area retain a foreign national identity. As a result of this, some display their homeland flag along-side the stars and stripes. This seems to be the shape of things to come for England.

It was Karl Marx who said, "The revolutions of Europe founder on the rock of England". Of course England then was a strong homogeneous society. The revolution of our time is to be seen in the shared policy aim of the European governing elites to create a European state. It is not being achieved by democratic means but by deception. England is no longer a rock on which such a revolution

---

[2] Gross Domestic Product (GDP) is the total monetary value of economic activity.

will founder because it is no longer a strong homogeneous society. The dogmas of multiculturalism and a united Europe have, perhaps deliberately, divided and weakened England and reduced it to the position where neither the EU nor UK government recognise it as a political entity. Our position is made worse by having a Scottish dominated Labour Party and UK government. Scottish interests have been well catered for at the expense of the people of England. This disproportionate Scottish representation is also found in the broadcasting media.

The people of the ancient land of Israel were in 70AD dispersed after bloody conflict with the Romans. The Jews were forced to seek refuge in other countries and survived as a nation by retaining their culture and communal identity within the host culture and its laws. Their identity was embedded in their religion and after two thousand years many were able to return to their homeland. There has of course been conflict because two nations laying claim to the same land. Each wants to govern itself and live by its own laws and the values that underlie those laws. Neither side is willing to embrace multiculturalism. The reason for this is that each knows that multiculturalism will either destroy each culture or lead to perpetual conflict between them. How can two nations live together in one democratic state? The nation with the fastest growing population will eventually dominate the other. The dominant nation will in one way or another impose its values and perceptions on the smaller nation. How can the smaller nation ever enjoy freedom and democracy in such a state? How can the larger nation ever be free of the tension and inhibition that comes from sharing the same land and political institutions with people of a different culture and outlook?

So I find it difficult to square the circle of multiculturalism with equal rights, freedom, and respect for other cultures. This is mainly because each culture is sustained by its own laws. How can you have two law codes within the same state? One culture may perceive criminal behaviour where the other sees none. Even when certain acts and omissions are perceived as crimes by both, each will be guided by a different set of values and seek different solutions to similar problems. No, you must have a mother culture with its laws intact. Any immigrant culture must live within the bounds of the mother culture's laws, only then can you have any sense of a unified and peaceful society. For this to happen the people of the mother culture must remain in control and be encouraged to work hard to maintain their culture. This is becoming much more difficult to maintain with the mass movement of populations and apparent lack of immigration control, or a lack of the will to deal with or even see the problem.

It was interesting to watch the last flights of Concorde into Heathrow airport. Obviously the technical and physical beauty of Concorde has captured the hearts of people and inspired them with that sense of pride, which we seem to have lacked in recent years. On seeing the last Concorde flight I recalled how, as a young boy in my early teens, I witnessed the Battle of Britain in the skies over Kent and South London. One day I saw a squadron of German bombers flying towards London. Suddenly a lone Spitfire dived on the German formation and I heard short bursts of the Spitfire's guns and saw one of the German bombers start to go down with smoke coming from it. The Spitfire then turned up and over, and again attacked the German squadron. This time only one burst of its guns was heard and the Spitfire broke off its attack, obviously out of ammunition, and was gone as quick as it appeared. I was held motionless with my young chest bursting with pride at the valour of that lone Spitfire pilot. It is at such moments in life that we can be truly inspired by a sense of love of country and pride in the actions of our fellow countrymen. Unfortunately, today, the English are virtually prevented from expressing such natural feelings and are, at best, asked to suppress them so as not to offend other ethnic groups. One of the ways in which this hostility to expressions of Englishness is shown is in the banning of England's flag by some authorities. It was, for example, deemed provocative for a student on a university campus to hang the St George flag from his window during the football World Cup.

The flags of Scotland and Wales are to be seen everywhere in those countries, with many flying from public buildings. In England such an act is seen to be offensive to other ethnic groups. Even on St George's Day there is a reluctance to fly the flag. Surely this cannot be right; I am fearful of the possible outcome from suppressing the expression of English national identity and the anger this generates.

The success in 2003 of England's rugby team, in winning the world cup, has shown that there is deep within us a sense of pride in our country, and that we have the right to demand a day of celebration. Such a day would allow our people to assert their existence and remind politicians that we should not be taken for granted. This day should be St. George's day, and it should have the full support of central and local government.

It is difficult to express in words those deep feelings of pride in one's culture which has a rich history, a beautiful language and many wonderful traditions, not to forget English literature, music, art and the theatre, and of course the sheer joy of the English country-side. It is not borne of any sense of superiority; it is simply the wonderful feeling of being home after a foreign trip; home and completely at peace with your kinfolk.

A School Photograph
Raymond Tong

It hangs forsaken on a store-room wall:
the Football First Eleven in thirty-nine.
How proud I was to play at last for the School,
slender perhaps but with the will to shine.

Six of that smiling team were killed in the War.
They all accepted what seemed an obvious truth:
it was their country they were fighting for,
the gentle English landscape of their youth.

Today this photograph brings only sadness.
Seeing those faces almost moves me to tears.
I recall that angry age of far-flung madness,
our political weakness in preceding years.

And thinking of all that has happened since then,
how little of what they fought for still survives,
it seems my friends were sacrificed in vain,
the outcome not worth the loss of their young lives.

The England Society – Keele University

Richard Chambers

Monday 6th October 2003. Seven days ago the England Society had officially launched as a Student Union society at Keele University in North Staffordshire. We were one society among many others, which covered a wide range of interests from music to martial arts, and the obligatory *saving the planet* and *stopping* those stood accused of ruining it. But for the first time ever, England was being represented by a brand new student society, a project that I felt needed to be started. Now I was sitting in the office of the Student Union president to explain myself.

I never expected an easy ride. I never wanted one either. And I didn't get one. My first objective had been achieved within the first week! The story of the beginnings of the England Society does document a struggle. But like many Englishmen before me, I saw a challenge and set forth to find a solution.

On the morning of the 28th of September 2003, I was sitting on our society stand at the Fresher's Fair watching the people come and go. I was not sure what kind of a reaction to expect from passers by. The Student Union is traditionally the domain of the socialist *burn all flags* type. Despite the peripheral positioning of the stand, which displayed the England Society title over a giant cross of St George, I stuck out like a sore thumb. Groups started to loiter at what could have been considered the outer marker on the approach to the stand. Not giving a wide berth and shaking heads in despair, but looking with interest with intrigued grins on their faces as if they were daring someone from the group to actually approach and ask what this is all about. And slowly but surely they did.

Concerns over being chased out of the building with torches and pitchforks dispelled, I was brought onto my second area of apprehension... How people would react to the literature. Our one and only leaflet at the time was a simple affair consisting of a welcome and thanks for interest before going on to give the basics about fair and moderate representation, a list of planned and provisional events over the first few months and a short piece on the current political struggles faced by England and the English, kindly provided by Julien Crighton from *wearetheenglish.com*.

After just over an hour had passed, I had to rush away to the Union's print shop to make more copies of the leaflet, such was the amount that had been taken. Some people took the leaflets and moved on. Others stopped to ask a few brief questions. Most encouragingly of all were the more than a few people who took the line "An England Society? About time too!". The vast amounts of positive interest came from people of many nationalities and races, all could see this was not to be an exclusive project, but something a lot of people could be involved in. The *sore thumb* of the event was becoming quite a point of interest, with people visibly and genuinely interested in this audacious little stand in the wings. Whether an England Society in England should or should not have been considered audacious is a different matter. The fact is that it was.

However, shortly before the clock struck midday, a young woman with a badge and a clipboard arrived. Despite the interest being experienced on and around the stand, a great deal of discomfort was being caused by our presence to someone *upstairs*. Someone involved in the running of the Student Union wanted the sore thumb amputated. The girl with the clipboard was the elected executive for communications at the Union. An attractive Northern Irish girl, she sat down and explained that a complaint had been made with regards to the content of our literature. More specifically, that someone had taken a dislike to one of our provisional events, which was to be a debate on multiculturalism. We were able to explain our different positions on the matter and, after about ten minutes in conversation, I was allowed to go about my business and she went away to continue hers.

But only another ten minutes had passed before a different girl with a different clipboard, who had drunk either too much or too little coffee that morning, marched up to the stand flanked by Union security. This girl failed to introduce herself (although I later found out she was another executive) and went straight into telling us that it had been decided that the England Society was operating in violation of Student Union policy and we had to pack up and leave immediately. This did our image no good at all.

And so there I was, sitting in the President's office seven days later explaining why I thought that I and my society should have the same rights to political expression and debate as was afforded other groups and individuals that operate within the Union. We were allowed to continue as a society, but the battle between the England Society and the policies of our own Student Union continued throughout the year.

The society operated successfully. We debated and supported many of the arguments expressed elsewhere in this book. But my purpose is not to put forward arguments but to record my experiences. And an experience it has been. When I conceived this project I knew it was something that I had to make a reality. I felt passionate about it and wanted it to disturb the uniform certainties of student politics. I also knew that such a project, in the current climate and possibly more so in the setting of a university, would not be met with universal approval, despite the aims being sensible and reasonable. I knew that we would have to be audacious.

The *England argument* is a relatively new one, and many people weren't sure what to expect from the England Society at its launch. Our removal from the event caused many more to wonder about our aims, which is understandable because there has been a widespread failure to properly distinguish between English and British nationalism, or indeed to know anything at all about *nationalism* and *nationalists*. The common presumption seems to be that nationalists are necessarily conservative/rightwing. This view conflicts with what is known of nationalist movements throughout the world or even within the British Isles. The Cross of St George has also come to be seen as a label for hatred. We must continue to inform people that this should not be so. It is the flag of England and anyone who wishes to display it should be free to do so without feeling shame. We cannot be blamed for the views and actions of those who bring it into disrepute.

Those of us who assert our English identity are seen by Unionists as a threat, not because we are extremists but because all Unionists (the three main political parties plus UKIP and the BNP) see the assertion of English national identity as a much more serious threat to the Union than that of Welsh or Scottish nationalism. Unionists have an interest in promoting a British identity and, to varying degrees, denigrating those who promote a competing English national identity.

We face a daunting challenge. But it is the English who saw unspannable gorges and spanned them. We must preserve our English way-of-life, which has at its core the belief that we should be fair and honest with each other so that all may enjoy freedom. We should not trade our freedom and autonomy for membership of Continental unions and a contrived stability. Since when have the English turned from a challenge and bought stability at the cost of freedom?

Rarely have the English been so politically quiet and docile as during the past few years. However, an English awakening is taking place. Students at this university now talk of an English Parliament versus Prescott's Regions in politics tutorials. Our existence outside the European Union is being seen as an ever more credible prospect by many. The political correctness lobby are finding it ever more difficult to convince the people of England that their re-engineering of society is what we wanted all along. People are learning that multi-culturalism and multi-racialism are not the same thing and that neither necessitates the other.

In view of what I have seen at this university, I can proudly say that the English are awakening.

When returning to the Potteries house in which I once lived, I occasionally got off the bus early and walked the last half-mile. I did this so that I could enjoy the fantastic views offered from the top of my road in Wolstanton. There I could see across the Potteries, over Longport and Etruria, towards Burslem and Hanley on the far side of the vale. The old potteries factories hugged the Trent and Mersey Canal, which long ago linked one of the birthplaces of the modern industrial age to the rest of an envious world. This cradle is still watched over on all sides by a thousand castles to a thousand Englishmen. Either bathed in the sun or under a blanket of streetlights, this real-life portrait of over a hundred years of history inspired me like nothing else. It made me see that England and the English had to be recognised and awakened, and that I should do what I could to play a part in the struggle.

In conceiving this project, I read widely about the problems facing England and the English. I am in no doubt that we are being pushed off the political carriageway. Fortunately, the English can, like no-one else, read a story of despair and turn it into a struggle for the victory of hope over despondency. From the moment I chose to act in a positive way rather than sit back and do nothing, I was being English and proud. And we do have so much of which we can be proud. I use the word *proud* to mean *assured*, *pleased*, and *confident*, not *arrogant* and *haughty*.

If to always struggle and hope in the face of daunting difficulties is the way of the English, then the English will never fade. Enjoy struggling to be English! Laugh, and try to make others laugh. The more we and other people enjoy what we do, the stronger we become. Parody of others and ourselves can sometimes be the best way to make a point and the English are renowned for being the best at it.

I know the struggle continues and I'm thoroughly looking forward to playing my part in it.

Modern Education and Political Correctness

Ken Howman

Nazi is not a word to be taken lightly by anyone with knowledge of 20th century history. Yet it was a word used to describe and, more accurately, insult me. It was used by many students in my particular high school/sixth form college as a means to try to make me feel ashamed of my beliefs and views - to make me feel different, wrong, defective. Why? Because I assert my English identity and express a desire to preserve the English way-of-life. In other words, I am an English nationalist.

I was astounded by the violent reaction when I expressed an opinion in a Sociology class three years ago. My teacher delivered a speech on the subject of nationalism. I won't refer to it as an argument because only one point of view was put forward. "Nationalism is like patriotism gone wrong", she said. I was stunned. Not just by the sheer ignorance of such a claim but more so by the complete absence of any critical response from any of my fellow students. I foolishly raised my hand to suggest a different view - to explain that it is natural for people to celebrate their national identity. I said that as I am English, live in England, and value English culture. I consider myself to be an English nationalist. Both teacher and class immediately set me upon, all unshakeable in their belief that I was wrong. I was shouted down, with no chance for a sympathetic hearing.

Not long after these events, during another *discussion* in class on the subject of crime and deviance, I was given the title, "Nazi". My crime once again was to express non-PC views – to be unorthodox. I was told that I was immature and inhumane. I had thought that a willingness to listen to the views of others was an integral part of being mature, and to shout at those with whom one disagrees and to call them a Nazi is not only immature but also a sign of an inability to discuss or think about ideas that conflict with the dominant ideology. Is that not a sign of totalitarianism?

Such is the power of state institutions - especially schools and colleges - to promote the *approved* state ideology that many people fail to recognise it for the propaganda it is. This ideology, which for convenience can be called Political Correctness, promotes intolerance of contrary views. It is a form of totalitarianism that is nearer to Communism than Nazism, in that it preaches that 'everybody must be treated equally' whether or not, by any commonsense consideration, they deserve to be.

Human rights is a phrase that trips off the tongue of the politically correct yet they fail to recognise the right to an ideologically-free education as one of these rights. An obsession with dogma takes precedent over everything else, including discipline. Many teachers have virtually no authority over their pupils because they aren't allowed to administer effective punishments. Children need show no respect for teachers yet feel free to demand it for themselves. I have witnessed such behaviour.

Those students who do pay attention are able to follow a thoroughly biased curriculum geared to indoctrination. The ignorance that results is appalling; this is especially so in history. Many pupils don't know who Admiral Lord

Nelson was, and they lack even basic knowledge of important English and British historical events. What's more, they don't seem to care. In fact, most history lessons seem tailored to promote this attitude. For example, when the subject of the British Empire came up, a negative atmosphere descended on the room. No one knew a thing about Drake or Nelson but much time was given to a long list of 'crimes against humanity' perpetrated by the British Empire. The GCSE history course included topics such as 'The Black Slave Trade' and 'The History of Native American Indians'! Both were interesting but what about my native English history?

Sociology and history are subjects where PC ideology might be expected but it affects (or infects) virtually every subject and every classroom, although some subjects are more prone to corruption than others, particularly the essay based ones, like English, in which 'suitable reading materials' can be easily decided upon by the Politically Correct education establishment. My current book in English, *The Handmaid's Tale*, is a feminist perspective novel which is thought provoking and very well written, but it is a *political* book of the type liked by PC ideologues. Its satirisation of religion is aimed principally at Christianity. No approved book, however thought provoking and well written, would be tolerated if it satirised Islam or any other religion except Christianity; to do so would be considered racist and an infringement of human rights. Insulting Christianity raises no such concerns.

In many countries, national flags are commonly seen in the classroom but not in England. There are no emblems or images of any kind to suggest that the school is in England. There is, however, no shortage of PC imagery and texts. In fact they are to be found on every available surface. Perhaps you can appreciate the terribly depressing atmosphere that one such as myself has to endure each day. The sense of isolation that I frequently feel is not something I should have to endure in my own country.

It seems to me that the education system is designed to function as a sieve that removes all traces of England and Englishness from the curriculum. Thus my homeland, my culture, and my identity are deemed not to exist. In this way, naturally rebellious youths become sheep. They are immersed in PC ideology until they bleat in the approved way.

But some survive. I am a free man – I am an English nationalist!

Notes from an English Town
eighteen months in the life of ...

T.P. Bragg

Entries taken from journals and other notes.

These entries do not span from the worst case to the least or vice versa, but as I have uncovered them and chronologically laid them out. I lived in this town for five and a half years. They show the wearying effect of continual disturbance through time and its cumulative effect. The psyche, the spirit is not untouched. But you have to live through constant noise, harassment and violence to really understand it. Some of you will have or currently experience far worse. In the time I lived in the top flat of an old, Victorian building in an old Georgian town, I rarely had an undisturbed sleep. The sounds that woke me would send adrenalin shooting through my body. Once woken it was hard to get back to sleep. The nature of the sounds was so very threatening. These recorded events happened to find themselves in my journals; they are by-products of and not the reason for keeping them, therefore they neither depict all nor particularly the worst cases. They are all things I have witnessed - seen or heard through my window or out on my street. During this time I attended university, wrote, composed music and played in various bands.

What you are about to read though is not the record of life lived in one of England's major cities. Not in a deprived town. Not in a notable "problem" area. Not in a sink estate or Northern conurbation. This town would - for most people - be considered affluent and 'middle-class'. It is the very ordinariness of this town - its quintessential Englishness - that adds to my witness. It is the kind of town in which so many English people now find themselves.

(Note) Sometime before:

Thu 21st - Party, awake till 3.00am.

Fri 22nd - lads from Kebab-House are throwing stones and/or rocks. Have they hit a car? Chased. Police arrive. Lads insult one officer, deny everything. Could hear them from my bedroom window. Woken 'till 3.30am.

Sat 23rd - Woke at 12.30am then 1.00am then regularly - Kebab-House patrons shouting. (Journal)

Jan 18th: - Despite the fact that things have got much better around here since the Kebab-House converted to a pizza takeaway, and I am no longer constantly depressed by what goes on outside, I just looked out of the window to see some men urinating against the wall. One had just finished but two policemen caught the other. Some other men walked by saying, "He's only going for a piss." They want to live here - to know what it is like. People urinating in your doorway, threatening you, vomiting on the doorstep (and cynically ringing the doorbell after so that you go downstairs to find it). I have seen it all; riots, firebombing, gang-fight, cars vandalised, girl attacked, rock-fight, robbery - so many things I've probably forgotten most of them. You have to learn to forget.

Feb 4th - Temporary stop (from writing diary entry) as I check un-human sounds from outside. It's students. They have tied their legs together in twos, threes fours and are busily going from one pub to another, urinating against the shop opposite. As predicted the outside wall is attracting more posters. And these are being pulled off. The wall looks dirty and ragged.

Mar 30th - Sometimes I feel so hopeless - hope-less and afraid to live where I do. I can feel the tension, anger, frustration that pervades the air. I wonder if I will ever find a way out...screams like shotguns pass over the roofs.

Apr 25th - What must it be like to live in peace in the countryside, surrounded by the smell of country air, not Indian meals or car exhaust or the rubbish gently rotting outside?

May 9th - Unearthly noises outside, an air of violence...a car alarm has gone off...insulted in the street by a young boy - no reason.

May 11th - From my window I can see a man urinating beneath a lamppost on a side road opposite. I left [****] and the smell of the night, dew-wet grass and the sound of sheep bleating beneath the open star-lit sky, to come back here with people vomiting outside the nightclub...girls' voices outside, a running figure...an alarm has gone off and a car is revving its engine. The smell of a taxi's diesel engine drifts by. An 'animal' grunt is heard. The time is 2.35am. Shouts from men in the distance. Heated voices, an argument. A whole group of lads have walked past and cars drive past the end of the road incessantly...car tyres squeal. More cars pass...I'm not depressed, I just wish I didn't live here...now more cars.

May 14th - Noise; there is always noise about me. Always noise.

July 6th - Outside a fight is about to happen or it has continued from somewhere else and spilt into our street.

July 12th - Just got back from [****] to find that some Asian guys have smashed the Indian restaurant's windows. They were drunk and hadn't been let in. When I asked some of the workers if it was the same lot from last week they said it was. Glass everywhere, police on the scene. Yes this is our street where it all happens.

July 15th - Looked out of the window to see the skips had been removed, a great pleasure, but then I saw the debris remaining. About 16 bags of rubbish, two dustbins and various odds and ends left from the skip flanking the front door...wrote letters to the nightclub and the Chief Constable complaining of nuisance and noise outside.

July 19th - Screaming and shouting. Two women screaming like banshees - went on and on. This is two o'clock in the morning. T... and me hang out of the window and listen. Is one of them pregnant? Has one stolen the other's boyfriend? T... cannot believe what is going on. The sound is barbaric. A... wakes up from below as the whole of the outside is filled with nightclub patrons. This is typical. I cannot sleep, it is unnerving. Early in the morning the council cleaning wagon makes a noise like a helicopter landing and wakes me up. Sounds like the helicopters of *Apocalypse Now* droning in to Wagner's *Ride of the Valkyries*. At about 8.00am workmen start drilling outside. No chance of sleep or peace.

July 26th - Midnight - man kicks road cone about, urinates on the street next to his car and continually spits at the same time. Asks his girlfriend to expose herself. Later a youth has the top part of a dustbin on his head and is wandering down B*** Street. He approaches a girl saying, "I am a Dalek."' Amusing if it wasn't so late.

July 29th - Today the workmen moved back into the street; the never-ending saga of the sewers in South Town continues.

August 9th - Some 'men' have just walked past and rang the doorbells of the flats.

August 10th - Looked out of the window in response to shouting and chanting and counted 33 Indian guys and 2 'Whites' walk past. I felt threatened by the air of violence.

August 12th - 11.35pm - Heard sound of breaking glass and then a hysterical woman's voice. Looked out to see a police car, policeman, man and woman. Man and woman arguing, woman screaming. Police car tears down the street and woman is arrested despite her violent disapproval.

August 15th - Sound of tambourine being played in the park (early hours) and a strange man walking about. Urine streaming down the road. (This is the park where I saw the female tramp defecating. Where some shaved-head man was training his savage looking dog.)

August 17th - The streets feel threatening, the usual Saturday night violence. Shouting. Urine stains on the pavement. It is so difficult to relax with that outside, unnatural, sharp noises. Whole bunch of Irish guys outside making a noise, one has gone to urinate. One just dropped his trousers and 'mooned' to the girl who lives next door.

August 21st − I live in an attic dungeon. It is always dark. Both yesterday and today I had no idea it was a beautiful, hot August day. I'm sure the lack of light tends to depress the spirit. 11.55am - Just saw a man mess about in the skip outside...he was trying to break a metal strip; he couldn't so he found a rock to help him. Pulled the strip and some contents from the skip, left them on the road and walked away.

August 23rd - I dream of getting away from the car horns, noise of people and smell of the town.

August 27th - Midnight: loud music has kept me up. Builders still working in the street.

August 30th - Came back home. A... noticed a shop window had been smashed. I went round to have a look and was trailed by the police. That evening a girl was swearing at the top of her voice, woke us up. She spelt out C U N T at the top of her voice. When I shouted to her to shut up I just received a barrage of obscenities.

Sept 2nd – Domestic violence erupts outside. Noises, voices raised. Outside W... looks up and insults me (an Indian guy I had had a lot of trouble from. I used to get back as late as I could to the flat but he would be there still with another man - sitting on my doorstep ready to insult me) but fortunately the Indian guy next door and a Black guy intervene. W... and another Asian guy start fighting. The Black and the Indian guy are trying to get in next door. Suddenly the girls' voices can be heard and there is the suggestion one of them has been beaten up regularly. Kid involved. Bad feelings, violence and tension. This has affected me badly, I'm still shaking.

Sept 12th - Sound of the weird mechanical voice from outside. Went down to look, everyone outside or hanging out of windows but the voice had disappeared somewhere.

Sept 13th (Friday!) - Robbery, window smashed. Lots of action. Police involved. (Possible cause of later harassment.)

Oct 6th - F.... had just witnessed a White guy head-butt an Indian.

Oct 7th - Church bells at night keep me from relaxing. Unholy row.

Oct 14th – Looked out of window because of the excessive noise - see a naked man stretched out over the pavement. Woken, as usual by the noise of the Indian restaurant staff. Despite asking them to be quiet on several occasions there is no response.

Nov 10th - Outside the air is damp and rain has collected in dirty puddles which drunken students jump in, laughing. The skip overflows with rubbish. Bags of rubbish, an old baby's chair, bricks etc. Next to the front door the vomit is gradually being washed away by the rain (and the slow drip of the leaking gutter). The Indian restaurant's car squeals violently every time it moves off. No point sleeping.

Nov 12th - Saw an old guy sitting in the weeds and mess by the council flats - out of his head.

Nov 13th - Guys hanging outside the Commonwealth Club. 2.30am woke to hear the maniacal shouting of a woman. A little later there was a loud smash that made me jump out of my skin. Car below had windscreen smashed.

Nov 25th - burglary. My flute is taken. I loved this flute - given as a gift and used all around Europe. Part of me stolen. Other stuff too, including bankcards etc.

Feb 28th - Two men huddle in the doorway below, urinating and stream of urine runs down over the pavement.

March 17th - Massive punch-up in the park to celebrate St.Patrick's day.

March 18th - The day of the court case (I am to be witness to burglary). Between 7.00am and 9.00am woken 7 times.

March 24th - Screaming from outside. The Indian guy was chasing the girl next door up our street. Girl rescued by neighbours.

March 25th - Found out that the girl had been quite badly beaten.

March 28th - Caught sight of boys running down the street trashing car headlights. Gave chase but didn't catch up. Perhaps I shouldn't ever look out of my window. But the outside is my 'world'.

April 10th - Bottom of the Parade a guy is laid out on the road. Kept awake by restaurant staff then a whole load of people gathers, standing in the street. Two guys with chips were spitting the contents of their mouths onto the windscreens of cars.

May 30th, May 31st, 'update' - Boy urinating against A....'s car, another boy drops his trousers and yet another takes a picture, another set of boys perform the 'chip eating and spitting on car windscreen' trick, the Indian restaurant's alarm goes off at all times of the day and night, the restaurant's staff 'mouth off' at night, the 'Rave Cave' draws in an unpleasant bunch, two youths thrown out of shop-yard opposite, car horns, burps, taxi horns, alarms.

June 17th - Outside the voice: **** is a wanker. Two girls threatened by an Indian man.

June 19th - Alarm went off from 3.15am till 10.15am. 7 hours. No sleep.

June 22nd - Girl urinates in street.

Further:

I witness a police shield and baton charge in B*** Street.
I see the attempted rape of girl in yard opposite.
There is a stabbing in neighbour's doorway.
Twice the local butcher's shop is firebombed.
Once Oxfam is firebombed.
My girlfriend is threatened.
I am threatened many times.

There is racial abuse. During riots elsewhere, Black people outside threaten to kill any White men they find. Me and a friend have to lay low for nearly an hour. Cars vandalised, including a friend's mini completely turned over. Oh yes I witness scenes of drunken, drugged behaviour and prostitution (one of the women is now dead). I am followed and harassed by two men. I am trailed by a car. Burgled twice and have mail stolen over a period of three weeks. Constant alarms, car horns. Girl pulled down street by her hair. Witness students dancing on the roofs of cars and denting them - dressed in 'penguin' suits. Funny? Woken constantly by the noise of radios in cars. Taxis regularly letting their engines rumble for over half an hour. Others I can now no longer - thankfully - remember. But in a sense everything has stayed with me. Everything will stay with me. For those of you who have suffered far worse - I know that everything you too have witnessed will always stay with you.

Why didn't I move? I couldn't afford to. No doubt there are many who live in our towns and cities that escape much of the low-level violence because they inhabit *genteel* areas. I feel embarrassed to use this word - *genteel*. Low-level violence is a dirty sea lapping at the shores of the middle-class. For the moment they can turn the other way. Perhaps soon they will feel water drenching their feet and its stench reaching their nostrils. One can only hope. One can only hope. And things can change.

The View from the West

Ian Holt

In May 2003 I returned to my home city, Gloucester, having lived for the previous fourteen years in the London Borough of Waltham Forest. I started to take an interest in Gloucester, even occasionally subscribing to the local rag *The Citizen*. I read with some interest plans to develop the area around Blackfriars, the largest extant Dominican priory in England. The city council have been discussing redevelopment in this part of the city for twenty-five years. When, however, I read that the city had been consulting with the South West Regional Development Agency (RDA) my antennae started twitching. When I read that the RDA had acquired land near the priory my antennae behaved like a pair of hyperactive Mexican beans on speed. I immediately wrote to the local paper saying that although redevelopment of the Blackfriars area was long overdue and very welcome, it could not be right that a body with no democratic mandate, or even an official existence, should be allowed to own property in the city of Gloucester. What is going on here?

In 1997 the government consulted the people of Scotland in a properly constituted referendum before embarking on the legislation for a Scottish Parliament. They followed the same procedure with Wales and London. Yet when it comes to the English regions, they have inverted the process, put the cart well and truly before the horse. Why? New Labour needed to undermine the position of the Scottish National Party and was sure that it could get the referendum result it sought. There was far less enthusiasm in Wales for an Assembly but the government worked hard to get the *right* result. New Labour is not at all sure of its ability to win support for English regions. They must surely realise that the vast majority of English people are at best indifferent to regionalisation, and at worst hostile. So why do they bother? Stranger still, why was John Prescott put in charge; do they secretly want a rejection of elected assemblies, preferring to stay with the present unelected variety?

In the first instance the answer lies in Brussels. In spite of the fact that governments of both political parties have lied to us about Europe for thirty years, we now know that there is a federalist agenda and that part of that agenda is a Europe of the regions. Whereas Old Labour, the party of Michael Foot, Tony Benn and Peter Shore, had an honourable tradition of opposition to the EEC and its successors, Blair's New Labour is even more enthusiastic about Europe than the Liberal Democrats. Blair wants to put us at the heart of Europe (a geo-political impossibility) and sign us up to both the Euro and the European Constitution, preferably without a referendum. The United Kingdom has been divided into twelve regions: Scotland, Wales, Northern Ireland and the nine English regions, including London. So whilst acknowledging Scottish and Welsh nationalism, government spokesmen, in any event not renowned for being over friendly with the truth, can claim that Scotland and Wales are merely regions. I wonder if the SNP and Plaid Cymru realise this. More to the point, most English people seem blissfully unaware of what will become of their country and its counties in the name of Europe.

Then there is the war against the counties and their councils. County councils, uniquely amongst existing statutory bodies, have certain powers to scrutinise planning. Municipal authorities do not have similar powers and neither will the regions. This is another instance of New Labour putting the interests of business above those of democracy and accountability. It also explains why our egregious deputy prime minister, John Prescott, is cheerfully contemplating turning the South East of England into a gigantic building site, with potentially horrific implications for the green belt, including ancient woodlands, hedgerows and wildlife habitats. The human implications are pretty serious too. At the very least there will be demographic overload, and the likely breakdown of public services, utilities and even infrastructure. Meanwhile, Mr Prescott is allowing the demolition of perfectly good houses in the north of England. Evidently the north of England will be allowed to stagnate as a post-industrial wasteland, blighted by systemic unemployment and lack of investment - a good base for the rise of the far right. Would it not make more sense to target investment on the north and to encourage people to move up there and, thus, helping to regenerate the north? I thought this government believed in joined up politics! Mr Prescott, however, probably has the same problems with that concept as he does with joined up speech.

There were to be referenda in the three northern regions but because it looked certain that the *right* result could not be obtained in two of them, it was decided to have just one – in the North East. Our compatriots in the north must resist Mr Prescott's blandishments and point out to his cohorts that they are part of England, not separate from the rest of us. Unlike Scotland, Wales, and Northern Ireland, the regions of England will not get massive extra funding from central government. Instead, the people of England will continue to be burdened with the Barnett formula, a device by which central government funds (about £10 billion a year) are used to bribe the people of Scotland to stay in the UK. Do the people of the north of England really believe that their regions and assemblies will get anything like the additional funds and powers that have been given to the Scottish Parliament or even the Welsh Assembly? If pigs could fly! In a real *united* kingdom, public money would be distributed according to need, not political advantage. The arguments for regions and regional assemblies should be rejected. Instead, the people of the north of England should question the government on the continuing existence of the indefensible Barnett formula and call for its abolition. They should also demand that they be given the same right as the people of Scotland to have a parliament for the whole of their country.

Contrary to government propaganda, regionalisation is not a means of devolving power, but of seizing it and taking it to Westminster and Brussels. Like everything else that John Prescott has been involved in, regionalisation will be a disaster. The regions will never be popular and it is likely that only a tiny minority will bother voting in the referenda or in subsequent assembly elections. Sooner or later the regions will be abolished and the counties restored. There will also be an English Parliament. The unfair and unwanted imposition of regions will prove to be a very expensive mistake.

This England

Tony Linsell

This England conjures an image of thatched country cottages, corn harvests, and ancient churches. It endlessly reminisces about the 1930s through to the 1950s as if that thin slice of English history is a virtual reality world we can bury our heads in. It is romantic treacle that sticks to those elderly expats who think that the England they once knew still exists. Well I've bad news for you, that England only exists within the pages of *This England*, where a confused Englishness is jostled by Britishness and Unionism. In reality the England of the English is being relentlessly destroyed. *This England* should be using terms like 'occupied territories' and 'colonisation', and showing the diaspora pictures of mosques and Hindu temples. They should be told that while the population of England increases and our country becomes an ever more crowded and unpleasant place in which to live, the number of English is declining as our birthrate plummets. The madness that makes all this possible goes by the name *liberalism* – a pseudonym for communal suicide - a dogma as shallow as the way-of-life it promotes. Watch a *soap*, watch the footie, cook frozen pizza; never mind the quality, feel the width.

The communal heart was torn from many English towns when, starting in the 1960s, Labour governments were intent on *redevelopment* - wreaking destruction and building concrete multi-storey car parks and dismal shopping centres. They cleared low-rise slums and built high-rise slums. Now we have another Labour government inflicting yet another wave of vandalism with its demand that a million or more new homes be built in the English countryside. Given such Soviet style directives, it is no wonder that many English people like to visit the French countryside and its towns. There they can enjoy those things that the French have so wisely preserved. In France, considerations of culture, tradition, and way-of-life are regarded as important. In England, economics (unit cost) and the needs of business are all that seem to matter. In provincial France the English can ponder on what has been lost and what might have been.

Some words and phrases have the power to conjure powerful images and thoughts - *the world's fourth largest economy* (doesn't that make your chest swell with pride) - *individualism - globalism - self-fulfilment - a career - representative democracy* (surely you're kidding – aren't you?) - *ideological monopoly - the civilised world - pre-emptive attack - making the world safe for freedom and democracy - a proud tradition of taking in refugees* (pure fiction) *vibrant - inclusive - too busy to have children - can't afford them - ego - oblivion.* The England I know is moving closer to Hell than to Heaven.

Yes (hand up) I watch footie on Sky and enjoy it. Yes I know it is an important part of English culture – I'm not decrying it. But it is no more than a brief distraction from the reality about me, it is not a way-of-life, not a permanent stupor. As the world fries and dies, and the last delirious Englishman expires, he will gasp some banality – *Who's Arsenal playing next week?*

And the liberal said

R. Henderson

And the liberal said,
With a moron's profundity,
All men are the same.
How strange that they
Should fight in our new world.

And the liberal said:
How ridiculous,
This is the twentieth century!
But the mass of men acted
As they always had.

And the liberal said:
This is medieval,
Reason will prevail.
But the mass of men shouted reason down,
As they always had.

And the liberal said:
It's only a matter of time,
Of men being shown the way.
But the mass of men refused to sit
On one legged ideological stools.

And the liberal said:
Just a little more time
Or another way.
But the mass of men refused to be
Bound in the ways of reason.

And the liberal said:

We know best, man can evolve,
Nurture is all.
But the mass of men still moved
In predestined genetic ways.

And the liberal said:

We need more money,
It's just a matter of education.
But the mass of men heard their words
And thought them empty vanity.

And the liberal said (privately):

How infuriating!
What lesser men are these!
But the mass of men refused
To see their fault.

And the liberal said:

These are but children,
Give them time to learn.
But the mass of men rose up
And no longer let the moments pass.

And the mass of men said:

What a thing is freedom!
How painful, so burdensome a state!
And oppressed the liberal
As he had oppressed them.

England - the mother of modern politics

Robert Henderson

I was tempted to entitle this essay "England - the mother of modern democracy", for the political structures of any state which calls itself democratic today owe their general shape to the English example. In addition, many modern dictatorships have considered it expedient to maintain the *form* of representative democracy without the *content*.

But democracy is a slippery word and what we call by that name is very far removed from what the Greeks knew as democracy. The Greeks would probably have described our system as oligarchy - rule by the few. Many modern academics would agree, for they tend to describe representative government as elective oligarchy, a system by which the electorate is permitted to select between competing parts of the political elite every few years, but which has little other direct say in how they are governed.

If democracy today is a debatable concept, the very widespread modern institution of elected representative government is an objective fact. It is the foundations and evolution of this institution that I shall examine here to the point at which modern 'democratic' politics emerged during the English Civil Wars of the 1640s.

Elected representative government is an institution of the first importance, for it is a truism that the more power is shared the less abusive the holders of the power will be. Imperfect as it may often be as a reflector of the will and interests of the masses, representative government is still by far the most efficient means of controlling the naturally abusive tendencies of elites and of advancing the interests of the ordinary man or woman, by imposing limits on what those with power may do, either through legal restraints in the form of constitutional law which is superior to that of the legislature, or through fear of losing office in an election. Indeed, no other system of government other than elected representative government manages that even in principle, for no other political arrangements place meaningful restraints on an elite. Whether democratic or not in the Greek sense, representative government is undoubtedly the only reliable and non-violent means by which the democratic will may gain at least some purchase on the behaviour of an elite.

Yet however much utility it has as an organising political idea, the fact that we have representative government today is something of a fluke, certainly a very long shot, for had it not developed in England we should probably not have it at all. In the non-European world nothing of its nature ever developed before the Western model was imported. Elsewhere in Europe the many nascent parliaments of the later Middle Ages either never went beyond their embryonic form or were crushed by autocratic rulers. In England we have had continuous parliamentary development for the better part of eight centuries.

Why did the English alone develope such a political system? It was a mixture of such traits and circumstances as the democratic spirit, egalitarianism, individualism and royal weakness. But before examining the detail of those traits, consider first the utterly abnormal political success of the English.

The political success of the English

The first genius of the Anglo-Saxon may reasonably be said to be political. Above all peoples they have learnt best to live without communal violence and tyranny. Set against any other country the political success of the English throughout history is simply astonishing. Compare England's political history with that of any other country of any size and it is a miracle of restraint. No English government has been altered by unconstitutional means since 1688. No Englishman has killed an English politician for domestic English political reasons since the assassination of Spencer Percival in 1811, and that was an assassination born of a personal grudge, probably aggravated by mental illness, rather than political principle. (The assassin, John Bellingham, believed he had been unreasonably deserted by the British Government when imprisoned in Russia and ruined by the economic circumstances of the war with Napoleon. He killed Percival after unsuccessfully attempting for a long time to get financial redress from the British Government.)

Compare that with the experience of the other major states of the world. In the twentieth century Germany fell prey to Nazism, Italy to Fascism, Russia to Communism. France, is on its fifth republic in a couple of centuries. The United States fought a dreadful civil war in the 1860s and assassinated a president as recently as 1963. China remains the cruel tyranny it has always been and India, which advertises itself as *the largest democracy in the world*, is home to regular outbreaks of serious ethnic violence, not least during elections which are palpably fraudulent in many parts of the country, especially the rural areas.

Why is England so different?

Why is England so different? Perhaps the immediate answer lies in the fact that she has been wonderfully adept in dealing with the central problem of human life - how to live together peaceably. A Canadian academic, Elliott Leyton, has made a study of English murder through the centuries in his book *Men of Blood*. Leyton finds that the rate of English (as opposed to British murder) is phenomenally low for a country of her size and industrial development, both now and for centuries past. This strikes Elliott as so singular that he said in a recent interview "The English have an antipathy to murder which borders on eccentricity; it is one of the great cultural oddities of the modern age." (Sunday Telegraph 4/12/1994).

This restraint extends to warfare and social disorder. That is not to say England has been without violence, but rather that at any point in her history the level of violence was substantially lower than in any other comparable society. For example, the English Civil War in the 17th Century was, apart from the odd inhumane blemish, startlingly free of the gross violence common on the continent during the 30 Years War, where the sacking and pillage of towns and cities was the norm. A particularly notable thing, for civil wars are notorious for their brutality.

The way that England responded to the Reformation is instructive. She did not suffer the savage wars of religion which traumatised the continent and brought human calamities such as the St Bartholomew Day's Massacre in France in 1572, when thousands of French protestants were massacred at the instigation of the French king.

It was not that the English did not care deeply about their religion, rather that they have been, when left to their own devices, generally loth to fight their fellow countrymen over anything. English civil wars have always been essentially political affairs in which the ordinary person has little say, for the struggles were either dynastic or a clash between Parliamentary ambition and the monarch. Even the persecution of the Lollards in the late fourteenth and fifteenth centuries and the persecution of Protestants under Mary I had a highly political aspect. The former was a vastly disturbing challenge to the established social order with men being told, in so many words, that they could find their own way to salvation and the latter an attempt to re-establish not merely the Catholic order in England, which had been overturned since the time of Henry VIII's breach with Rome, but also what amounted to a new royal dynasty with Mary's marriage to Philip of Spain.

Even the prohibitions on Catholics and non-Conformists after the Reformation had a fundamental political basis to them, namely, they were predicated on the question of whether such people be trusted to give their first loyalty to the crown.

The treatment of foreigners

Compared with other peoples, the English have been noticeably restrained in their treatment of other peoples residing within England. A few massacres of Jews occurred before their expulsion from England in 1290, but from that time there has not been great slaughter of a minority living within England. Since 1290 there have been occasional outbreaks of anti-foreigner violence. During the Peasants' Revolt London-based Flemings were murdered. In later times an anti-Spanish *No Popery* mob was frequently got up in London and the influx of Jews and Huguenots in the 17th and 18th centuries caused riots, one so serious in 1753 that it caused the repeal of a law naturalising Jews and Huguenots. But these riots did not result in great numbers of dead, let alone in systematic genocidal persecutions of any particular group. Most notably, the English fonts of authority, whether the crown, church or parliament, have not incited let alone ordered the persecution of a particular racial or ethnic group since the expulsion of the Jews. They have persecuted Christian groups, but that was a matter of religion not ethnicity, the persecuted Christians being English in the main. The only discrimination the English elite have formally sanctioned against an ethnic group for more than half a millennium was the inclusion of Jews within the general prohibitions passed in the half century or so after the Restoration in 1660 which banned those who were not members of the Church of England from holding a crown appointment such as an MP or election to public offices such as that of MP.

Peaceableness and constitutional development

Is this comparative lack of violence a consequence of England's political arrangements, or are the political arrangements the consequence of the comparative lack of violence in the English character? Probably the answer is that one fed the other. But there must have been an initial exceptional tendency towards reasonableness which started the long climb towards settling disputes without violence.

Perhaps the fundamental answer to English peaceableness lies in the fact that the English enjoyed a level of racial cultural homogeneity from very early on. Long before the English were united in one English kingdom, Bede wrote of the English as a single people. The English have never killed one another in any great quantity simply because one part of the population thought that another part was in some way not English. That is the best possible starting point for the establishment of a coherent community. The favoured liberal view of England is that it is the mongrel nation par excellence. In fact, this is the exact opposite of the truth. The general facts of immigration into England are these. The English and England were of course created by the immigration of Germanic peoples. The British monk, Gildas, writing in the sixth century, attributed the bulk of the Saxon settlement to the practice of British leaders employing Saxons to protect the Britons from Barbarian attacks after Rome withdrew around 410 A.D. The English monk Bede (who was born in A.D. 673) attributed the origins of the English to the Angles, Saxons and Jutes who came to England in the century following the withdrawal of the Romans at the request of British war leaders.

Archaeological evidence suggests that substantial Germanic settlement in England had a longer history and dated from the Roman centuries, perhaps from as early as the third century. What is certain is that in her formative centuries following the exit of Rome, the various invaders and settlers were drawn from peoples with much in common. They were the same physical type, there was a considerable similarity of general culture and their languages flowed from a common linguistic well.

When the Norsemen came they too brought a Teutonic mentality and origin. Even the Normans were Vikings at one remove who, if frenchified, were not physically different from the English nor one imagines utterly without vestiges of the Norse mentality. Moreover, the number of Normans who settled in England immediately after the Conquest was small, perhaps as few as 5000.

After the Conquest, the only significant immigration into England for many centuries was that of the Jews. They were expelled from England in 1290. There was then no really large scale and sudden immigration from outside the British Isles until the flight of the Huguenots after the revocation of the Edict of Nantes (which granted limited toleration to the Huguenots within France) in 1684 by Louis XIV.

There was other immigration in the period 1066-1650, but it was small and highly selective. Craftsmen of talent were encouraged to settle here, particularly in the Tudor period. Italian families with trading and banking expertise (such as it was in those days) appeared after the expulsion of the Jews. Foreign merchants were permitted, but for much of the period on sufferance and subject to restrictions such as forced residence within specially designated foreign quarters.

The upshot of all this is that for six centuries after the Conquest, England was an unusually homogeneous country, both racially and culturally. This is reflected in the absence since the Norman Conquest of any serious regional separatist movement within the heart of English territory. There has been meaningful resistance at the periphery - Cornwall, the Welsh marches and the far north, but even that has been effectively dead since the sixteenth century. Englishmen have fought but not to create separate nations.

The Free-Born Englishman

It may have taken until 1928 for full adult suffrage of English men and women to arrive, but the essential sentiments which feed the idea of democracy - that human beings are morally equal and enjoy autonomy as individuals and a natural resentment of privilege and inequality - are ancient in England.

If there is one outstanding trait in English political history it is probably the desire for personal freedom. This might seem odd to the modern Englishman who sees the large majority of his country men and women consistently welcoming the idea of the most intrusive forms of ID cards and who stand by dumbly as many of the age-old and ineffably hard-won rights which protect the individual, such as the abridgement of jury trial and the right to silence, are being swept away by modern governments. But it was not always so and that "always so" was not so long ago. The great Austrian political and economic thinker Friedrich Hayek put it forcefully during the Second World War:

> It is scarcely an exaggeration to say that only in English society, and those societies deriving from it, is the notion of individual liberty built into the social fabric. The English have been free not primarily because of legal rights, but because it is their evolved social nature. They accept liberty because it seems natural to them. (*The road to Serfdom* - chapter *Material conditions and ideal ends*)

In short, individual liberty has been and is part of being English and part of England. It would be going too far to claim that the English masses have ever had any highly developed sense of liberal with a small 'l' sentiments, but throughout English history there has been both a widespread resentment of interference, either public or private, in the private life of English men and women and an acute awareness that privilege was more often than not unearned and frequently cruelly used to oppress the poor.

Most importantly, over the centuries the elite gradually adopted the ideal of personal freedom into their ideology. Here is the elder Pitt speaking on the notion of the idea that an Englishman's home is his castle:

> The poorest man may in his cottage bid defiance to all the forces of the Crown. It may be frail - its roof may shake - the wind may blow through it - the storm may enter - the rain may enter - but the King of England cannot enter! - All his force dares not cross the threshold of the ruined tenement! (Quoted in Lord Brougham's *Statesmen* in the time of George III)

The desire for liberty and a freeman's due is seen in the constant demand by medieval towns for charters which would free them from aspects of royal control, most particularly taxation. In some respects it helped fuel the barons' demand for Magna Carta. It drove the Peasants' Revolt. It provided the emotional engine for the decline of serfdom once circumstances were propitious after the Black Death. The Levellers made it their ideological centrepiece in the 1640s, their leader, John Lilburne, revelling in the name of "Freeborn John". "Wilkes and Liberty" was the mob's popular cry in that most aristocratic of centuries, the eighteenth. The Chartists held tight to the ideal in the nineteenth.

Equality and privilege

Intertwined with the desire for personal freedom was a strain of those seeking material equality and opportunity. It also had its expression in the organisation of society, most notably in the widespread use of common fields which were a natural source of egalitarian feeling. These were a form of agricultural organisation whereby a group of farmers worked strips on a large common plot of land, with the strips being rotated regularly to ensure that no one had the best land permanently.

Prime examples of the egalitarian mentality are found in the Peasants' Revolt of 1381 (which I shall deal with shortly in some detail), the sixteenth century has Thomas More's Utopia, while the Digger, Gerrard Winstanley writing in the 17th century spoke of "The cheat of men buying and selling" (The Law of Freedom 1652).

We also have the literary evidence. The English who people the pages of Langland and Chaucer show a medieval England where commoners would not as a matter of course willingly touch their forelock or allow their lives to be circumscribed by those with social status. Later, Shakespeare's lowlifes and the characters in Ben Johnson's Bartholomew Fair often show a rumbustious lack of deference for their social betters. It is improbable in the extreme that the worlds depicted by these authors would not have reflected the societies in which they lived. Traits were exaggerated for dramatic effect doubtless, but the cultural story they told was fundamentally rooted in the England in which they wrote.

Langland's *Piers Plowman* is especially interesting because the work begins with a catalogue of the people who inhabited the world he knew (Prologue - The plain full of people). Here are the worldly and the devout, the high and the low. The cleric and the noble jostle with minstrels, tramps, beggars, merchants, tradesmen, and the honest ploughman who tills "the soil for the common good". Langland's clerics are often corrupt, the nobles capricious, the merchants avaricious, the workmen shoddy and cheating in their work, the beggars dishonest and the minstrels bawdy, but they are balanced by honest men in their various callings. In other words, it is a world not so different in terms of human personality to that we inhabit.

The medieval elite ideology

There was also in the medieval world the idea that although men were unequal in material wealth or social status, nonetheless society was a co-operative enterprise, that all had a place and that all were entitled to that place, which was what God had called them to. Not egalitarianism but a recognition that men whatever their status had a right to life. The ideal was of course frequently breached but it nonetheless had a basis in both the attitude of the elite, especially in the Church, and in the organisation of society.

The ideas that men should just be left to buy and sell as they chose or that economic activity should be the lodestone of a man's life was admirable or moral, were alien concepts. Usury was officially banned for many centuries and the example of the poverty of the early Christians was given fresh focus by the Friars of St Francis and Dominic. More mundanely, there was also the concept of the just price, the price of staple foods such as bread, being fixed by magistrates. As a matter of social course it was accepted that the rich and great, and especially the Church, had moral and material obligations to the less fortunate. *Noblesse oblige* was not an empty term.

Turning men out of their homes and off the land for profit crashed through this medieval moral standard. That was what the grazing of sheep in particular accomplished, for it greatly reduced the need for agricultural workers. By the early years of the 16th century the problem of landless men was becoming acute. Some members of the elite rebelled against the cruelty of leaving thousands of men and their families without a means to live honestly and the alarming disruption of the medieval social order. Thomas More addressed the question most famously in his satire Utopia (1516). More complained that it was now thought moral to "buy abroad very cheap and sell again exceeding dear". He wrote of the mania for sheep as that which, "consume, destroy and devour whole fields, houses and cities". More also asked of those who turned men and women off the land to feed sheep, "What other thing do you do than make thieves and punish them?" and castigated the rich for a "strange and proud new fangleness in their apparel and too much prodigal riot and sumptuous fare at their table" while the poor starved or turned to crime or begging.

The Peasants' Revolt

Nothing demonstrates the Englishman's lack of deference and desire to be his own man better than the Peasants' Revolt in 1381. General resentment of privilege and particular hostility to the imposition of a tax (the Poll Tax) considered to be both unreasonable and illegitimate, was given unambiguous voice. For a brief period the fog of obscurity which ordinarily covers the masses in the medieval world clears. A remarkable scene meets the eye for we find not a cowed and servile people but a robust cast of rebels who far from showing respect for their betters display a mixture of contempt and hatred for everyone in authority bar the boy-king Richard II.

Perhaps most surprising to the modern reader is the extreme social radicalism of their demands which might, without too much exaggeration, be described as a demand for a classless society. The Revolt may have had its origins in the hated Poll Tax but it soon developed into a series of general political demands. One of the revolt's leaders, the hedge-priest John Ball, reputedly preached "Things cannot go right in England and never will until goods are held in common and there are no more villeins [serfs] and gentlefolk but we are all one and the same", and the anonymous and revolutionary couplet "When Adam delved and Eve span/who was then the gentleman?" was in men's mouths. The medieval chronicler Jean Froissart has Ball preaching:

> Are we not descended from the same parents, Adam and Eve? And what
> can they sow or what reason can they give why they should be more
> masters than ourselves? They are clothed in velvet and rich stuffs
> ornamented in ermine and other furs while we are forced to wear poor
> clothing. They have wines and fine bread while we have only rye and
> refuse of straw and when we drink it must be water. They have handsome

manors...while we must have the wind and rain in our labours in the field and it is by our labours that they...support their pomp. We are called slaves and if we do not perform our services we are beaten and we have no sovereign to whom we can complain...let us go to the King and remonstrate with him; he is young and from him we may obtain a favourable answer, and if not we must seek to amend our conditions ourselves. (Simon Schama, *A History of Britain*, p.248)

Whether or not these words bore any resemblance to Ball's actual words, whether or not they were black propaganda (on behalf of the elite) by Froissart to show the dangers society faced from the Revolt, we may note that the sentiments are compatible with the demands made by the rebels in 1381.

When the Kentish men led by Wat Tyler, an Essex man, met the 14-year-old king Richard at Mile End on 14th June, they demanded an end to serfdom and a flat rent of 4 pence an acre. The king granted the plea. When the king met the rebels a second time Tyler shook the king's hand and called him "brother". Tyler demanded a new Magna Carta for the common people which would have ended serfdom, pardoned all outlaws, liquidated all church property and declared that all men below the king were equal, in effect abolishing the peerage and gentry. Richard, much to the rebels' surprise, accepted the demands, although cunningly qualifying the acceptance "saving only the regality of the crown". A few minutes later Tyler was mortally wounded, supposedly after he had attempted to attack a young esquire in the royal party who had called him a thief. His death signalled the beginning of the end of the revolt for without Tyler the Revolt lost direction and those who remained willing to resist were pacified in the following few weeks.

During the Revolt the rebels did not run riot, but acted in a controlled manner, attacking the property of tax collectors, other important royal servants and any property belonging to the king's uncle, John of Gaunt. Any identifiable Exchequer document was ripe for destruction.

The revolt began in Essex when the commissioners attempting to collect the Poll Tax were surrounded by a hostile crowd on 30th May 1381. Physical threats were made against one of the commissioners, and the commissioners retreated from the immediate task of attempting to collect the tax. This brought in the Chief Justice of the Court of Common Pleas to restore order. He was captured by an even larger crowd and made to swear on oath that no further attempt would be made to collect the tax in the area. The names of informers who had provided names to the commissioners was discovered and the culprits beheaded.

The spirit of rebellion soon spread. By 2nd June a crowd in the village of Bocking had sworn that they would "have no law in England except only as they themselves moved to be ordained".

The rebellion had infected Kent by the end of the first week in June. By the time Wat Tyler, an Essex man by birth, had been elected to lead the Kentish men the demand was for the heads of the king's uncle John of Gaunt, the Archbishop of Canterbury Simon Sudbury and the Treasurer Sir Robert Hales. After Tyler's first meeting with Richard, Sudbury and Hales were captured and beheaded by the rebels. No deference or want of ambition there.

The extent to which the Revolt frightened the crown and nobility can be seen in the violence of Richard's words when he addressed another group of rebels at Walthamstow on 22nd June, by which time the danger was felt to have largely passed:

> You wretches, detestable on land and sea; you who seek equality with lords are unworthy to live. Give this message to your colleagues. Rustics you were and rustics you are still: you will remain in bondage not as before but incomparably harsher. For as long as we live we will strive to suppress you , and your misery will be an example in the eyes of posterity. However, we will spare your lives if you remain faithful. Choose now which you want to follow. (Simon Schama, *A History of Britain*, p. 254)

Anti-clericism

There were two great sources of general authority in medieval England. The Crown was one, the other was the Church. Yet, before the Reformation the English were renowned throughout Europe for their anti-clericism - a good example of this attitude was the response to Sudbury's warning to Wat Tyler's rebels that England would be put under an interdict by the Pope if he was harmed. This was met by hearty laughter followed by the grisly dispatch of the unfortunate cleric soon afterwards, whose head did not part from his shoulders until a goodly number of blows had been struck.

The contempt in which many of the servants of the Church were held can be seen in both John Wycliffe's complaints against clerical abuse in the latter half of the 14th century and in Geoffrey Chaucer's Canterbury Tales and William Langland's Piers Plowman, both written in the same century in which the Peasants' Revolt took place. Both works are full of jibes at fat illiterate priests and cheating pardoners who peddled absolution from sins with their indulgences sold for money.

Wycliffe's doctrine contained the fundamental ideas which were later realised internationally in the Reformation. He questioned the reality of transubstantiation (the Catholic belief that the bread and wine at Communion turn literally into the body and blood of Christ), he attacked the authority of the pope, he railed against the abuses of simony and indulgences. He advocated a bible in English and either he or his followers, the Lollards, produced a complete translation before the end of the fourteenth century.

Implicit within Wycliffe's thought was the democratic spirit, because it is a short intellectual step from the belief that each man could be his own mediator with God to the idea that he should have a say in his earthly life.

The Black Death

The Peasants' Revolt has to set in the context of the dramatic social changes wrought by the plague. When the Black Death came to England in 1349 it was a source of both immediate misery and future opportunity for those who survived. Estimates of the numbers who died range from a quarter to a half of the population, but whatever the true proportion it had the most dramatic effect on the organisation of society. The immediate result was a widespread transfer of property and consolidation of wealth as the lucky survivors inherited. This consolidation aided people a long way down the social scale, for a man inheriting no more than a couple of oxen and a plough was considerably better off than a man with none.

Most importantly, the country went from being one with an oversupply of labour - England prior to the Black Death was probably as well populated as it was in any time before 1700 - to a country where labour was scarce. Landowners were suddenly faced with a new economic world. They had either lost many of their workers through death or were faced with serfs who were no longer obedient and frequently absconded, often lured to work as free men by other landowners, or drawn to the anonymity of the towns. Landowners had to employ free men who demanded what were considered extortionate wages. The Statute of Labourers of 1351 was a forlorn attempt to keep things as they had been before the Black Death by restricting wages but, like all attempts to buck fundamental economic forces, it failed.

It is probably not overly sanguine to see English society in the late medieval period after the Black Death as a golden age for the common man. Not only was labour scarce and land plentiful, but the great enclosure movement was still in the future and a very large proportion of the population were, to a large extent, their own masters as they worked their land. Even where labour services were still performed, they were not crushing, being commonly 40 days work in a year. Moreover, agricultural work is seasonal, especially the arable, and for substantial parts of the year there is relatively little to do on a farm.

Beyond agriculture, many people had a large degree of control over their daily lives. This was the time before industrialisation, before the wage-slave and the factory. Skilled craftsmen were often their own masters, and even those who worked for a master will have organised their own time because they worked from their homes. Indeed, most English men and women today almost certainly have far less control of their time than the average medieval inhabitant of England.

The limits of state power

The hand of the state was also light by modern standards, especially so during the century long struggle of the Houses of Lancaster and York and partly because medieval kingship was of necessity very limited in what it could do administratively because of a lack of funds, the power of the peerage, primitive technology, poor communications, administrative naivety and a radically different view of what government and society should be - apart from looking after their own privileges and estates, kings were expected to defend the land, put down rebellions, provide legal redress through the royal courts, maintain the position of the church and lead in war against other rulers. And that was about it.

But there was also a further check on the monarch. Perhaps the most important practical adjunct of this desire for freedom, has been that the English long hated and mistrusted the idea of a standing army as the creature of tyrants. The English were eventually content to have the strongest navy in the world because it could not be used against them, but a substantial army was not accepted as reasonable until the experiences of the Great War accustomed men to the idea. Soldiers were held in contempt before then. "Gone for a soldier" was little better than "taken for a thief". The needs of Empire produced more ambivalence into the English view of soldiers as Kipling's poem *Tommy* shows: "Oh, it's Tommy this an' Tommy that, and chuck him out the brute! But it's 'Saviour of 'is country' when the guns begin to shoot." But the old resentment, fear and contempt remained until the stark democracy of experience in the trenches during the Great War tempered the English mind to tolerance of the soldier.

Because of a lack of a large standing army, English kings were ever dependent on the will of others, be it their nobles, parliament or the gentry. Even the most practically tyrannical of English kings, Henry VIII, was very careful to use Parliament to sanction his acts.

The consequences of this weakness was that power was localised. Incredible as it may seem today, the practical governance of day-to-day life in England until well into the nineteenth century lay largely in the hands of private gentlemen occupying the post of JP, whose powers were much greater than they are today. Indeed, the central state impinged very little on the ordinary Englishman before 1914. George Bowling, the hero of George Orwell's *Coming up for air*, reflecting on how the arms of the state touched an honest citizen before the Great War could think only of the registration of births, deaths and marriages and the General Post Office.

By keeping the king dependent upon the will of others, the English ensured that a despot such as Louis X1V could not arise in England and in so doing underwrote their general liberties. Without that, it is improbable that parliamentary government (as opposed to a parliament) would have arisen. England would almost certainly have been involved in many debilitating wars for the aggrandisement of the king. In those circumstances it is unlikely that England as a modern state would have arisen.

The medieval good times end

The comparatively good times for the poor of the post-Black Death world did not last forever. The enclosure movement began in earnest in the fifteenth century. Men were driven off the land and their place taken by graziers of sheep. The Tudors put an end to serious dynastic strife and expanded the power of the state. Gradually the population recovered. Trade grew and towns thrived, but it was also, by medieval standards, a time of high inflation caused by a mixture of a debased currency under Henry VIII, the economic consequences of the Dissolution of the Monasteries, population growth and the influx of gold and silver from the recently discovered New World.

The way to political success

Whatever its cause, England's political development is unparalleled. If political success lies in the general tenor of English society, the institutions through which it was achieved were cultivated from the thirteenth century. The start of the long climb towards representative government and the neutering of monarchy may reasonably be set in the reign of John. In 1215 he was forced by many of his barons to sign a charter which granted rights to all the free men of the kingdom. This charter, the Magna Carta, was of immense significance because it formally restricted the power of the king in an unprecedented way. The pope of the day thought it such an abomination he granted John absolution for its repudiation. Perhaps for the first time since the end of the classical world, a king had been forced to acknowledge unequivocally that there could be legal limits to his power.

Long regarded as a revolutionary document by historians, the fashion amongst them in recent times has been to treat the charter as little more than an attempt to preserve and enhance the position of the barons or to restate existing English law and custom. Of course it did that but it did much more. Had it done nothing beyond circumscribing the power of the king it would have been revolutionary, but it went far beyond that by explicitly extending rights that we consider fundamental to a free society of free men. Perhaps its two most famous clauses show its importance in the development of the future sharing of political power:

Clause 39. No free man shall be seized or imprisoned, or stripped of his rights or possessions, or outlawed or exiled or deprived of his standing in any other way, nor will we proceed with force against him or send others to do so, except by judgement of his equals or by the law of the land.

Clause 40. To no one will we sell, to no one will we deny or delay right or justice.

Until the security of a man and his property are secured, there can be no sustained spreading of power, for if a king may imprison and dispossess at will no man is safe. All merely live at the will of the monarch. By providing both, Magna Carta created the necessary legal and ideological infrastructure for the political development which culminated in parliamentary government.

Perhaps the most intriguing clause of Magna Carta was clause 61, which gave a committee of 25 Barons legal authority and practical power over the king. It is long clause but worth quoting in full:

Clause 61. Since, moreover, for God and the amendment of our kingdom and for the better allaying of the discord that has arisen between us and our barons we have granted all these things aforesaid, wishing them to enjoy the use of them unimpaired and unshaken for ever, we give and grant them the underwritten security, namely, that the barons shall choose any twenty-five barons of the kingdom they wish, who must with all their might observe, hold and cause to be observed, the peace and liberties which we have granted and confirmed to them by this present charter of ours, so that if we, or our justiciar[1], or our bailiffs or any one of our servants offend in any way against

---

[1] Chief political and legal officer who deputised for the king in his absence and presided over the king's courts.

any one or transgress any of the articles of the peace or the security and the offence be notified to four of the aforesaid twenty-five barons, those four barons shall come to us, or to our justiciar if we are out of the kingdom, and, laying the transgression before us, shall petition us to have that transgression corrected without delay. And if we do not correct the transgression, or if we are out of the kingdom, if our justiciar does not correct it, within forty days, reckoning from the time it was brought to our notice or to that of our justiciar if we were out of the kingdom, the aforesaid four barons shall refer that case to the rest of the twenty-five barons and those twenty-five barons together with the Community of the whole land shall distrain and distress us in every way they can, namely, by seizing castles, lands, possessions, and in such other ways as they can, saving our person and the persons of our queen and our children, until, in their opinion, amends have been made; and when amends have been made, they shall obey us as they did before. And let anyone in the country who wishes to do so take an oath to obey the orders of the said twenty-five barons for the execution of all the aforesaid matters, and with them to distress us as much as he can, and we publicly and freely give anyone leave to take the oath who wishes to take it and we will never prohibit anyone from taking it. Indeed, all those in the land who are unwilling of themselves and of their own accord to take an oath to the twenty-five barons to help them to distrain and distress us, we will make them take the oath as aforesaid at our command. And if any of the twenty-five barons dies or leaves the country or is in any other way prevented from carrying out the things aforesaid, the remainder of the aforesaid twenty-five barons shall choose as they think fit another one in his place, and he shall take the oath like the rest. In all matters the execution of which is committed to these twenty-five barons, if it should happen that these twenty-five are present yet disagree among themselves about anything, or if some of those summoned will not or cannot be present, that shall be held as fixed and established which the majority of those present ordained or commanded, exactly as if all the twenty-five had consented to it; and the said twenty-five shall swear that they will faithfully observe all the things aforesaid and will do all they can to get them observed. And we will procure nothing from anyone, either personally or through any one else, whereby any of these concessions and liberties might be revoked or diminished; and if any such thing be procured let it be void and null, and we will never use it either personally or through another.

The extreme nature of the concessions the king made - he gave permission for his subjects to act with force to remedy any Royal failure to observe the charter - is a graphic example of the inherent weakness of the medieval monarch. King he might be, but not a tyrant because he did not have the resources to dominate utterly.

This committee was never actually formed, but the clause has great interest. Once such a council of nobles to restrict the behaviour of the king is accepted as reasonable and possible, it is not such a great leap to the idea of a larger assembly which might do the same. That idea was realised before the century was out in a parliament.

Magna Carta is not as is commonly said the first formal restriction on the powers of a monarch. The coronation oaths of medieval kings regularly contained promises to observe the laws and customary freedoms of England, but there was no means of enforcing the oaths other than rebellion. There was even a previous occasion when Ethelred was forced to agree to formal restrictions on his powers in 1014, but that had no practical effect because of his death and the Danish conquest in 1016. Magna Carta, unlike coronation oaths, was both specific enough to usefully form the basis of law and in 1215 England did not fall under foreign rule. Instead, in modified form, it quickly became part of the statute books which developed in the thirteenth century. More importantly it acquired a mythological quality which lasts to this day. Every important English rebellion and political movement from 1215 until the Chartists in the 1840s has cited Magna Carta in their defence and derived their programme from it. The Levellers in the 1640s constantly cited it. It was a benchmark which allowed the powers of the king to be progressively whittled away. Never again could an English king convincingly claim that such restrictions on the prerogative were unthinkable or unprecedented.

Parliament

The distinction of the English Parliament is not that it is the oldest such assembly in the world (although it is one of the oldest), nor that it was unusual at its inception, for parliaments were widespread in medieval Europe. The English Parliament's distinction lies in its truly national nature - it was a national not federal assembly - its longevity and the nature of its development. No other parliament in a country of any size was meaningfully maintained by regular meeting through seven or eight centuries, its only competitors for endurance being the tiny Icelandic assembly and the federal arrangements of the Swiss. Most importantly, before England created such an institution to act as a model, no other parliament in the world developed into a fully fledged executive as well as a legislature.

The English Parliament made a very gradual progression to the place we know today. It began as an advising and petitioning body in the 13th century and before the end of the 14th century had come to exercise considerable power over any taxation which was considered over and above the king's normal and rightful dues, such as the excise. Gradually, this power transmuted into what was effectively a veto over most taxation. Parliament also added the power to propose and pass laws subject to their acceptance by the monarch. These developments meant that executive power gradually drained from the King. From this came cabinet government as the monarch was more and more forced to take the advice of his ministers and by the end of the 18th century the struggle between Crown and Parliament for supremacy had been emphatically decided.

As Parliament gained power, the Lords gradually diminished in importance and the Commons became by the 19th century, if not before, the dominant House. The final act in the play was a century long extension of the franchise culminating in a government dominated by an assembly elected under full adult suffrage from 1928 onwards.

A corrupted Parliament

By 1600 Parliament had become important enough to the governing of the country for Guy Fawkes and his fellow plotters to think it necessary to blow it up rather than simply killing the king and his ministers. In any other major European country of the time, the idea of destroying Parliamentary representatives rather than just the monarch and his more powerful friends would have seemed rather odd, either because a parliament did not exist or was considered of little account because European monarchs had been generally very successful in abolishing or curtailing the powers of medieval assemblies and preventing their political development.

But Parliament, although growing in power and ambition, was suffering the ills of any ancient institution. There were accretions of privilege and it had failed to keep pace with the changing times. In 1600 it neither represented the country as it was nor satisfied the growing wish of its members, especially the elected ones, to have a greater say in the management of England. At the heart of the dissatisfaction lay the unsatisfactory nature of the Commons' franchise. I shall examine this question in some detail because it will demonstrate the historical political backdrop against which the democratic radicals of the 1640s acted.

The question of the franchise

Serious disquiet with the Commons' electoral qualifications, provisions and practices began in Elizabeth's reign and reached its highest pitch, prior to the 1640s, during the years 1621 to 1623.

The discontent was provoked primarily by the situation in the boroughs rather than the counties. Since 1430, the county electorate had been restricted to the forty shilling freeholder, which qualification had become almost sacrosanct by the end of the sixteenth century - only one proposal before the 1640s (in 1621) was made to raise or lower it. Tudor inflation had greatly lowered the barrier it represented (40 shillings in 1600 was worth perhaps 15 shillings at 1430 values) and it is reasonable to suppose this considerably increased the rural electorate. Also, there is evidence to suggest that the qualification was not always enforced and some county electorates may have had a very broad manhood franchise indeed prior to 1640.

Borough franchises were anything but uniform. In some the whole 'commonalty' (all householders) or even all 'potwallers' (men with their own hearths) voted. In others the vote was restricted to all taxpayers ('scot and lot'), freemen of the town, or those in possession of burgage property. In extreme cases the vote might be restricted to the ruling corporation. Such discrepancies of representation were aggravated by a distribution of borough seats which took insufficient account of the demographic changes of the past two centuries, during which time England's population increased very substantially, especially during the 16th century, perhaps by as much as a third. These facts prepared a well mulched political soil for agitation for more equal borough representation, both in terms of the breadth of the franchise and in the number of seats.

Tudor monarchs, not unnaturally, did not favour larger electorates. The existence of 'rotten boroughs' was a source of patronage and, if the monarch could control the oligarchies who returned the MP, a means of reducing opposition to the Crown. As there was a significant number of such boroughs, this was no small advantage to the monarch.

The attitude of Parliament to the franchise was mixed. The Lords had a similar interest to the Crown in distrusting broad franchises. The peers often effectively controlled seats in the Commons. They also had a natural inclination to deny the 'commonality' any voice in the affairs of the kingdom. Conversely, it was obviously in the Commons' interest to increase electorates, where such increases reduced the Monarch's' and the Lord's opportunities for patronage.

There is particular evidence that the Puritans favoured larger electorates, at least in so far as it suited their own purposes. At Warwick, in 1586, Job Throckmorton was elected after he threatened to invoke the right of the 'commonality' to vote. In 1587 John Field remarked to a colleague 'seeing we cannot compass these things by suit or dispute, it is the multitude and people that must bring the discipline to pass which we desire.' (J.H. Plunb, *The Growth of the Electorate 1600-1715*) As Puritans displaced many court nominees and the creatures of aristocrats, this is significant in view of the attitude of the Commons towards electoral qualifications between 1621 and 1628.

By 1621, the Commons had gained the right to decide disputed elections and to revive lapsed borough seats and even make new creations. The tendency until 1628 was to decide in favour of a wider franchise and to allow all the 'commonality' to vote. At Bletchingly (1624) and Lewes (1628) 'all the inhabitants were to be electors', and at Cirencester (1624) all 'resients'. In the case of Pontefract in 1624 a general principle was formulated:

> There being no certain custom nor prescription, who should be the electors and who not, we must have recourse to common right which, to this purpose was held to be, that more than the freeholders only ought to have voices in the election, namely all men, inhabitants, householders resient [resident] within the borough.
>
> (J.H. Plunb, *The Growth of the electorate 1600-1715*).

Further, in the case of Boston (1628) it was asserted that the election of burgesses belonged by common right to the commoners and only prescription or 'a constant usage beyond all memory' could rob them of this. (K. Thomas, *The Levellers and the Franchise*, p.62)

It is true that when the Commons revived or created borough seats, they concentrated, as the Tudors had done, on small towns to promote their own advantage. But, even so, they granted 'scot and lot' franchises in every case (except Weobley) which meant that even small towns such as Great Marlow or Hilbourne Port had electorates of around 200.

Bills were introduced to regulate elections and standardise the franchise in 1621, 1623, 1625, 1628 and 1640. The 1621 Bill is of particular interest because it proposed that the 40 shilling freeholder qualification be increased to £4, and to admit £10 copyholders by inheritance, which would have narrowed the franchise in one respect (the freeholders) and broadened it in another (the copyholders).

The borough proposals did not extend the franchise in general terms beyond what had already been established by the various decisions on individual cases and in one respect reduced the franchise, for all electors were to be freemen of the borough except where they numbered less than twenty-four, in which case all inhabitants not in receipt of alms were to be included within the franchise.

In 1640 the franchise was raised again by Sir Simonds D'Ewes. It was he who first uttered the idea later made famous by Rainsborough 'that the poorest man in England ought to have a voice, that it was the birthright of the subjects of England and all had voices in the election of Knights etc. previously'. (K. Thomas, *The Levellers and the Franchise*, p.63)

In 1641 a bill had reached second reading but was then lost. D'Ewes favoured its contents except that he 'desired that whereas it was provided in the bill that none that took alms should have voices in elections, which I well allowed, we would likewise provide that no more monopolizing elections might be in cities and boroughs, that all men resients might have voices.' (K. Thomas, *The Levellers and the Franchise* p.64)

It is also noteworthy, both for its own sake and the part it played in Leveller literature, that many believed that the Statute of 1430 had disenfranchised people. William May, in 1621, said 'Anciently, all the commonality had voice, but because such a multitude made the election tumultuous, it was after reduced to freeholders'.

The religious radical William Prynne put it even more plainly,

> Before this Petition and Act every inhabitant and commoner in each
> county had voice in the election of Knights, whether he were a freeholder
> or not, or had a freehold only of one penny, six pence or twelve pence by
> the year as they now claim of late in most cities and boroughs where
> popular elections are admitted.
>
> (K. Thomas, *The Levellers and the Franchise*, p.64)

It is a sobering thought that if the Statute of 1430 did disenfranchise large numbers of county electors, the county franchise may have been wider in medieval England than it was to be again before the end of the nineteenth century and conceivably wider than the franchise before the 1918 Representation of the People Act.

What of the position of those deemed to be dependents: the servants, wage-earners and almstakers? Resident household servants were generally considered beyond the electoral pale, although 'servants' were said to have voted in the Worcestershire county election of 1604. Wage-earners certainly did so, for those in the 'potwaller' and 'scot and lot' constituencies were granted the right to vote. Almstakers were excluded in the 1621 and 1640 bills, yet at Great Marlow in 1604, 77 of the 245 voters were said to be almstakers, nine of them inmates of the almshouse. In 1640 the right of the Bember inmates to vote was said to have been sustained and in 1662 the St. Albans almsmen were said to have 'had voices time out of mind'.

It is clear from all this that those who promoted the radical or democratic cause in the 1640s, most particularly the Levellers, did not enter untilled ground. There are also three points of particular interest. First, the Commons, or at least an influential part of it, was not unduly disturbed by the prospect of an enlarged electorate. Second, those deemed to be dependent such as servants and almstakers - were included on occasion in the franchise long before the Civil War. Third, that there existed even gentlemen (such as Sir Simonds D'Ewes) who had an active and unambiguous democratic spirit. The latter point is particularly pertinent because the chief Leveller, John Lilburne, was also of gentle-birth, albeit *small gentry*, a fact he never ceased to emphasise. Clearly, democratic ideas and feeling were not foreign political bodies suddenly introduced by the Levellers and others in the 1640s.

The English civil war, Commonwealth and Protectorate

Stuart society was a world on the physical, economic and intellectual move and waiting to move faster if the right engine appeared. The civil wars of the 1640s was that machine.

Representative government is one thing, democracy quite another. That did not come to England in its formal form of a full adult franchise until the twentieth century. But for a brief period in the 1640s a franchise for the House of Commons broader than any used before the late nineteenth century was more than a pipe dream.

The Civil War and its republican aftermath, the Commonwealth and Protectorate, changed English politics utterly. It brought the end of claims by the English crown to Divine Right and absolute monarchy. It promoted the political interests of the aristocracy and gentry as a class. It forced those on the Parliamentary side to exercise power on their own responsibility. It created a political class which saw politics as something they could control rather than merely be part of as an adjunct to the crown. It raised the idea that there should be a law superior to that which even a parliament could pass. It began the constitutional process which resulted in cabinet government. It laid the foundations for the formation of political parties as we know them. In short, it planted the seeds of modern representative government.

Into this new world were cast men whose political philosophies ranged from acceptance of the divine right of kings to unyielding *communists*. In the middle were those, such as Cromwell, who though socially conservative, realised that power and political interest had shifted not merely from the king to Parliament, but also in some sense to an appreciably broader circle of people than before. Such people were willing to extend the franchise to a degree, although still restricting it to those with property for fear that the poor would dispossess the haves if they had the power to elect and that those with no material stake in the country would have no sense of responsibility and duty.

But that was insufficient for many, especially those who fought on the Parliamentary side in the wars, and something else occurred which was to be even more momentous in the long run. The belief that men generally should only be ruled by those they had themselves elected became a serious political idea.

That the notion should find expression as a serious political idea in the 1640s was, of course, partly a consequence of the disruption of society by civil war, but that was more an opportunity rather than a reason. Innumerable civil wars all over the world have come and gone without the democratic spirit being given rein. What made England of that time unusual was the long-existing ideal of individual freedom which had reached a high degree of sophistication, including the notion that free debate, the *sine qua non* of democracy, was of value in itself. Here are two passages which give a taste of the way minds were working in the 1640s. First, John Milton writing in the *Areogapitica* in the 1640s:

> And though all the winds of doctrine were let loose upon the earth, so truth be in the field [and] we do injuriously by licensing and prohibiting to misdoubt her strength. Let her and falsehood grapple; who ever knew truth put to the worse, in a free and open encounter...

The second statement comes from the Leveller Richard Overton's, *An Arrow against all Tyrants* (19th October, 1646). It contains as good a refutation of the power of authority without consent over the individual as you will find:

> No man hath power over my rights and liberties, and I over no man's...
> for by naturall birth all men are equally and alike borne to like propriety,
> liberty and freedom, and as we are delivered of God by the hand of nature
> into this world, everyone with a naturall, innate freedom and propriety...
> even so are we to live, every one equally and alike to enjoy his birthright
> and privilege... [no more of which may be alienated] than is conducive to
> a better being, more safety and freedome... [for] every man by nature
> being a King, Priest and Prophet in his own naturall circuit and compasse,
> whereof no second may partake, but by deputation, commission and free
> consent from him, whose naturall right and freedome it is. (*An Arrow
> against all tyrants*)

These were not odd voices crying out in the wilderness. The democratic spirit was widespread in the 1640s. By this I do not mean that men were commonly calling for full manhood suffrage, much less the emancipation of women. Even the most democratically advanced of the important groups which evolved during the Civil War, the Levellers, were unclear as to whether those who were deemed dependent in the sense of not being their own masters - servants and almstakers - should be given the vote or, indeed, who counted as a servant or almstaker.

Rather, there was a sense that the social order had been rearranged by the war, that men were on some new ground of equality and had a right to a public voice. In particular, there was a belief that those who had fought for Parliament had won the right to enfranchisement. There was also a widespread feeling, which penetrated all social classes, that the existing franchises (which as we have seen varied greatly) were frequently too narrow and that the towns, particularly those most recently grown to substantial size, were grossly under-represented.

Ideas of social and political equality had, as we have seen, existed long before the Civil War, but never before had large swathes of the masses and the elite seen anything approaching representative democracy as practical politics under any circumstances. The political and social elite of the period after 1640 may have been desperately afraid of a general representation of the English people, but they did not say it was impossible, merely feared its consequences. They may have loathed the idea of every man his own political master but they were forced by circumstances to admit that a Parliament elected on a broad franchise was not a fantasy.

The Putney Debates in 1647 provide a vivid record of the political fervour and mentality of the times. Parliamentary and Army leaders including Cromwell and his son-in-law Henry Ireton, met with a variety of people on what might broadly be called the democratic side. A substantial part of the debate was taken down in a shorthand. It is a most intriguing and exciting document, despite its incompleteness and some confused passages. The sheer range of political ideas it displays is impressive. It shows clearly that the 1640s experienced a high degree of sophistication amongst the politically interested class and that this class was drawn from a broad swathe of English society. The ideas discussed run from the monarchical to the unreservedly democratic, epitomised in Col. Thomas Rainsborough's famous words:

> ... I think that the poorest he that is in England hath a life to lead, as the richest he; and therefore truly, sir, I think it's clear, that every man that is to live under a government ought first by his own consent to put himself under that government; and I do not think that the poorest man in England is not at all bound in a strict sense to that government that he has not had a voice to put himself under...
>
> (Col. Thomas Rainsborough, *Puritanism and Liberty.*
> *The Putney debates,* p. 53)

Democracy, the revolutionary idea

Why was the idea of every man being an elector so revolutionary? There was of course the age-old traditional fear, known to the Greeks, that the masses would dispossess *haves* if they had control of who was to hold power. But the matter went much deeper than that. The enfranchisement of a wide electorate is perhaps the most fundamental political change a society can undergo. It forces the elite to take note of the masses in a way that no other system does. Even the humblest man must be considered as a man in his own right, a person with a vote and needs and wishes. Those needs and wishes may be heeded and met to varying degrees according to the success an elite has in subverting the representative process through such tricks as international treaties and the development of disciplined political parties, but what the majority needs and wants cannot as a matter of course be ignored completely when each man has a vote.

A form of male-only democracy existed in the ancient world, but it was never inclusive because the citizens were only a part of the population of a Greek civis and the large numbers of unfree men and free men who were not citizens were excluded. The Roman Republic had enjoyed in varying degrees at various times democratic expression through plebeian institutions such as the concilium plebis and offices such as that of tribune. But that was a class based representation which arose to oppose the Patrician class, not a self-conscious representation of individual men.

Received wisdom it may be now, but the idea that every man (but not woman then) should have an active voice in choosing those who would represent and govern them was to most people, poor and rich, a truly novel and disturbing concept in the middle of the 17th century.

The Levellers

The group which gave the strongest voice and effect to democratic feelings in the 1640s was the Levellers. They were a disparate and ever shifting crew, drawing their support primarily from the ranks of the Parliamentary armed forces (especially after the New Model Army was formed in 1645), small tradesmen, journeymen and apprentices. However, they also included those from higher social classes, their most famous leader, John Lilburne, being the child of minor gentry.

The Levellers time was brief. They were a serious political force for, at most, the years 1646 to 1649 and that is probably being a mite too generous. They failed utterly in the end, not least because they were unable to carry the army, especially the junior officers, with them. But they were important both for giving voice to the ideas and creating many of the practices on which modern politics is founded.

Their opponents attempted to portray the Levellers as social revolutionaries who would take the property of the rich, most particularly their land, and give it to the poor. Hence the epithet of Leveller which originated as a term of abuse. But the Levellers consistently denied that they had any such programme and were staunch defenders of the right to property. They might best be characterised as radical democrats with a very strong libertarian streak. Indeed, so far were they from being proto-communists that they had an almost sacramental belief in the individual's right to personal property.

Intellectually, they started from the view that all Englishmen had a birthright which entitled them to have a say in who should govern them, although at times they accepted that the birthright might be breached through dependence on a master or by receiving alms. More importantly, their ideology contained the germ of the idea of a social contract between the people and those who held power, an idea which was to come to dominate English political thinking for the next century or so through the philosophy of Thomas Hobbes and John Locke.

The Levellers were, with one or two exceptions such as Richard Overton, who was a deist at best and an atheist at worst, or John Wildman, who was a libertine and chancer, religious. But their belief had a strong vein of rationalism in it. They saw God not as the often cantakerous and domineering supernatural being of traditional Christianity, but as a rational intelligence who entered every man and allowed him to see what was naturally just and reasonable. For the Levellers, it seemed a natural right - a rational right - for a man to have a say in who should hold power and what they should do with the power.

The Levellers were happy to use historical props such as Magna Carta and the legend of Norman oppression when it suited them, but their rationality led them to question how men were governed from first principles. One of the Leveller leaders Richard Overton actually called Magna Carta a "beggarly thing" and went on to comment:

> Ye [Parliament] were chosen to work our deliverance, and to estate us in natural and just liberty, agreeable to reason and common equity, for whatever our forefathers were, we are the men of the present age, and ought to be absolutely free from all kinds of exorbitancies, molestations or arbitrary power.
>
> (*A Remonstrance. Tracts on Liberty in the Puritan Revolution*)

More balanced was his fellow Leveller William Walwyn:

> Magna Carta (you must observe) is but a part of the people's rights and liberties, being no more but what with much striving and fighting, was wrested from the paws of those kings , who by force had conquered the nation, changed the laws and by strong hand held them in bondage.
>
> (*England's Lamentable Slaverie.*
> *Tracts on Liberty in the Puritan Revolution*)

To call the Levellers a political party in the modern sense would be misleading. Yet they were the closest thing to it both then and, arguably, for several centuries. Their tactics and organisation were modern - the use of pamphletering and newspapers, the ability to get large numbers of supporters onto the streets (especially in London) at the drop of a hat, the creation of local associations. Much of this was the work of Lilburne, a man of preternatural obstinacy, courage and general unreasonableness. It says much for the restraint of the English elite of the day and respect for the law that he was not killed out of hand. It is difficult to imagine such behaviour being tolerated anywhere in Europe in the seventeenth century.

Lilburne by every account of him was a most difficult man - it was said that his nature was so combative that he would seek a quarrel with himself if he were alone - 'Jack would fight with John'. Yet this man, who came from a very modest gentry background, remained alive despite challenging the authority of first the king and then during and after the civil war, Parliament, Cromwell and the Commonwealth. He thus carried on this mortally dangerous behaviour for almost a generation. To the end of his life in 1657, he was thought dangerous enough to imprison.

Lilburne first came to notice for seditious speeches and writings in the 1630s. For that he was whipped from the Fleet to the Palace Yard where he was stood in the stocks. Whilst in the stocks, he removed copies of the pamphlets which had caused his punishment and threw them to the crowd. That little episode will give a good idea of Lilburne's general mentality. He was an extreme example one of those necessary unreasonable men without whom nothing great gets done.

From the time of his flogging onwards, Lilburne's career was one of studied defiance of authority. He was one of the most potent pamphleteers England has ever seen. For more than a decade, he produced a flood of writings guaranteed to inflame virtually anyone in public authority in the land. He faced down judges in the most powerful courts in the land. He controlled the London mob consummately. He treated the greatest men in the land as equals. In any other place on the planet at that time, he would have been dead meat before his career as an agitator began. But not in England. He might be flogged. He might be put in the stocks. He might be imprisoned. He might be tried twice for his life. But what 17th century England would not do was unreservedly murder him.

The Levellers developed an increasingly sophisticated political programme in a series of documents known as *The Agreements of the People*. These Agreements dealt extensively with political representation and structure. They were also very successful in creating a sense of historic grievance and an enemy. They did this by portraying 1640s England as having declined from a golden age of freedom to an oppressed land and people under the heel of the Normans and their various foreign successors.

The Levellers and the franchise

The Levellers changed their position on the franchise throughout their existence, tending to compromise when they thought that some accommodation with the likes of Cromwell could be made and became ever more radical as political power slipped away from them, although there were times and places throughout their existence when this general tendency did not hold true.

What the Levellers did retain always was a belief that all Englishmen were born with the same birthright. However, they accepted more often than not that certain parts of this birthright could be forfeited under certain conditions. Religious, civil and even possibly economic rights could not be alienated justly, and as such should be protected constitutionally. The right to elect, however, could be forfeited by entering into a condition of dependence, either by taking wages or alms. In such cases, a just dependence resulted and the subservient individual's voice was deemed to be included in that of his master or benefactor, as far as a voice in elections was concerned, just as that of a wife was deemed to be included in that of her husband. An idea of how the Levellers' position changed can be gained from these extracts from Leveller tracts:

> That the People of England,... ought to be more indifferently
> proportioned according to the number of inhabitants.
> > (The first article of the First Agreement.)

> [electors] shall be Natives, or Denizen of England, not persons receiving
> Alms ... not servants to, and receiving wages from any particular person.
> > (The Second Agreement - D.H. Wolfe, *Leveller Manifestoes*, p.403)

> Whereas it hath been the ancient liberty of this nation, that all the
> freeborn people have freely elected their representers in Parliament, and
> their sheriffs and Justices of the Peace, etc. and they were abridged of that
> their native liberty by a statute of the 8.H.6,7. That, therefore, the
> birthright of all English men be forthwith restored to all which are not, or
> shall not be legally disenfranchised for some criminal cause, or are under
> 21 years of age, or servants or beggars.
> > (The franchise clause (section ll) of the Petition of January 1648
> > D.H. Wolfe, *Leveller Manifestoes*, p.269)

By the time political opportunity had long passed the Levellers by, we find in 1653 a pamphlet which is Leveller in tone - *A Charge of High Treason exhibited against Oliver Cromwell summoning all the people of England to the polls as well masters, sons of servants.*

Constitutional restraint

The Levellers did one more thing which was to have great influence in the future: they created the idea of constitutional law acting as a restraint on a parliament.

The Agreements of the People placed restrictions on what Parliament might do, removing the power from Parliament to repudiate debts it had incurred, interfere with the operation of justice, destroy the rights to property or diminish the liberty of the individual. The Levellers even included provision granting the electorate the right to resist Parliament if it acted beyond its powers. They also called for annual parliaments, i.e. a general election every year, which would have been a great restriction in itself on what those with power might do.

In 1648 the Levellers attempted but failed to convene a Constitutional Convention of the type which more than a century later produced the American constitution. However, the idea of restraining Parliament by superior law was given form in the Instrument of Government which set up the Protectorate. The idea of such constitutional restraint disappeared in England after the Restoration and the novel doctrine of Parliamentary supremacy eventually won the day after the "Glorious Revolution" of 1689, when the monarch became king not by right of birth but by gift of Parliament.

Other radicals

The most uncompromising of the democratic and egalitarian forces in the 1640s were the so-called Diggers or, "True Levellers" led by William Everard but best known through the writings of Gerrard Winstanley. In many ways the Diggers, probably unwittingly, reiterated the most extreme egalitarian sentiments of the Peasants' Revolt, such as the reputed words of John Ball, and reached back to the medieval idea of society as a communal enterprise.

They believed that the land belonged to no one saying "None ought to be lords or landlords over another, but the earth is free for every son and daughter of mankind to live upon". (*Works*, ed by Sabine p289) For the Diggers the *natural* state of man was one of common ownership and the root of evil the egotistic desire for individual advantage including the "cheating art of buying and selling" by which king's live. (Winstanley's, *Law of Freedom*,1652)

In 1649 a small group of Diggers attempted to put their philosophy into practice camped on St Georges Hill near Walton on Thames in Surrey and attempted to cultivate common land. Further Digger attempts were made at Cobham in Surrey and at Cox Hall in Kent and at Wellingborough in Northamptonshire. All met with a mixture of legal and physical harassment by local landowners and even attracted the attention of the Council of State, which sent troopers to repress them. The Diggers were brought twice to court.

Their numbers were small, probably amounting to no more than a hundred or so at most and they had no lasting direct legacy. Yet they are a reminder that many Englishmen have never accepted willingly the unearned privileges of social rank or vast differences in wealth while the masses struggled to feed themselves.

The Diggers are also significant for giving voice through Winstanley to the novel idea that the end of politics should be the well-being of the common man and for the clear recognition that liberty rests on the economic state of society.

Exporting *Representative Government*

After Cromwell's establishment of the Protectorate, democratic ideas did not gain serious political currency in England for more than a century, but the example of England's continually evolving parliamentary government proved a potent one.

The Restoration did not result in serious legal abridgements of the power of the monarch, but Charles II was in practice much restricted by a Parliament unwilling to adequately open the purse strings for a monarch who was, ironically, expected to do more and more as the formal power of the state grew.

The *Glorious Revolution* of 1689 produced a true constitutional sea-change. From then on the English monarch ascended the throne only with the acceptance of Parliament, and the Bill of Rights (1690) placed further restrictions on the monarch. Amongst the long list of things the king was forbidden to do were:

- Dispense with and suspend laws, and the execution of laws, without consent of parliament.

- Levy money for and to the use of the crown, by pretence of prerogative, for another time, and in other manner, than the same was granted by parliament.

- To raise and keep a standing army within England in time of peace, without consent of parliament, and quartering soldiers contrary to 4.

- To violate the freedom of election of members to serve in parliament.

- To demand excessive bail of persons committed in criminal cases, "to elude the benefit of the laws made for the liberty of the subjects".

- To impose excessive fines and illegal and cruel punishments.

The abuses of power by the crown listed in the Bill of Rights are described as being "utterly and directly contrary to the known laws and statutes, and freedom of this realm". Again that old reliance on the law and the traditional freedoms of the Englishman.

From 1689 began the century long decline of the monarchy as an executive power. The American War of Independence sealed the fate of the monarch and the Americans forged a new version of the English political model, with a formal separation of powers and a written constitution to restrict what governments and legislatures might do.

The received academic opinion on the American constitutional settlement is that it was the offspring of John Locke. In fact, it had at least as much affinity with the ideas of the Levellers. There is no direct intellectual link, but the most important popular propagandist on the American side, the Englishman Tom Paine, shared much of his ideology with the Levellers. The Constitution is a balancing act between Locke and Paine, granting a large degree of popular involvement in politics, whilst tempering it with restrictions such as electoral colleges and granting through the Bill of Rights (which was inspired by the English Bill of Rights of 1690) constitutional protections for the individual against the state.

If the American Revolution owed its shape and inspiration to England, the French Revolution was inspired by both English constitutional development and the American revolutionary example. Most political revolutions resulting in an attempt at representative government, have been touched, consciously or not, by the legacy of the American and French revolutions.

England through control of the British Empire, ensured that the Westminster model of government was transplanted with widely differing success, to approximately a quarter of the world's population, when the empire dissolved in the twenty years after 1945.

The astonishing upshot of the English example, the American and French Revolutions and the British Empire, is that the political structures of most modern states are broadly based on the English constitution of King, Lords and Commons, the overwhelming majority having a head of state plus two assemblies. In addition, the widespread practice of a written constitution derives from the example of the United States, which of course drew its form and inspiration from English settlements in North America, English history and political practices. These political structures apply as readily to dictatorships as they do to liberal democracies.

Of course, the balance of power between the head of state and the assemblies varies widely and there is much difference between Parliamentary and Presidential government, but they all have their ultimate origin in the example of the English system of representative government.

One last thing. Look around the world. How many countries can be said even today to have accepted elected representative government and the rule of law as a banal fact of life, the norm of their society? Britain, the USA, Australia, Canada, New Zealand certainly, Switzerland and Scandinavia possibly. But where else? Not France which as recently as 1958 overthrew the Fourth Republic. Not Germany which embraced Hitler nor Italy the land of Mussolini. Not Spain so recently loosed from Franco. As for the rest of the world, that tells a sorry tale of elites who generally have such a lack of respect for the individual and a contempt for the masses that the idea of shared power with and for the people is simply alien to them.

The fact that the only really stable examples of elected representative government in countries of any size are in those countries which have their origins in English colonisation strongly suggests that it was no accident that it was in England that the institution evolved. There must be something highly unusual about English society for it both to develop in a manner so different from any other country and to export this rare and valuable difference to its colonies.

William Cobbett
A rebel for honesty, for country people and for England

Edward Canfield

Our nation is under attack. It is under attack by those who wish to subvert our democracy and to subordinate the English people to the jurisdiction of foreign courts and institutions. And not simply that; it is under attack by those who aim to fragment our country into regions and to destroy our sense of common culture and identity. At a time like this, English patriots find ourselves compelled to fix our eyes on the arrogant and reckless forces of destruction. We certainly should be grateful to all patriots who have entered the political battle and thrown their energies into resisting those who scheme our national destruction. Yet if we are to be steadfast through the storms of repeated battle, we shall need more than energy and enthusiasm, more than just valid information of the immediate plans and tactics of our enemy. We shall need the long-lasting determination that springs out of a deep fondness for our country and out of an awareness of our national past, of the strengths and achievements of our people. Our history matters. It is an essential resource to inspire us and to harden our will in the struggle against those who are constantly worming away to erode and suppress the independence and integrity of our nation.

Who are they that act so traitorously? Overwhelmingly they come from within the elites of the political class, the media and the civil service. As we find ourselves confronted by a contemptuous British state and political establishment coldly ignoring our interests, loyalties and deep identity, we need to investigate the past relationships between that contemptuous ruling order and the thoughts and aspirations of our English ancestors. How well have they served each other? Has the British state defended well in the past the interests of our people or has the quisling frame of mind that now permeates elite circles in fact been a trait lurking within the thought of our dominant classes for many generations? What has been the real relationship between the British state and the English people over the last two centuries, the real history of our island, the real history of the rulers and the ruled?

We face difficulty in the task of recovering our history. Facile and superficial accounts of our national past have too often suppressed a record of tension and dissent and have sought instead to set up a narrative of cosy celebration of the British state. Other historians have recognised critical strains of thought and feeling but have distorted them, incorporating them within historical narratives that have changed meaning and ignored original objectives.

The narratives that incorporated the radical and dissident Englishness have been those of 'Labour' and 'Working-Class' history. These schools of history were successful over much of the twentieth century, explaining our past in terms of a developing progress or forward march. Historians of these schools have claimed that the English working class appeared as a conscious social class during the opening decades of the nineteenth century when an explosion of radical and democratic thinking and action swept our country. It was at that time, according to their narratives, that a newly industrialising society polarised into antagonistic classes. The Labour and Trades Union movement emerged. It campaigned on social issues and grew stronger. A forward march developed leading to the establishment of the Labour Party, the triumphant election of Labour governments and the creation of a welfare state. Working people, in the course of this march, not only benefited in health, diet and physique but in consciousness and understanding. From the original crude mentality of 'primitive rebels' they evolved into class-conscious, urban-minded workers. According to the Labour or social democratic school, the working-class movement was able to capture the British state and use it for its own purposes. This was a class not a national struggle and the issue of Englishness didn't come into it.

So let us look at these histories and investigate their 'truths'. In their survey of this two hundred year march, G.D.H. Cole and Raymond Postgate recognised the radical journalist William Cobbett as a pivotal figure in the emergence of an identifiable working class. They comment:

> The time when the British common people first, en masse, show a political mind of their own, separate from their rulers, is probably not earlier than the days of Cobbett.[1]

According to Cole and Postgate, Cobbett and his fellow-fighter, Henry Hunt, became in the turbulent years following the Napoleonic Wars: 'the outstanding leaders of working-class Radicalism'.[2] Raymond Williams, a New Left Marxist of the '60s and '70s, maintained a similar tone of approval towards Cobbett in his fascinating but tendentious study of English country writing, *The Country and the City*.[3] In his brief chapter on Cobbett, he exploited Cobbett's strident concern over the living conditions of the rural poor as a foil with which to highlight Jane Austen's near-total erasure of lower orders from the plot or background of her novels. So Williams was able to grant Cobbett his approval for his 'social questioning' and his 'class viewpoint' at a time of 'a developing capitalist order in the land'.[4]

Yet all these comments make the assumption that Britain was passing through a stage in social development that involved an inevitable progression towards an urban class-divided society. They assume, too, that complex political voices, such as that of Cobbett, can be judged as part of this process of modernisation and that their validity lies in the extent to which they adopted the norms of the social conflict of that pre-destined future. Writing about agrarian riots and rick-burning of 1830, Williams asserts grandly:

> Such disturbances had necessarily to be succeeded by the organisation of class against class, in trade unionism, and in its associated political movements. The structure of feeling that had held in direct appeal and in internal moral discrimination ... was now necessarily transformed into a

---

[1] GDH Cole & Raymond Postgate, *The Common People,* 1949, p.686
[2] ibid p.247
[3] Raymond Williams, *The Country and the City*, 1985 p.108-119
[4] ibid p.112

different order of thinking and feeling. The maturity of capitalism as a system was forcing systematic organisation against it.[5]

But what if that old-established 'structure of feeling' did not need any such transformation? What if it retained, and retains, within it a perfectly valid perception of the individual's social and political environment? What if it was Williams and not Cobbett who was mistaken and what if it was Williams who had misinterpreted as 'the maturity of capitalism' one particular and passing phase of our national experience?

At first sight the left-wing interpretation seems credible. William Cobbett was born in 1763 in the heart of southern England destined apparently to be a farmer's boy but died in 1835 a Member of the House of Commons representing Oldham, a town in the forefront of the new industrialisation. He certainly did play a major role in radical history, particularly in the years between 1816 and 1835. He became an enormously influential voice for the discontented and the unenfranchised poor after 1816, when he decided to issue a cheap edition of his *Political Register* for two-pence. Samuel Bamford, the Lancashire weaver and militant democrat recalled;

> The writings of William Cobbett suddenly became of great authority; they were read on nearly every cottage hearth in the manufacturing districts. ... This influence was speedily visible; he directed his readers to the true cause of their sufferings – misgovernment; and to its proper corrective – parliamentary reform.[6]

Cobbett continued to campaign until his death nearly twenty years later, touring the impoverished agricultural districts during the 1820s, renewing his call for parliamentary reform in 1829 and 1830, facing trial in 1831 accused of inciting the Swing Riots of agricultural labourers and finally taking a stand as a newly elected MP against the New Poor Law of 1834.

When, however, we investigate Cobbett's ideas, he does not appear so readily as a father-figure of the later socialist or social democratic politicians. Some left-wing historians were honest enough to admit this. E.P. Thompson, the most creative thinker of the 'New Left', was eager to give his approval to Cobbett's political activism but not to his actual political demands. Thompson writes approvingly that;

> he was willing to challenge the received social order ... This is why Cobbett and John Fielden, his friend and fellow Member for Oldham after 1832, came so close to being spokesmen of the working class.[7]

Thompson, however, then concludes uncertainly that Cobbett;

> nourished the culture of a class whose wrongs he felt but whose remedies he could not understand.[8]

---

[5] ibid p.112
[6] Samuel Bamford, *Passages in the Life of a Radical,* 1859, p.6
[7] E.P. Thompson, *The Making of the English Working Class*, 1968, p.836

Thompson, as a New Left Marxist, was uneasy with Cobbett's remedies because they did not fit into the accustomed programme of the socialist Left. To Cobbett the roots of conflict lay not within the productive process of industry, in a clash between workers and employers, but within the relationships between the state and civil society, between those on the one hand who lived off their labour and those on the other who consumed taxes and lived off the interest of state debt. Cobbett described the system that produced this as 'The Thing', a bloated leviathan of state power entwined with high finance. Writing about the consequences of the growth of the National Debt, Cobbett declares;

> I saw how it had been the instrument of putting unbounded power into
> the hands of the Government; I saw how it had drawn the wealth of the
> country into masses, how it had destroyed the lower and middle classes of
> farmers, how it had added to the list of paupers, how it had beggared and
> degraded the country.[9]

So Cobbett's target was not the capitalist system in which, according to Marx, the worker's labour power is exploited by the employer but 'The Thing' under which all productive classes are exploited by the tax-eaters and their government. According to this viewpoint the socialist call for the nationalisation of the commanding heights of the economy would provide no remedy to the problems afflicting the common people. It would in fact worsen them by inflating the opportunities for patronage, corruption and waste.

That Cobbett was no early pioneer of socialism has been obvious for years. As long ago as 1945 H.J. Massingham, the great defender of the traditions of rural England, pointed out that Cobbett always upheld;

> the inalienable rights of private property. He stood foursquare for private
> property as a means to freedom and for freedom as only to be secured by
> private property.[10]

We need discuss this issue no further. The traditional socialist programme for the state ownership of industry is of course now abandoned as unconvincing by all except the most ancient of old leftists.

The programme of old red socialism may have withered away but that of its pink social democrat rival, with its goal of a state-regulated 'social market economy', still remains to haunt us. The commitment to increasing the interference of the state into wider and wider areas of economic, social and personal life has not only survived but has been given added assertiveness by the interventionist obsession of the bureaucrats of the European Union. Needless to say, the working people who eagerly read Cobbett's papers did not find in them any arguments for any great interference of the state in personal life, for he observes;

---

[8] E.P. Thompson, *The Making of the English Working Class*, 1968, p.837

[9] ed. William Reitzel, *The Autobiography of William Cobbett: the Progress of a Ploughboy to a Seat in Parliament* (an edited selection from the writings of Cobbett), 1947, p.129

[10] H.J. Massingham, *The Wisdom of the Fields,* 1945, p.23

> Something must be left and something ought to be left, to the sense and reason and morality and religion of the people. There were a set of 'well-meaning' men in the country, who would have passed laws for the regulating and restraining of every feeling of the human breast and every motion of the human frame.[11]

Cobbett believed that the common people had a better sense of how to conduct their lives than the 'bleeding heart' experts of his time.

Cobbett and his supporters were utterly opposed in their economic programme, too, to the growth in the power of the state. Within years of his return to England from America in 1800 he began to denounce what he called the 'Pitt-system' or 'the funding and taxing system'. He bitterly attacked the ruling elite that was imposing heavy taxation on the people while paying substantial interest to those who had been able to subscribe to the state debt. The Pitt system can be characterised as the grafting together of high finance and the state. Cobbett denounced the consequences the system brought, noting that;

> the tendency of the funding and taxing system was to draw the produce of labour into unnatural channels, into the hands of upstart cormorants, and to deal it back again in driblets, under the name of relief or charity, just to support the life of those from whose pores it had been drained.[12]

From the current contemporary perspective such intense distaste for the intervention of the state into social life can often appear strange. We have been conditioned into this response by the experience of the first half of the twentieth century when the state's intervention helped to handle the acute problems of unhealthy housing, inadequate sanitation, endemic disease and impoverishment in old age. But this heroic age of state intervention has passed away, its achievements seemingly secure by the mid-twentieth century but fading and tarnished thereafter. The viewpoint, favoured by social democrats, that the state (good) and private wealth (bad) are two antagonists has become dated. Too often what we experience now is the collaboration of state and big business to impose their wishes and advance their interests at the expense of the rest of our national community.

Examples of this collaboration abound. The mid twentieth century state deliberately and consciously financed a vast nuclear power programme which natural economic channels would have made unviable. Just as it deliberately and consciously laid out an infra-structure which made the triumph of the motor-car over the railway fixed and unalterable, it is now promoting the interests of the airline industry by a range of tax subsidies and by backing the expansion of airport facilities. The directives and edicts we are receiving from the European Commission act in exactly the same direction, suffocating the small entrepreneur in regulation while giving the advantage to big multi-nationals that have the capacity to absorb sudden increases in costs. The EU's Common Agricultural Policy is the most striking example of how the intervention of the state, in this

---

[11] Reitzel, p.92-3
[12] ibid p.94

case the European state, has cut across natural economic development and provided subsidies to fuel massive over-production by vast agri-businesses. Natural economic channels, if allowed to flow freely, would by now have long seen a collapse in the price of low-grade intensively produced foodstuffs. This would have removed the incentives to farm in this destructive manner and left the way clear for small producers of organic and speciality produce to take an increasing, and perhaps even a predominant, role within English rural life.

So it seems that it is Cobbett's critique, rather than that of later socialism or social democracy, which is now proving more useful in helping us to interpret the society in which we live. The state and private wealth are not opposed forces as the social democrat dogma asserts. Instead big business and the state are working together to subordinate the rest of us and to advance their own interests. We are still facing the 'Pitt-system', or its equivalent. English radicals of our age must take up Cobbett's programme and oppose the alliance between the interfering, regulatory state and the cushioned, privileged tax-eaters and market-manipulators, the alliance that is stifling small enterprise and distorting and reducing the choices available to the ordinary consumer.

So if Cobbett, a father figure of English radicalism cannot be seen as a fore-runner of modern socialism or of social democracy, what does he represent? Cobbett always saw himself as a traditional countryman and not as a cosmopolitan and urbane inhabitant of the city:

> I have always most loved and cherished the people employed in the cultivation of the land... Born amongst husbandmen, bred to husbandry, delighting in its pursuits even to the minutest details, never having, in the range of life, lost sight of the English farm-house and of those scenes in which my mind took its first spring, it is natural that I should have a strong partiality for country life, and that I should enter more in detail into the feelings of labourers in husbandry than into those of other labourers.[13]

Cobbett looked back fondly to his early boyhood when he was employed to scare the birds from the turnip seed. He revelled in country sports and pursuits and looked back with nostalgia to his youth when farmers provided board and lodging to their labourers, when the rural community acted as an organic whole. He deplored the spread of enclosures, which sacrificed the beauty of the land and the common welfare of the country people to the advantage of those who pursued the crude expansion of production and the maximisation of profit. If Cobbett were alive today, he would be one of the most vigorous defenders of country life, opposing the wilful neglect of its vital interests and the hostility of this government towards it.

What else does Cobbett represent to us now? Many historians have pointed to the year 1809 as a great turning point in Cobbett's life, dividing it into two halves. Before 1809 he had gained his fame as a journalist, who was campaigning vigorously against the democratic cause, first in the USA and then in Britain.

---

[13] Reitzel, p.234

After then he won his reputation by doing the exact opposite, campaigning for parliamentary reform and the democratic extension of the franchise. Yet it seems unlikely that Cobbett underwent a complete and drastic transformation in his fundamental beliefs. There were strong continuities in Cobbett's life. Corruption, injustice and the abuse of power were constant targets of his rage both before and after 1809.

Patriotism was the great constant in his life. From his love of the countryside sprang his love of country, of England. He proudly admitted that:

> All that I can boast of in my birth is that I was born in Old England.[14]

The truth is that before 1809 Cobbett was motivated by a burning hatred of those who were mocking and sniping at his country in the USA and in Britain and that after 1809 he was motivated by a burning hatred of those who were ruining his country by increasing state debt and excessive taxation.

It is true that the focus of his patriotism did change. His love of our country first emerged as an instinctive reaction rather than as an intellectual consideration. He swung his immense energy into play with an emotional defence of the superficial emblems of our nationhood. Explaining why he took up his pen in the USA to rebut the enemies of his homeland, he writes:

> the first object was to contribute my mite toward the support of the authority of the Sovereign, whom God had commanded me to honour and obey. The uniform intention of my writings was, and is, to counteract the effects of the enemies of monarchy in general, and of the monarchy of England in particular.[15]

If this had been all there was to Cobbett's patriotism there would be little to make this combative and lucid journalist so outstanding and so relevant to us today.

True patriotism involves a loyalty to more than just the upper emblems of nationhood. It involves loyalty to the folk of the nation and when the upper classes did not listen, as they did not listen to Cobbett's denunciation of the funding system, the true patriot must look out to the folk, the common people. In 1809 that moment came for Cobbett. It was not a transformation of his beliefs, but a development, a necessary development, a development from loyalty to the emblems of nationhood to loyalty to the living nation as a whole. It was a moment when Cobbett realised that the common people of England were not only corruptly misgoverned but were also unjustly oppressed. He describes in his own clear, forthright style:

> In 1809 some young men at Ely, in what was called the 'local militia', had refused to march without the 'marching guinea', which the Act of Parliament awarded them. This was called Mutiny; and a body of Hanoverian horse were brought from Bury St Edmunds, to compel these young Englishmen to submit to be flogged! They were flogged, while surrounded by these Hanoverians.[16]

---

[14] Reitzel, p.10
[15] ibid p.87
[16] ibid p.116

So a group of young English men who had volunteered to serve their country in the militia had been corruptly and dishonestly cheated of their earnings. For the offence of complaining about this, they had been punished by flogging at the hands of foreign mercenary troops. This was a cause to inflame Cobbett's heart.

> I, in my Register, expressed my indignation at this, and to express it too strongly was not in the power of man. The Attorney-General, Gibbs... harassed me for nearly a year, then brought me to trial. This took place on the 15th of June 1810 when I was found guilty of treasonable libel by a Special Jury.[17]

Rather than accept that it had unjustly oppressed some young Englishmen, the ruling elite turned on the journalist who had exposed the injustice! Imprisoned in Newgate for two years, Cobbett was financially ruined and obliged to sell his beloved farm at Botley. He was now set on his ultimate career as the clarion of radicalism and the tribune of the common people that was to last until his death in 1835. But he was the same Cobbett throughout. It was the same patriotism that was now driving him to radicalism that had inspired his earlier defence of the country and his King.

Cobbett's sense of English patriotism shines out of his writings, such as when he was explaining his views on political reform:

> All I wished, and all I strove for, was the Constitution of England, undefiled by corruption... There was so much good in the institutions which we had inherited from our fathers, that I always looked at any change in them with great apprehension. But, with regard to the monstrous encroachments of the aristocracy and the usurers, within the last fifty years especially, it was impossible for me not to wish for a change.[18]

It shines out, too, when he was considering the objectives that had inspired his life of political struggle:

> If I have one wish more ardent than all other, it is this; that I, enjoying my garden and few fields, may see England as great in the world, and her industrious, laborious, kind and virtuous people as happy as they were when I was born.[19]

It shines out when he was looking back late in life on what that life of struggle had achieved:

> Some generations, at least, will pass away before the name of William Cobbett will cease to be familiar in the mouths of the people of England; and, for the rest of the world, I care not a straw.[20]

---

[17] Reitzel, p116
[18] ibid p214
[19] ibid p236
[20] ibid p235/6

During his life Cobbett witnessed the zenith of the British state, when that state was at its most effective in mobilising the English, Scottish and Irish peoples to wage war, to build empire and to advance vigorous economic growth. Cobbett was not swayed by those apparent successes. His loyalties were to England and the English people and when he saw the ruling elite oppressing his people, he had no qualms about where his duty lay and how he should respond.

In our day we find the British state long sunk in decadence, demoralisation and decay. The ruling elite has now no determination for any objective but that of managing an orderly decline which it regards as the inevitable fate of our nation. The ruling elite indeed has no longer any faith in our people as a nation with a defined and cherished homeland and with a right of self-government. The loyalties of the elite now lie elsewhere and its goals involve the destruction of our own English culture and sense of identity. So with the ruling elite the people of England no longer share common loyalties and common goals. There is now a yawning gap between the interests of the British state and the interests of the English nation. How much easier it should be, and how much more impellent it is, that we now follow Cobbett's example and campaign tirelessly against the injustices and oppressions which the industrious, laborious, kind and virtuous folk of England are now enduring at the hands of the government of our time, a government so fatuous, so dishonest and so utterly beneath our contempt. We have great figures of courage in our English past. We in this generation must now be steadfast in taking up the path they so heroically and vigorously pioneered before us as patriots and Englishmen.

Too late, too late!

Robert Henderson

All around is heard the whisper -
Bend your mind towards the wind,
Our rulers are effete
And none new to be found.
Soon the world will shake
Before never altered truths
Of blood and land
Which hide behind
The scapegrace clothes
Of selfish fools
Who mewl upon an idea
Thinking wishing is reality.

A Parliament for England

Robert Henderson

Let me put my cards on the table: I view devolution as a most pernicious and reckless act which has gratuitously destabilised what was arguably the best-established and most harmonious political arrangement in the world, namely, the United Kingdom. But the deed is done and cannot be realistically undone. So the question the English must now of necessity address is not how to put the union back together again, but how best to guard their own country and interests. This is a matter of urgency, indeed simple self-preservation, for the Blair government has made it clear that English interests will not merely be casually neglected, but placed under active attack. Behind the domestic threat and linked to it through New Labour ambitions, are the Federal ambitions of the European Union.

Why do we need an English Parliament?

The short answer is that an English Parliament is needed to achieve a stable constitutional settlement following devolution within the rest of the UK and to protect the interests of England.

The sense of national identity and the political power of the Scots and the Welsh is enhanced by devolution. It gives them significant control over their domestic affairs, strengthens their ability to deal directly with non-British agencies such as the EU and, most importantly, provides assemblies for the expression of their national aspirations.

England, on the other hand, merely loses by devolution. Scots, Welsh and Northern Irish members continue to vote on all English matters. On the other hand, English MPs are denied an opportunity to vote on many important areas of Scots, Welsh and Irish legislation and English ministers are prevented from forming policy on domestic Celtic matters.[1]

It is also unlikely that Scotland, Wales and Northern Ireland will be satisfied forever with their current devolved powers. As they develop confidence, each national political class will seek more control over their domestic matters. Scotland will push for greater tax raising powers and the removal of what remains of Westminster's power to interfere in their domestic life: Wales will continually seek equality with Scotland. Northern Ireland will do the same if they ever get their assembly up and running again. That is human nature. The inexorable and natural trend will be towards greater and greater autonomy.

In short, England requires a parliament to defend her own interests without the distraction of the domestic needs of the rest of the UK or the interference of politicians sitting for non-English constituencies.

Behind the domestic reasons for an English Parliament lurk the federalist aspirations of the EU.

---

[1] For the sake of convenience I shall refer to Scotland, Northern Ireland and Wales collectively as *the Celts* and their doings and interests as *Celtic*. I offer an apology to Lowland Scots and the Protestants of Northern Ireland.

The Eurofederalists

The Eurofederalists fear English interests being realised and defended. They understand that a strong, self-confident England would spell the end of their plans to embed Britain within the EU. That Scotland, Wales and Northern Ireland should have a means of national political expression is nothing to them, because these countries are, in their eyes, too insignificant and above all too poor to resist the march of Eurofederalism. England with fifty million people and the third or fourth largest economy in the EU is a different kettle of fish. It is also a fact that opinion polls show the English to be considerably more Eurosceptic than the rest of the UK.

The Eurofederalists' preferred means of preventing England from realising her political potential is the institution of Regional Assemblies. Here Brussels works hand-in-hand with the Blair Government, which is both emotionally committed to Eurofederalism and sees regional English assemblies as a means to emasculate England politically – Labour, never having had a substantial overall majority of English seats in their history, is heavily dependent on non-English constituencies for a majority at Westminster. Finally, from the Labour viewpoint, English regional assemblies also divert attention from the imbalance of the constitutional arrangements as they stand.

The groundwork for Balkanising England has already been done through the institution of eight publicly funded Regional Development Agencies (RDAs) and the creation of unelected consultative bodies which roughly correspond to the physical areas covered by the RDAs. Interestingly, these divisions of England correspond to the English regions planned by the EU.

The process of formal English political regionalisation began with the creation of a mayor and assembly for London. That was followed by a promise from the Government that referenda would be held during 2004 in at least three of the English regions. That was subsequently reduced to one region – the North East.

The political regionalisation of England would provide the EU with an opportunity to advance its interests. The tactic of the Eurofederalists will be to create, through competition, conflict between the English regions at RDA level before referenda are arranged for elected regional assemblies. Those arguing for a YES vote in such referenda will point to the negotiating advantages gained by Wales and Scotland, whilst giving the English regions the false impression that they each will get more from both Westminster and the EU if they have a political voice. It is classic divide and rule.

Regional assemblies in England would not utterly destroy English national feeling, but they would lead to the development of regional political classes which would, out of self-interest or ideological conviction, actively work to create bogus divisions within England. In the absence of a national English Parliament, such regional voices would be difficult to counter.

Why does England not already have a parliament?

To a foreigner it must seem curious that the English of all peoples should be denied a Parliament. Why, they would ask, is the country in which parliamentary government evolved now deemed unfit to rule itself?

Even stranger to the foreigner would be the fact that of the four countries of the United Kingdom, England should be the only one to be denied national political representation. The foreigner would note in particular that even the implacable factions of Ulster are deemed fit to run their own affairs if they can but remove their hands from one another's throats, while England, the country which has been free of civil war for longer than any other state on earth, must place its fate in the hands of others.

The foreigner would become most bemused when he contemplated the existing arrangements between the four countries of the UK. He would see that an English Parliament is not merely the most just, but also the most obvious and economical solution to the inequality of democratic representation and opportunity wrought by devolution. He would marvel that such an imbalanced and unstable constitutional settlement could ever have been engineered by politicians.

If it is so obvious, so just, so economical, why do we not already have a parliament? The obnoxious truth is that our political elite - not merely the present government alone - understand that it is the only solution which would deliver fair treatment to the five sixths of the UK population which is presently disadvantaged by devolution, but oppose an English Parliament for various anachronistic or disreputable reasons.

The anachronistic reason, almost wholly on the Tory side of politics, is the good old cause of unionism, the desire to maintain the UK as a single national and political entity. A good old cause, but not a good present cause because devolution has destroyed it utterly by cracking the political shell which held Britain together. Those politicians who support it are simply living in the past, unable to overcome the inertia of their experience and emotional commitment.

The most obvious of the disreputable reasons is pure electoral fear by the Labour Party, which throughout its history has relied heavily on its dominance of Scots and Welsh constituencies for a majority in the Commons. Labour realises that it is most unlikely that they would ever be able to control an English Parliament in the way they can control the Commons.

There is also a dread, shared by all parties, of English interests being realised and fought for because England is so dominant within the UK.

England has five sixths of the UK population. She has more than five sixths of the wealth, commerce and industry. An English Parliament with the same powers as that of the Scots would account for well over half of total UK state expenditure.

With such a preponderance of population and wealth, it is improbable that an English Parliament would long remain subordinate to the Westminster parliament for reasons of human nature. Solemn agreements and treaties mean nothing if they do not serve the needs of the moment or the powerful. Thus once an English Parliament was in being, it would in practice have a great deal of power regardless of the initial theoretical limits of its authority.

But it would in any case make little political sense to have what would be in effect a federal UK parliament (the UK government as it is now, less any devolved powers to an English Parliament) collecting the vast majority of tax revenue, while controlling only a minority proportion of public expenditure.

To these domestic reasons must be added the knowledge of Euroenthusiasts - who exist in all the major parties - that a strong self-confident England would subvert their Eurofederalist plans.

The Anglophobia of our political elite

The reasons given so far for the failure to give England a parliament are obvious enough. But there is something deeper, more subtle, more poisonous, whose acid growth has slowly corroded our entire public life, namely the elite Anglophobia which exists in all parties.

Here is William Hague, an Englishman born and bred, during his time as Tory leader declaring in the Daily Telegraph (8/7/98) "I am not an English nationalist" and stated that he "is determinedly British rather than English" and was "dismayed to see so many St George Crosses at the world cup".

Jack Straw when Home Secretary (reported in the Daily Telegraph 17/7/2000) in an interview with GMTV made the following statements:

"There is a particular problem with some people's view of Englishness..."

"There is a distorted, incomplete idea of what it is to be patriotic for those in England, which is different from that in Wales or Scotland or Ireland..."

"The sense of nationality that these smaller nations within the United Kingdom have is partly defined by the fact that they are smaller, "They have had to express their culture in order not to be overwhelmed by England..."

"We have not had that. We have also had all the global baggage of the empire and a lot of jingoism here. And I think it is very important that we redefine not only what it means to be British, but also what it means to be English..."

"It is the responsibility of people who have a leadership position in our society, like me, to try to change that..."

The same Telegraph piece (17/7/2000) also quotes from an article by Simon Hughes, the Liberal Democrat home affairs spokesman, "It seems beyond doubt that England particularly has a severe and continuing problem with a consistent current of aggression and violence...".

"Football thugs, domestic racial and homophobic abuse, Friday-night fights after closing time, more and more road rage are all very obvious signs of an easy tendency to violence with which we will undermine any chance of becoming a country at peace with ourselves."

The statements of Hague, Straw and Hughes all display the same mentality: a fear of English national feeling and a libellous view of the English and their society. They actively fear and despise what England is and wish to both keep English feelings caged and to subvert the very idea of what those interests are and what England is.

A Federal UK

England is faced with two options for resolving the constitutional imbalance, a federal settlement within the UK or complete independence. Either would be sustainable. Let us examine the federal solution first.

The first quality that any political settlement should seek is stability. As the UK is comprised of four peoples who think of themselves as nations, the only system with any hope of long-term survival as a stable political arrangement is a federation in which each constituent part is legally equal and responsible for its own domestic affairs. That means home rule in each of the four home countries and expenditure on all domestic matters in each country being raised from within each country.

The federal government would be restricted to general matters such as defence, foreign policy, the issuing of currency and the servicing of government debt. Payment by each country for these matters would be proportionate to the population of each country. Any other system, which in effect could only mean England subsidising the rest of the UK must mean one of two things: English political dominance, which would incite the age old Celtic hatreds of England, or ever growing English resentment of the Celts. Both would be a road to the dissolution of the UK.

Those who oppose English self-determination argue that England is so large in comparison with the other parts of the UK that a Federation would be unbalanced. The argument about federal imbalance can be simply shown up for what it is, a demonstrable nonsense, by referring to the examples of the USA, Canada and India. There are sixty Californians to every Alaskan; seventy bodies in Ontario for each person in Prince Edward Island and one hundred and eleven inhabitants of Uttar Pradesh for every human being in Goa.

How would the change to a federal system be made? The simplest solution would be to remove all MPs sitting from non-English constituencies from the House of Commons which would them revert to its historic role of an English representative assembly, abolish the House of Lords and institute a new body to represent the four nations at federal level.

The administrative arrangements could be simple. Each of the four home countries would elect their own parliament. The members of these parliaments would also be members of the UK Parliament. This would have three advantages:

(1) it would substantially reduce the number of politicians by removing the current duplication resulting from the election of both devolved assembly members and MPs;

(2) the members elected to the national assemblies would not be able to shirk responsibility for the effect of their national decisions on UK federal issues - this would act as a brake on irresponsible domestic political decisions which could clash with the federal interest;

(3) it would remove any cause for legitimate complaint from any part of the UK.

There would be no need for any new building. The Westminster Parliament could act both as the English Parliament and, as required, the federal UK Parliament. Because all domestic issues would be with the national assemblies, the UK Parliament would need to sit only a few days a month.

Because the responsibilities of the national and UK federal governments would be clearly demarcated, members of the UK federal government would not find themselves constantly at odds with their national government. The federal government would be formed as it is now, by gaining a majority in the federal parliament.

There is also a sound case for creating a second chamber in each of the four national parliaments, because a single chamber parliament is all too prone to reckless behaviour and corruption, political and financial, from within and without. The danger of corruption is particularly strong in very small assemblies such as those in Wales and Northern Ireland for the simple reason it is easier to control and bribe a few people than it is to control and bribe a large number.

For the same reason of preventing elite abuse, a written constitution is desirable.

The arguments for a two-chamber parliament and a written constitution applies equally to an independent England.

If England was a sovereign state again

For England it is difficult to envisage any insuperable disadvantage in the break up of the UK, but easy to see definite and substantial advantages. Her very considerable population, wealth and general sophistication would ensure that she could maintain without any real difficulty the present levels of government provision from the welfare state to the military. Moreover, England would be able to act wholeheartedly in her own interests.

The only important disadvantages for England could be balance of payments deficits (primarily from the loss of oil, gas and whisky production) and ructions in the international institutional sphere. Happily, adverse balances of trade are (eventually) self-correcting even if the correction, as is the case with America, can seem an age coming. Moreover, with the free global currency market and a floating pound, an adverse balance of trade does not hold the horrors it once did, for international borrowing is infinitely easier than it was and devaluation of the currency is not viewed as a national humiliation. England might be temporarily embarrassed by a substantially increased trade deficit, but there is no reason to believe that it would be prolonged or seriously affect the English economy.

As for international upheaval, it is conceivable that England would be unable to sustain a claim to Britain's privileged position on international bodies such as the UN Security Council and the board of IMF. However, this is unlikely for a number of reasons. To begin with there is the precedent of Russia which assumed all of the Soviet Union's international entitlements. Britain is also the United States' only halfway reliable ally on most of these international boards. To this may be added Britain's position as one of the larger international paymasters and providers of reliable military muscle. None of these facts need essentially change with the substitution of England for Britain. Perhaps most importantly, the denial to England of any of Britain's institutional places would pose the awkward question of who was to take any vacant position. This could (and almost certainly would) in turn raise the whole question of whether the constitutions of most world bodies are equitable or suited to the modern world. (The constitutions were after all created approximately fifty years ago, reflect the balance-of-power at that time, and are in no sense equitable). To deny England could mean the opening of a can of worms.

Conversely, it could plausibly be argued that membership of such international bodies represents a liability rather than an advantage and England would be well shot of them.

The alternatives to an English Parliament

These are all insufficient, impractical or unnatural. The Tories' preferred solution is to allow English MPs a veto on matters which effect only England. This is impractical because it ignores the position of the executive. Such a system would mean in effect that no party elected without an English majority could govern. Suppose for example that the party divisions in the Commons were as follows: for the entire UK (659 seats) - Labour 339, Tories 280, others 40: for England alone (525 seats) - Labour 230, Tories 280, others 15. The UK wide Labour majority would be robbed of any say over the expenditure of approximately three quarters of all public expenditure in the UK. Further complications would arise if the English component of the Commons was *hung*, that is no parliamentary party had a majority of English seats. The worst possible situation would be a Commons in which the overall House and the English component were both *hung*, but with radically different balances between the parties. For example, suppose that Labour and the LibDems had an overall majority in the Commons, but did not have an overall majority between them of English seats.

There would also be the question of who would make policy to present to the Commons. Obviously it could not be a party without an English majority for that would be pointless. It would have to be the party with a majority of English MPs. This would mean in effect an English government within Westminster, which would have more practical power and patronage that the UK government.

The other alternatives on offer are an English Grand Committee, an English Secretary in the cabinet, a reduction in the numbers of non-English MPs and Regional Assemblies. An English Grand Committee would solve nothing for of itself it would decide nothing. The Scottish, Welsh and Northern Irish Grand Committees were of importance prior to devolution, if at all, because each of the

Celtic parts of the UK had a cabinet minister with the powers of a viceroy, a budget to meet most of their domestic expenditure under the control of the cabinet minister and a bureaucracy to carry out ministerial policy. An English Secretary with similar powers would be an absurdity, because he or she would exercise more power than the prime minister for most of UK government expenditure and patronage would be under his control.

I have already referred to English Regional Assemblies when dealing with the Eurofederalists and the danger they represent to our national independence of action. But there are also daunting practical difficulties in the creation of such assemblies. There is no natural division of regions in England. Even those parts which are most commonly cited as having a strong regional identity - the South West, Yorkshire and the North East - are far from being homogeneous. There is an emotional division between Cornwall and the rest of the South West. Yorkshire is extremely diverse, the south with its large cities and very substantial immigrant population having little in common with the North Riding, which is largely rural. As for the North East, anyone who knows the area will realise that the people are far from seeing themselves as a single entity and often display considerable rivalry, for example between Sunderland and Newcastle. As for the rest of England, there is no obvious division anywhere. Moreover, traditional regional loyalties are much diluted by internal migration. In Cornwall, for example, less than forty percent of its population was born in the county. There are local loyalties in England, but they are precisely that, local, being based on neighbourhoods, towns, cities and villages.

If elected Regional Assemblies are set up, all the complaints which are now levelled at Westminster will be replicated and most probably amplified, because local animosities are greater than national animosities. There will be accusations of remoteness - the likely representative regions would be physically large - complaints of unequal spending within the region and disputes about the distribution of centrally raised taxation. There is also the problem of subsidies. The richer regions would come to resent paying for the poorer. Eventually this dissatisfaction would be given a political voice. Already there are political stirrings in London about the amount of money which is redistributed to the rest of the country. On 22/7/99 the London local paper, the *Evening Standard*, carried an article by the chair of the Association of London Government, Toby Harris. It began: "For too long the taxpayers of London have been bank-rolling the rest of the UK. Too much of the tax revenues generated by our households and businesses are recycled to the supposedly more needy regions of the UK, while too many of the capital's own needs go unmet." As London and her environs has an economy larger than the combined economies of Scotland, Wales and Northern Ireland, a reduction in her willingness to pay tax would have very serious implications for the poorer parts of England. Regional Assemblies would lose whatever appeal they might have once it became clear that subsidies from the wealthier parts of England might cease or be reduced.

There is also the question of what powers Regional Assemblies could be reasonably given. The natural tendency for Westminster will be to give them as little power as possible, indeed to produce bodies which are little more than local councils. Yet this will be easier said than done. The Scottish Parliament controls most domestic matters other than major tax raising. Even the Welsh Assembly deals with a great deal of domestic legislation - those who doubt this should tune into Welsh Questions in the Commons. Time and again questions are rejected because they deal with matters now outside Westminster's competence. It is difficult to see how English Regional Assemblies could be given anything less than the Welsh and improbable that they could be denied that which has been granted to Scotland. Indeed, it is improbable that the Welsh will be satisfied with a lesser status for long. This has profound implications. That Scotland or Wales may institute new laws which differ from those in England is one thing because they can claim to be a national governing entity: for English Regions to do the same quite another. To take an example, we could end up with different laws on abortion in the South West and Yorkshire. Even more problematic would be regional differences with commercial implications, such as different rates of tax or safety regulations. In effect, we would have not one system of English law but many.

Reducing the number of non-English members at Westminster is a non-solution. It is true that there is an imbalance which should be addressed. At the 1997 election it took an average of 69, 577 electors to form an English constituency. In Scotland it was 55,563, in Wales 55,338. Significantly, Northern Ireland - which could put forward at least as good (or bad) a case for over-representation as Scotland and Wales - matched England with an average of 66,122 electors. However, even if the imbalance is remedied, and the situation has still not changed, it would not address the Scottish Labour MP Tam Dayell's West Lothian Question, namely why should MPs representing Scottish constituencies vote on English matters when MPs representing English constituencies may not vote on Scottish matters?

There are those who argue that no change is necessary because English MPs are always in the majority. This argument is bogus because it ignores the reality of party discipline. It is highly improbable that English MPs of any political colour would regularly breach three line whips. Most particularly, it is difficult to imagine Labour and Tory MPs sitting for English seats combining to defeat a Labour government. But the difficulty goes beyond the obvious. Any future Labour or LibLab coalition government would probably be substantially dependent on non-English seats. Consequently, such a government would never introduce policies driven solely by what is best for England.

What could an English Parliament do?

What could an English Parliament do if it were given full powers? In practice, almost everything that Britain can do. Moreover, it could declare independence from the other parts of the UK. That would give England the same freedom of action which Britain enjoys. If the parliament withdrew England from the EU, her sovereignty would be greatly increased. An independent England free of the EU could do such immensely useful things as controlling welfare expenditure by restricting the benefits of the welfare state to English citizens, repudiate disadvantageous treaties which have no time limit and insist on work permits for any person without English citizenship.

Even within a federal UK, much could be done. It would be reasonable for the English to put in place a system whereby money raised in England was spent solely in England or spent on matters such as defence and foreign policy. That would force the Celts to follow suit.

An English Parliament could even introduce English citizenship alongside British citizenship. Anomalous? Not at all for that is precisely what the EU has done by designating member states' citizens as EU citizens. Such citizenship could be used even within the confines of the EU to give preferential treatment to those with English citizenship.

The demand for an English Parliament

What demand is there for an English Parliament? Our political elite state baldly that there is no desire amongst the English for a parliament, a proposition which they are strangely unwilling to put to a ballot.

The reality is that the elite fear the English would welcome a parliament. That explains the fervour with which the proposition is publicly attacked. No one expends much energy belittling something which does not exist or which is not feared.

There is not of course any great public clamour at present. It would be amazing if there was, because no mainstream political party advocates such a parliament and the national media makes a positive fetish of screaming nationalism or racism whenever one is publicly mooted. The media are also most assiduous in censoring and abusing those in favour of a parliament. Without mainstream political leadership and access to the mass media, it is next to impossible for a political idea to make headway. Come the rise of a credible political movement with English interests at heart and things will look very different. The media will not then be able to censor so effectively and there will be a focus for dissent.

Once mainstream political leadership is given, it would be extraordinary if the English did not favour control over their own affairs. But even if the English have at present no great desire for a parliament, circumstances might make one a necessity simply to safeguard English interests.

If democracy means anything, any responsible British mainstream political party would adopt an English Parliament as a matter of prime policy. They are meant above all to represent the interests of their constituents. In this case the large majority of the constituents are English. It is clearly to their disadvantage to have no independent political representation.

As with complaints of English nationalism, the bogus nature of the claim that the English should not have a parliament because they do not clamour for one publicly can be shown by the treatment of the rest of the UK. Support for a Welsh Assembly was muted in the extreme: approximately 25% of the total electorate voted for it and 50% didn't bother to vote. This did not prevent the government from hastily granting such an assembly. Even in Scotland, only 60% of the electorate voted and a parliament was granted on a YES vote of only 45% of the total electorate. Scarcely rampant enthusiasm.

How do we get a parliament?

This is the most daunting question of all. It would be heartening to think that a new English party advocating an English Parliament could arise which would sweep rapidly to power. Sadly, that is a romantic fantasy. The British political system is so constructed that the sudden rise of a party is next to impossible. Any new party would have to find 650 or so suitable candidates to stand for election. It would have to be prepared to lose 650 deposits. It would need time for credible leaders to emerge. It would have to overcome the sociological inertia of electors - the large majority of voters are still not floating voters. The media would have to be persuaded to give considerable airtime and space to the party and its doings. That and a hundred other political bridges would have to be crossed. If it could be done at all, it would be the work of a generation. By then England would in all probability be Balkanised with regional English assemblies and Britain itself so enmeshed in a United Sates of Europe that its status would be no more than that of a state in the USA.

Any party advocating an English Parliament would have to achieve a Commons majority on English seats alone, because electors in Celtic seats could not be expected to vote for a party which they knew would ultimately remove English subsidies. Achieving such a majority is difficult at the best of times: even in the landslide of 1997, Labour won only 329 English seats. It means gaining 330 out of 525 English seats for a bare majority. A working majority would require 350-360 seats. If the Labour vote stays constant in Scotland and Wales, Labour can achieve an overall majority by winning a mere 230 English seats.

As things stand, there is very little prospect of an English Parliament coming about through mainstream political action. What might be done to alter matters? The ideal should be to frighten the entire political mainstream into believing that it is in their electoral interests to support an English Parliament. More realistically, the strategy should be to persuade the Tory Party to adopt an English Parliament as a policy and to cause enough concern in the other mainstream parties to get them to offer some concessions to English national feeling and interests, such as an English Grand Committee. Although such concessions would have little practical effect, they would be an admission of the need to observe English interests and a recognition of an English desire to govern their own affairs. Those would be important propaganda gains.

The most vital task for the English in the immediate future is the breaking of the public censorship of the subject. This might be done by a new political party advocating an English Parliament. Although it would stand no chance of forming a government, with a decent electoral showing it could place considerable pressure on the major parties to change their policies. The grotesqueries and injustices of devolution must be constantly put before the public through the media of petitions, demonstrations, public meetings, pamphletering and the use of the Internet.

Such a party would be most effective if it offered a full range of policies rather than standing on a single issue. It might have a platform which included, for example, not only English self-government, but such policies as withdrawal from the EU and a national rather than an international defence policy.

An English constitutional assembly set up by private individuals could also have a part to play. It would undoubtedly raise the public profile of the campaign. But such an assembly could also be the means of creating a pro-English party with some electoral punch. The primary problem for any Englishman or woman wishing to work for an English Parliament is knowing where to start in the absence of a mainstream party taking the lead. An English constitutional assembly would provide a means by which likeminded people drawn from across the country to meet and clarify their ideas, but there is a clear difficulty in gaining support for such an idea because of the media antipathy towards giving publicity to any attempt at English political organisation and the need for large amounts of money to mount an effective PR campaign.

There is also civil disobedience. This includes such non-violent actions as illegal demonstrations and occupations, a mass refusal to pay tax and a General Strike. Breaking the law en mass does not come easily to the latterday English, but there are times when it becomes necessary. Those times are when the political system develops a constitutional bottleneck. Examples from English history are the civil war, which destroyed the notion of the king as sovereign, the "Glorious Revolution" which created the conditions for parliamentary government, the agitation for the Great Reform Bill which made the first breach in the concept of parliament as an aristocratic club, and the fight for women's suffrage which completed the transition to full adult suffrage. All involved criminal acts as defined by the law of the time.

It is important for a democratic society that any breach of the law should be made within the moral context of restoring meaningful democratic control. I suggest that to do this a breach of the law must meet the following criteria: the matter must be of great importance and the political and social system must offer no meaningful opportunity to challenge the status quo.

Urgency and the difficulty of reversibility also come into the equation when assessing whether a breach of the law is justified. The action is given greater moral force if (1) a policy is being pursued which will cause either great damage or immense change, (2) a policy cannot be legally reversed, (3) a policy cannot be practically reversed and (4) a policy can be reversed only with immense difficulty.

What if there is no English Parliament?

English resentment will inevitably grow and have nowhere to go within the political system. The danger will be that people will turn to violence because they have no democratic means of gaining national representation. Suppose no mainstream party takes up the cause. Suppose that English majorities committed to an English Parliament were elected to Westminster, yet were never able to form a government because an English minority allied to the Celts always formed a Commons majority. Suppose that Proportional Representation was introduced and practically removed forever the opportunity for a single party to form a government. Some would think that no meaningful constitutional or non-violent opportunity was left.

The most obviously inflammatory constitutional position would be where an English party advocating an English Parliament gains a majority of English seats in the Commons but did not gain an overall Commons majority. Using parliamentary procedures and keeping their behaviour within customary bounds, they could inconvenience the business of government but little more. They might boycott Parliament but that would be an impotent ruse unless linked to massive demonstrations. They might set up a self-declared English Parliament but it would have no power. The best tactics in such a situation would be for the party with the English majority to take the lead in organising civil disobedience and to announce before the election that they would do so if an English Parliament was denied.

Then there is Europe. Our enmeshment in the EU may become so advanced that we could not legally set up an English Parliament. Fanciful? Suppose that the EU at some future date insists on Regional Assemblies throughout the EU and this is accepted by a British government. Such Assemblies might then be set up in England without referenda. Suppose further that the EU insists that the only representation for domestic matters rests with the Regional Assemblies.

The existence of the EU is in itself a powerful argument for an English Parliament because the EU already so controls Add to that the possibility of entry into the euro and the likelihood of the adoption of an EU constitution which promises EU control over such fundamental matters as foreign relations, defence, and tax harmonisation, and it would be constitutionally impossible for England to set up a meaningful parliament for it could decide nothing. The only non-violent answer to such a situation would be to elect a UK or an English Parliament to declare independence from the EU.

Conclusion

The English should not be afraid of national feeling. Let them ask themselves why should all peoples except the English be encouraged to celebrate and defend their ethnicity? The oft-cited dichotomy between patriotism and nationalism is contrived. Both words have at their core a sense of "tribe" and a desire to protect and celebrate the nation and culture.

Nationalism is a synonym for patriotism. The true difference is between non-aggressive and aggressive patriotism; between those who wish to celebrate and protect their nation within their existing territory and those who wish to invade and compromise the culture and territories of others. The modern English of all peoples can be trusted to remain within the limits of non-aggressive nationalism.

What the English must understand is that they cannot afford to simply sit on their hands and let matters drift. If they do they will find themselves within ten years divided by regional assemblies and arguing interminably amongst themselves about who should get what while those who are actively hostile to their interests obtain their ends by default.

The Arbiters
Raymond Tong

Here there are no whips raised in anger,
no thought-criminals or though-police,
only the feeling of being manipulated.

Here the blandly smiling arbiters decide
how to present the awkward and unacceptable,
what should be disclosed and what withheld.

Most of the media, unlike a Ministry
of Love, does not persuade us what to think,
but much more subtly, what not to think.

Seeking to help us find enlightened answers
they make omission an equalising virtue,
obscuring every subject deemed taboo.

UnEnglish Madness

P. Scrivener

Throughout England's history there has been an undercurrent of individualism. At the same time, the English have been adept at suppressing their individualism by keeping their opinions private (called *reserve* and *understatement*) which encouraged a team spirit that produced efficient and professional military, civil service etc. The English had a keen sense of what was fair, and sneaks were despised.

The assertion of the freeborn nature of the English is proclaimed in *Piers Plowman* (Langland) in the chant *When Adam delved and Eve span, Who was then the gentleman?* John Ball used this quote to introduce a sermon on the same theme in 1381, which sparked off the Peasants' Revolt.[1] He said:

> From the beginning all men by nature were created alike, and our bondage or servitude came in by the unjust oppression of naughty men ... And therefore I exhort you to consider that now the time is come, appointed to us by God, in which ye may ... cast off the yoke of bondage, and recover liberty.[2]

The Bishop of Norwich (the Church of England being then, as now, part of the ruling class) acted swiftly to quell the revolt.[3]

Queen Elizabeth I believed in freedom of conscience, saying that there should be no windows into men's souls.

Gerrard Winstanley, leader of the Diggers, declared in 1649:

> the earth was not made purposely for you, to be Lords of it, and we to be your Slaves, Servants, and Beggers ... mankinde in all his branches, is the Lord of the Earth and ought not to be in subjection to any of his own kinde.[4]

In 1643 Oliver Cromwell said:

> I had rather have a plain russet-coated captain that knows what he fights for, and loves what he knows, than what you call a gentleman, and is nothing else.

For *plain russet-coated captain* read a modern ordinary patriotic Englishman, and for *gentleman*, read the ruling class today.

People who believe that England had rigid social classes welcome the end of that *system* and the deference that went with it. They have so far been unable to recognise that there are now in England new classes. Deference to the upper

---

[1] http://www.wwnorton.com/nael/middleages/topic_1/uprise.htm
[2] http://www.bbc.co.uk/radio4/history/voices/voices_reading_revolt.shtml
[3] http://www.umilta.net/anchor.html
[4] http://www.bilderberg.org/land/poor.htm

classes is demanded, but there is little of the mutual respect that was often given in the old ways. The members of the new ruling class are drawn from all sectors of society and they organise themselves to crush the way we think and act into a very narrow mould. They include teachers, journalists, the BBC and other broadcasters, religious officials, trades unions, *community leaders* (which means representatives of ethnic minorities), and chief constables, as well as politicians. But whatever their origin, their thinking is alien to us, the common people of England. *Race* is the new *class* but unlike in the previous system, the ruling class ensures that no one can escape his race. As with apartheid, the ruling class fits everyone into a racial category and treats those it rules not as individuals but as members of a racial group. The lowest class (caste?) is the only one which can be insultingly stereotyped and disadvantaged through institutional racism with impunity (untouchables?), because the higher classes of rulers and races are protected by racial *privilege*.

The insulters – regardless of their origin - appear to have no understanding of, or sensitivity to, the English cultural trait of reserve and understatement. These traits are often interpreted as *tolerance*. For the English, living in a small and comparatively crowded country, it has been more difficult to escape objectionable neighbours, unlike, say, the pioneering days of the West in America, where people could pack their belongings into a wagon and set out to find virgin land. The English of that time shared with those settlers a cultural instinct for self-reliance, minding your own business, and fair-dealing. These cultural characteristics remain strong in some English people, producing a paralysing reluctance among them to claim any political rights for themselves as a group – a racial class. But the conditions which brought about these characteristics become more and more demanding as England becomes more and more crowded. The ruling class invokes English tolerance to forbid the English from talking about the cause of the overcrowding. Ever more tolerance is required to put up with ever more overcrowding. The English sense of fairness is continually offended by the gross injustices against them perpetrated by the political class. The only ways they can deal with it are either by emigrating to escape this madness, or by internalising their rage and frustration. At present, there is no safety valve.

This dire situation has been imposed on the English by an alien code. The devil comes in various guises, such as *multiculturalism* (now accurately referred to as the Multi Cult); *diversity* (though everyone knows diversity is divisive); the deceitful claim of *anti-racism*; and political *correctness*. The claimed sensitivity of politically correct speech cannot be compared with the understating type of speech traditionally practised by the English. Political correctness is instead the use of language to exclude the unfavoured class by only using sensitivity when dealing with the favoured classes. These new attitudes are illogical, inconsistent, shallow, unfair, and their holders cannot recognise the harm they do. They have forgotten their duty to the people they govern. *Anti-racism* has been described as "a psychosis impervious to reason". Popular usage has indicated that normal people are beginning to see the hidden truth of the condition – "political correctness gone mad" they say, but perhaps it always was mad.

Sandwell was one of the first local government authorities in England to be accredited by the Commission for Racial Equality with the preliminary-level mark of approval, *Promoting Racial Equality Through Sport*. It received the award for its claim to tackle "racism" and promote "racial equality". The standard was developed to break down barriers in sport. The borough was commended for its racial equality policy, designed to "create an environment where everyone can enjoy sport without facing discrimination of any kind". Officers took part in the regional launch of National Anti-Racism Week *Kick Racism out of Sport* - showing off work by the Sandwell *Ethnic Minority Football Group,* which supported the *Shaheedi Games.* The team was also recognised for supporting a new *Asian Academy.*[5] The perpetrators of this contradictory monstrosity boast their *anti-racist* credentials not only at the very same time as proclaiming racially exclusive sport but using racially exclusive sport as proof of their *anti-racism,* the verbal equivalent of claiming that 2+2=5 which is so typical of today's inanities.

> Dramatic new evidence of the under-performance of *white* pupils from impoverished backgrounds was published by the Government in July 2003 ... Throughout their schooling, deprived *white* children languish at, or near, the bottom of a league table of progress by ethnic group. ... The figure for Black Caribbean pupils - whose achievements have lagged behind other groups - also beat poor whites ... Schools are to be given more help to boost the achievement of pupils from *ethnic minorities.* [The Government]... is also launching a scheme to boost the performance of *Black* Caribbean children at secondary school.[6]

For the first time the performance of *ethnic minority* pupils was to become part of the performance targets laid down for schools, the performance of poor White children apparently being of no interest to the government. Schools Minister Stephen Twigg claimed "*Every child matters, whatever their background*".[7]

Rather worryingly, some of the most serious examples of discrimination have been committed by the police, who are no longer citizens in uniform. This is evident from pronouncements such as that from Chief Superintendent Paul Pearce of Sussex Police who said, "Sussex Police is overtly hostile to those who discriminate on the grounds of race, religion, skin colour, sexual orientation, disability, gender, social class or any other inappropriate factor".[8] Law and order should be their business, not *discrimination* – not even discrimination on the grounds of social class!

An investigation of *Stop-and-search* by police, set up to see whether *ethnic minorities* were unfairly targeted, discovered that the police were "not biased against blacks and Asians". Instead, there was an over-representation of *Whites* among those stopped and searched. This fact was held to show that the police were *not* racist. Being biased against Whites is of no significance and not deemed to be *racist*. The only concern was to show that there was "no general pattern of bias against people

[5] *Sport services are given equality award,*
   http://www.expressandstar.com/artman/publish/article_44335.php Oct 15, 2003
[6] *Ethnic minority pupils get more help*, The Guardian, October 23, 2003
   http://www.guardian.co.uk/race/story/0,11374,1068766,00.html
[7] *Deprived White pupils are bottom of ethnic group pile*, BBC, 24 October 2003
[8] http://news.bbc.co.uk/2/hi/uk_news/england/southern_counties/3228833.stm,

from *minority ethnic* groups either as a whole or particular groups".[9] The possibility of bias against Whites is of no relevance or concern for them.

A newspaper claimed that a £700,000 investigation of 13,000 prosecutions "failed to establish whether there is racial bias or discrimination in the Crown Prosecution Service". But the article went on "It found that Afro-Caribbeans were more likely than White defendants to have their cases discontinued before trial, suggesting that the police were more likely to charge those who ought not to be prosecuted. Confusingly, Asians were less likely to have their cases dropped than White defendants". Having implied that the discontinuance of Afro-Caribbean cases was due to racism, the writer is then presented with the problem of avoiding having to say that the discontinuance of White cases, compared with Asian, is also due to racism. Any sleazy port in a storm will do as a refuge for a PC scoundrel, so he lamely resorts to saying that this is "confusing". The other problem for the compilers of the report was that the investigation had "*failed*" to establish whether there was racial bias. Sir David Calvert-Smith said it was a "*difficult*" and "*uncomfortable*" day for the service. They had been longing for the investigation to find discrimination and it seems they were disappointed. And yet they had – against Whites. Sir David said: "I don't believe there are any grounds for saying that this service is consciously biased against members of the black and minority ethnic communities."[10] They didn't look for unconscious bias against members of the White community, but when they found it they either didn't recognise it or didn't care, thus demonstrating their conscious or unconscious bias against Whites.

Of the Macpherson Report (The Stephen Lawrence Inquiry), Frank Ellis writes:

> Having attacked the iniquities of 'colour-blind policing', Macpherson,
> with no sense of any embarrassment, notes with obvious approval, the
> summing up made by Mr. Justice Curtis ... 'The burden and standard of
> proof and the legal principles involved govern all cases, and there must
> never be differential rules or standards applied because of the horrendous
> nature of a case'.[11]

Shortly after the publication of the Macpherson Report, which blamed helpless natives for institutional racism, the *Sunday Times* published a breathlessly enthusiastic article which purported to show that British society was *not* institutionally racist. As proof, it stated that while in 1999 ethnic minorities comprised around *5.5%* of the British population, *25%* of those enrolling on the bar vocational course to become barristers were Black or Asian, *23%* of those entering medical school to train as doctors were non-White, *12%* of all students registered as British were Black or Asian, of solicitors entering the profession, *15.8%* were Black and *8.5%* of all barristers were non-White. In London, where *20%* of the population was Black or Asian, *29%* of nurses and *31%* of doctors came

---

[9] Stop-and-search police are 'rude but not racist', *Times*, 21st September 2000

[10] *Inquiry finds little race bias at CPS*, Joshua Rozenberg, Legal Editor, Daily Telegraph, 22nd October 2003

[11] *The Macpherson Report: 'Anti-racist' Hysteria and the Sovietization of the United Kingdom*, Dr. Frank Ellis, booklet published by Right Now!, 2001

from ethnic minorities. There followed many other examples of what, if the races had been reversed, would have been taken as proof of institutional racism, yet the writer of the article concluded by suggesting that the feelings of Black and Asian people would be hurt because their share in these activities was not even more advantageous. White readers were clearly meant to welcome these examples of discrimination against themselves.[12]

Two Asian drivers who had been fined for not wearing their seatbelts – an offence they admitted - had their fines refunded by Chief Superintendent David Baines - because a BBC programme had supposedly exposed the policeman to whom they admitted the offence as a *racist*.[13] We are fortunate – no thanks to the police - that their offending behaviour was not more serious. Can I have a refund on my parking ticket please? I'm sure the traffic warden must have been a racist. And what proof do I have of this? Well, Macpherson assures us that any incident must be considered to be racist if anyone perceives it to be so – and I do!

Sussex Police suspended a detective for complaining about racism in the promotion of a colleague. He was *white* and the colleague was *brown*. What the political class calls *racists* are uppity Whites like the detective who dared to speak up. Presumably there was no sense of embarrassment when officers in the force were asked to sign a declaration that they believe in values such as *fairness* and *justice*.[14] Empty words from blinkered minds.

As mentioned earlier, in 1999 it was reckoned that around 5.5% of the UK population was non-White. If Whites and non-Whites were equally racist, then around 5.5% of the victims of racial attacks would be White, and 94.5% non-White. However, in 1999 the Commission for Racial Equality reported that of the 373,000 people who said they had been the victim of racial offences, 62% were White. Even when we allow for the fact that official figures greatly understate the size of the non-White population, it is clear that non-Whites were on average far more likely to commit a racial offence than Whites. This should be of concern to everyone. However, the facts do not fit the prejudices of the ruling class, and we are continually given the false impression that Whites are proportionately more guilty of racial attacks than are non-Whites. It seems that the racism of so-called anti-racists is so ingrained that they are unable to see what the figures mean. A further insult to our intelligence came when the then Chairman of the Commission for Racial Equality, Herman Ouseley, grotesquely distorted the findings by saying that Whites are being prejudiced if they interpret an attack as being racially motivated.

In perhaps the worst example of institutional racism yet in the police, particularly in view of the figures quoted above, there is evidence that at least some police forces have a policy of putting White victims on a lower priority than non-White. Devon and Cornwall Police have instructed their officers to "give priority to black victims of crime". Police candidates sitting their exams are advised to "distinguish between White victims and those from ethnic minorities" when

---

[12] *Is Britain really a nation of racists?* Sunday Times, 28th February 1999

[13] http://www.manchesteronline.co.uk/news/stories/Detail_LinkStory=71527.html

[14] http://news.bbc.co.uk/1/hi/England/southern_counties/3233505.stm Saturday, 1 November, 2003, 15:14 GMT

responding to calls for assistance. If two identical crimes are reported the Black victim should be given precedence.[15] In another police area, a dedicated special constable who decided to become a full-time police officer was failed in his examinations because when presented with a hypothetical situation of two very similar incidents happening at the same time, which had to be prioritised, he had failed to put the White victim on a lower priority and used a criterion other than race. Because the police recruit concerned subsequently retook the examination and was admitted to the force, the names of those concerned and the force must remain confidential. In an attempt to find out how widespread is this practice, a telephone call to West Sussex police, who had recently issued a pompous statement about eliminating discrimination, elicited the telling response that Whites would not be put on a lower priority "unless it was a racist incident". The woman on the other end of the telephone, despite being prompted several times to think about what she had said, was unable to understand that a victim is a victim regardless of colour and regardless of the type of crime. Similarly, after another attempt to investigate this issue, a Home Office respondent wrote that the Home Secretary had said, "*ethnic minorities* should be protected from discrimination". In both cases the assumption had been made that White victims are not worthy of consideration.

The Race Relations (Amendment) Act 2000 makes it unlawful for any public authority to discriminate on the grounds of race. Each organisation will have passed a resolution declaring something like; "it acknowledges the general duty placed upon it by the Race Relations Act 2000. [It]...will continue within its functions and policies to promote equality of opportunity and promote racial equality between people of different racial groups". Yet in every case, as far as we can tell, these public bodies, including the police, carry on with exactly the same racist policies as they had before. There are hundreds, if not thousands, of special lobbying organisations and government-backed schemes exclusively for the benefit of the non-English, in education, training, recruitment, mentoring, promotion, charities, housing, old people's care, and so on. All of them either expressly or implicitly exclude the English, who are thus disadvantaged, and yet it is largely the English taxpayer who pays for this discrimination. There is no moral principle which dictates that a nation should have money removed from it, by what amounts to legalized theft, and passed on to other peoples whose presence was not sought and which is not only of no advantage to the people paying the money but in many cases is actually to their detriment. Wandsworth Council uses council tax payers' money to fund an Asian Women's Association Elderly Project giving advice on welfare rights and benefits, housing, social services, help with form filling, and lunch club and day and weekend trips. When asked the address of any English Women's Association the enquirer was directed to a particular webpage. There was no mention of any English association on that page and a search under the word *English* produced only a mention of a special council-run facility for Asians. We said to Wandsworth that there must be something wrong with their search because we still could not find the association for elderly English. The reply was, ah well, there isn't *actually* a club for *English*

---

[15] Daily Mail, 26th August 2000

people, but anyone can go to the Asian club. We pointed out to them that in that case why call it an "Asian" club and didn't they think it would rather put everyone else off from going, and were they not worried that they were in breach of the Race Relations Act? Apparently they were not. All the hypocritical sanctimonious outpourings from the political class about combating racism simply induce disgust. What has happened to that fabled English quality of fairplay? The weirdest thing is that this type of discrimination comes mostly from Englishmen doing it to their fellow English. What has happened to English manhood that they shirk their duty to repel conquest and instead vigorously impose conquest on their fellow English?

At a country fair at Frampton-on-Severn, Gloucestershire, in September 2002, well-known writer and broadcaster Robin Page made a speech defending the rights of countryside dwellers. He said "In case any of you are of a fragile disposition and easily offended, please go for a walk round the lake and come back when I have finished. If there is a Black, vegetarian, Muslim, asylum-seeking, one-legged, lesbian lorry driver present then you may be offended at what I am going to say, as I want the same rights that you have got already". A humourless collaborator chose not to take Mr. Page's advice, chose to listen to what he had to say, thus chose to be offended, and informed the police. Gloucestershire Police thought it was acceptable to waste taxpayers' money making a 200-mile round trip to Mr. Page's home in Cambridgeshire (when the police notoriously can't be bothered to go round the corner to a burglary) just because he said he wanted equal rights. Mr. Page was detained in a cell with dried faeces on its walls. Gloucester thought-police, in the person of Detective Sergeant Geoff Clark, of Stonehouse Police Station, near Stroud, Gloucestershire, compounded the harassment of Mr. Page by inserting an advertisement in the local newspaper accusing him, in their words, of "bombarding" visitors with what they described as "pro-hunting propaganda". Hunting is not a crime and consequently neither is bombarding anyone with "propaganda" about it a crime. The police were obsessed with a triviality and failed in their duty to uphold the law without fear or favour.[16]

At the end of September 1999 an announcement appeared in the *Daily Telegraph* and other newspapers, of a prize for a journalistic piece that would tell an "unpalatable truth, validated by powerful facts" and which would expose "establishment conduct and its propaganda", or "official drivel". The announcement was signed by various well-known contemporary journalists, including John Pilger. J F Cronin was thus inspired to write an article about *The forgotten victims* – White victims of violent crime with a racial element which, had the victims not been White, would have made headline news. He submitted the article to Mr Peter Wilby, John Pilger's editor at the *New Statesman*. Mr Wilby denounced it, saying, bizarrely, that this article – "about victims of violent crime" - would be *"grossly offensive"* to virtually all his readership. *The Spectator*, the *Sunday Times* and the *South London Press* also chose to ignore these victims. *Right Now!* magazine published it.

---

[16] The 'Robin Page thought crime case': a summary of relevant facts, T Bennett, 5th November 2002

A prison officer, a former Coldstream Guardsman with a 21-year unblemished record in the Prison Service, was sacked for noisily throwing some keys into a metal chute at the prison gatehouse and then saying "There's a photo of [a terrorist] there". This throwaway remark about the terrorist was alleged to be insulting, because three people *might* have heard it and *might* have been offended by this "insensitive" remark. No one established whether they had heard it, let alone been offended. However, one Andrew Rogers, the assistant governor, did indeed take offence, informed the prison governor, Jerry Knight, who suspended and then sacked the prison officer. Why did they take this wholly disproportionate action? Were they closet fans of the terrorist, or were they making culturally inappropriate judgments? Of this over-reaction to a trivial incident, the Sun's columnist Richard Littlejohn wrote:

> One of the great joys of this job is the hate mail ... It all came pouring in on Friday after my defence of the prison officer sacked for slagging off Osama bin Laden. You might wonder how on earth anyone could take offence at my sticking up for someone who was rude about a mass murderer, responsible for the slaughter of thousands of innocent people. Not so. Apparently this made me a Muslim-hating, racist, BNP, blah, blah, no better than a terrorist, who deserved to die a painful death ... But I should point out that none of these insane e-mails came from anyone called Shah or Sheikh or Ali. In fact, every single one was sent by someone with an English surname. Where do they find these people?[17]

In 2003, the Trades Union Congress produced a report called *Black voices at work*. It recommended that "black and ethnic minority" workers should not feel the need to "blend in" – presumably with their ethnic majority colleagues. No account was taken of the cultural sensitivities of English workers, who are likely to consider this advice to be snobbery at best (*stuck-up* would be one of the more polite colloquial English words), and racism at worst. The report also recommended that "black and ethnic minority" workers be allowed time off for their own religious holidays. A query to the TUC asking whether those workers would in return be required to work over the traditional Christmas and Easter breaks produced, of course, no response. Again, English cultural sensitivities are trampled on, and the ideals of classlessness and fairness are thrown out the window. Bafflingly, on the TUC's press release web page for this report there was a link to an "anti-racism festival" called *No Racism: No Them And Us*. Which philosophy does the TUC recommend? Is it the inclusiveness of "no them and us", or is it the exclusiveness of no blending in and special holidays for certain categories of worker? And when is the TUC going to produce a report on English voices at work? No doubt it would make interesting reading, especially after the implementation of the recommendations in the other report.[18]

Christmas time nowadays always produces a rich store of stupidities. In 2003, Tessa Jowell, a NuLabour minister, distributed a card – which can only be described as a Christmas card because it was timed for Christmas – which contained no reference

---

[17] http://www.thesun.co.uk/article/0,,43-2003570407,00.html
[18] http://www.tuc.org.uk/equality/tuc-6519-f0.cfm

whatsoever to anything connected with Christmas (for fear of offending ethnic and religious minorities of course) yet included a picture of a mosque minaret and Hindu dancers. The feelings of the majority of course don't count. The public library in High Wycombe held a party to celebrate a Moslem festival, at the same time as banning a poster for a church carol service – in case it offended religious minorities. This policy had been put in place by the Conservative controlled local council. Richard Littlejohn wrote in the Sun newspaper "The councillor responsible, Margaret Dewar, said she was 'appalled at the attitude of so-called Christians making a fuss about this policy. We have a policy which aims to be inclusive and to respect the religious diversity of Buckinghamshire'. Except, of course, Christians — *so-called* or otherwise." Richard Littlejohn went on "What better illustration could there be of the extent of the *diversity* tyranny? Perhaps Michael Howard could have a quiet word with this preposterous prodnose. If this is typical of Tory councils in Middle England, the game is well and truly up."[19]

The examples given above are just some of the bits of scum that float on the top of the whole repellent mess concocted by the twisted minds of the ruling class. The grossest example of their incoherent spewings – an essentially racist one - is that for decades this class has subjected us to nauseating propaganda denouncing imperialism and colonialism, at the same time as inflicting both imperialism and colonialism on their own people, and declaring that *this* colonialism and imperialism brings with it the *enormous benefits* (always unspecified) of a *vibrant diversity* that we must all *celebrate*. One of the more ludicrous examples of this hypocrisy was a BBC Radio 4 Holiday Programme panel discussion of British tourism in India. The panel was unanimous in agreeing that this was a *bad thing* because, they claimed, it caused "cultural pollution". The panel was equally unanimous in agreeing that it would be *a jolly good thing* if Indian immigration into Britain made Britain become more culturally Indian.

I doubt whether many of the individuals mentioned above would consider themselves members of the ruling class. But the ruling class comprises all those people who make and implement the rules dictating how we must think and act. This class does not itself suffer from the consequences of the madness described, being overbearingly smug about it. It is inflicted on the rest of us, and it is altering the English character. Before, the English were, for the most part, down-to-earth, courageous, humorous, and comradely. In clichés worth repeating, it was seen in the spirit of the Blitz, Dunkirk, and the Battle of Britain. Now, far too many English are becoming mean-minded humourless sneaks, who provide a conduit for the tentacles of the great PC diversity monster that probes into every private corner of their fellow-Englishmen's lives. They are notable for their delusional thinking, insincerity and complete loss of all sense of proportion. The political class now has more of other people's money than sense, and can use it to impose their madness on ordinary people. It pretends to a *moral high ground*, but the more it's cornered the more it blusters and you know that their high ground is really just sand. They and their dogma are essentially weak. They are bullies who use the strength of an organised and aggressive minority to intimidate and control a disorganised majority.

---

[19] http://www.thesun.co.uk/article/0,,2003580758,00.html

Why are there so many English followers of this alien cult? Are they weak-minded, or ignorant, or evil, or mentally ill? Those who control and manage the state - the ruling class - should always be conscious of the fact that the state has no money of its own. Its financial resources come from the people, and those who govern have a duty to use that money only in the people's own interest. The state should use the money, on behalf of the people, to protect the country from invasion, to protect the people from imported diseases that threaten the people's health and lives. Every action of government should be directed to the maintenance of the welfare, peace and happiness of the people who temporarily lend it the power to do so. Since almost everything done by British governments and their agents for more than half a century appears to have been with the opposite intention, they must be insane.

Richard Fuerle has written on a similar phenomenon in the United States. [20] He believes that *liberals*, in general, profess to be altruistic. Liberals, although of European heritage, nevertheless express contempt for "dead White European males" and their works of genius. Liberals work for "affirmative action", though it will make it more difficult for them and their children to enter college, find a job, and get promoted. The altruism of liberals is not natural. It is a suicidal altruism, an altruism that, if practised to its logical extreme, would result in the extinction of the genes held by the people who practise it and, more important, the nation to which they belong. There is something phoney about it. It very often does not actually help those people it is supposed to help. Moreover, much of the help that liberals want to bestow on others is not help that they, themselves, offer. Rather, their help consists of using the government to force their enemies to help others, with little or no personal sacrifice from liberals. Their outrage is selective and peculiar, and the hypocrisy of liberals is legendary. They proclaim that morality is just a manifestation of culture, but bitterly denounce their opponents as "evil". Insincerity and hypocrisy are the hallmarks of an underlying psychological disturbance. Fuerle suggests the genesis of this psychosis is in childhood, resulting from a state of terrible tension, a conflict that the child desperately wanted to win, and that the conflict must have been with the child's parents. The future liberal is a destroyer, driven by hatred. He may not allow himself to consciously hate his parents, but he will allow himself to hate everything about them. If he is White, of European heritage, his hatred may extend to classical music, art, architecture, maths, science, law, free markets, and all the magnificent accomplishments of White Europeans. He may hate White people and work for their extinction. But over millennia the morality of liberals cannot survive. "For those who would commit suicide, nature is quick to oblige," someone said. The liberal will be displaced by those who spurn his morality.

Fuerle is describing homogenophobic racism, of which the British government is guilty. It accords ethnic status to all sorts of disparate peoples - including motley bands of travellers – but not the English. By such tricks they are able to avoid any consideration of such things as English children's educational achievements while those of ethnic minorities are celebrated and rewarded. Expressions of Englishness, such as including what was referred to as "White" culture in multiculturalist education have been banned - on the grounds of "inclusiveness", they said.

---

[20] *What Makes Liberals Tick?* Richard D. Fuerle, http://home.adelphia.net/~rdfuerle

Robert Henderson calls any individual with this condition a *liberal bigot*. Liberal bigots have character traits of hypocrisy; the wish to create the world in one's own image; paternalism; a sense of moral superiority; a desire to gratuitously interfere with the lives of others; false humility; self-indulgent masochism; and a pathological refusal to accept evidence which contradicts emotionally based beliefs. The liberal bigot, he says, "pretends to support freedom of expression whilst being a willing censor". The liberal bigot "acknowledges no sense of belonging or cultural indebtedness". Liberal bigots are parasites who "enjoy benefits gained at the expense of the host, in this case Anglo-Saxon society. But parasites can only be successful in the long run if they do not so weaken the host so that it is eventually unable to support them".[21]

Sean Bryson has likened this condition to the lemming effect. Lemmings are small rodents – not native to England - who are reputed to follow each other as they charge to their deaths into raging rivers or off cliffs.[22] *Lemminghood* is an innate psychological phenomenon, present in most mammals and observable in ordinary people as well as the most sophisticated and educated elites. A grant-seeking university scientist can be a lemming just as much as a fashion obsessed teenage girl. One blindly follows the latest trendy theory while the other blindly follows the latest trendy clothing style. This lemming effect can afflict entire segments of a society with a collective loss of judgment. For lemmings, denial is a basic psychological defence mechanism used to not only shield themselves from unpleasant realities, but also to reassure themselves that they will still fit within the acceptable range of opinion held by their peer group. Lemmings simply cannot bear the burden of responsibility, or the discomfort, which comes with thinking independently.[23]

Is the English trait of individualism powerful enough to overcome the lemming effect, or will that other English trait of polite, self-effacing tolerance prove to be so overwhelming that the ordinary English, ever-anxious to prove their tolerance, will hurl themselves over the cliff, along with their suicidal compatriots, in an act of communal suicide?

Three common drugs of abuse, LSD, PCP (*angel dust*) and amphetamine, produce the same schizophrenic-like behaviour.[24] Clear signs of schizophrenia can include fundamental and characteristic distortions of thinking and perception. The most intimate thoughts, feelings, and acts are often felt to be known or shared by others, and explanatory delusions may develop, to the effect that natural or supernatural forces are at work to influence the afflicted individual's thoughts and actions in ways that are often bizarre. Irrelevant features of ordinary things may appear more important than the whole object or

---

[21] Robert Henderson, http://www.anywhere.demon.co.uk

[22] Lemmings do not willingly throw themselves off cliffs but the myth helps to make a point.

[23] Sean Bryson

[24] *'Master molecule' could be pathway to treating schizophrenia*, Roger Highfield, Science Editor, Daily Telegraph, 24/11/2003

situation and utilized in place of those features that are relevant and appropriate to the situation. Thus thinking becomes vague and obscure, and its expression in speech sometimes incomprehensible. These symptoms can be summarized as persistent delusions that are culturally inappropriate and completely impossible, such as religious or political identities, breaks or interpolations in the train of thought, resulting in incoherence or irrelevant speech, or neologisms.[25] Amphetamine and cocaine induce euphoria[26] - perhaps this explains why the political class is notorious for its total lack of any embarrassment or shame over its treatment of the indigenous population.

Many years ago I was invited to a friend's house for dinner. I was ushered into the drawing room and introduced to her husband. This *man*, whom I suppose some might have described as the head of the family, was lolling in his armchair giggling vacantly. I saw at once that, through weakly following fashion and succumbing to mind-altering drugs, he had abandoned his role of host. So I felt under no obligation to play my role as guest, and ignored him ever after. I feel the same contempt for the ruling class today, and the same release from any obligations to it.

---

[25] http://www.mentalhealth.com/icd/p22-ps01.html

[26] *Getting the giggles is addictive*, Roger Highfield, Science Editor, Daily Telegraph, 04/12/2003

Dear Mr. Phillips

Robert Henderson

Mr Trevor Phillips
Chairman
The Commission for Racial Equality
Elliott House,
10/12 Allington Street
London SW1E SEH

2nd February 2004

Dear Mr Phillips,

Now that you have had time to settle into the job, I have a few questions for you.

1. How can a target for ethnic minority participation in an activity be achieved without positive discrimination which is illegal under the Race Relations Act (RRA)? Logic suggests that ethnic numbers could only be seriously increased from one level to another by deliberately choosing people on the grounds of their ethnicity.

2. The CRE workforce has a racial split of approximately 60% Black, 20% Asian and 20% White. What steps are you taking to ensure the CRE workforce is broadly in line with the racial composition of the UK population: 92% White, 5% Asian and 3% Black? What targets have you set to achieve this?

3. The CRE has commissioners for Scotland and Wales but not England. Thus approximately 83% of the UK population are denied the special representation of their interests which is granted to the remaining 17%. What steps will you be taking to end this anomaly?

4. The BBC has announced (Sunday Telegraph 1/2/2004) that ten per cent of their staff are now from an ethnic minority and that they intend to increase this to 12.5% As ethnic minorities form only 7.8% of the population according to the 2001 census, action is clearly required by the CRE to ensure that the White population are not under-represented. Please let me know what action you will take to ensure this happens.

5. Whites are seriously under-represented in the law and medicine, both at the level of training and practice. Please let me know what action you will take to increase the number of Whites in these professions.

6. There are approximately 80 housing associations in the UK which restrict tenancies to Blacks or Asians - see enclosed list. There are none which restrict tenancies to Whites. Please let me know what steps you will be taking to ensure that either the Black and Asian housing associations are disbanded or a number of White-only housing associations, proportionate to the number of Whites in the population, are set up.

Your earliest reply please.

Yours sincerely,

Robert Henderson   [No reply was received]

Nations and States: Nationality and Citizenship
Tony Linsell

What is a Nation?

The word nation is commonly used in the following three ways:

As a synonym for *state*. For example, when the European Union is discussed, mention is often made of its member nations pooling and sharing their sovereignty. The members of the EU are in fact states.

As a term for the citizens of a state. For example, reference is often made to the British nation when what is meant is citizens of the UK or the British people. Also, at the time of the coming to power of Nelson Mandela there was much talk of the people of South Africa being one nation; a rainbow nation. What was meant was that the people of many nations shared the same citizenship.

As a term for a group of people who share a common descent, culture, history and language. For example, the Kurds, Zulus, Palestinians and Tibetans are all nations, as indeed are the English.

Those who are careless with their terminology, which includes many journalists, tend to use the words *state* and *nation* as if they are interchangeable. Those who study global society (International Relations) or are involved in inter-state relations have to be more precise with their terms and better appreciate the need to distinguish a state from a nation.

The misuse of the terms is mostly due to ignorance but sometimes it is a deliberate act by those who wish to promote an inclusive civic identity in place of an exclusive national identity. They believe that the state should be central to the identity and loyalty of those who live in it. They further that aim by merging national identity into a civic or state identity. Thus, *nation* and *nationality* are used in a way that implies that they are political rather than cultural terms. *Nationality* is equated with *citizenship*, which can be constitutionally defined and bestowed by the state. For example, if a person is a citizen of France they are deemed to be French and to owe loyalty to the French state.

A very different view is that a nation is a community of people with a communal name, ancestry, culture, history and language. Those who take this stance believe that nations exist independently of states, and that nationality is determined by membership of and loyalty to a cultural and kinship community; a nation. For example, an Algerian who becomes a French citizen remains an Algerian. It is this fundamental difference in outlook that is explored below.

It is widely recognised that it is difficult to define a nation but that does not mean that nations do not exist. A fairly simple definition, or collection of guidelines, as to what constitutes a nation is that it is a group of people who share all or most of the following: a collective name; a perceived or real common ancestry; a history; a culture; a language and sometimes a common religion. There is nearly always an association between a nation and a specific territory that is regarded as its homeland. A nation has myths, legends, heroes and loyalties. It is a community with a sense of solidarity and common identity; there is a *we* sentiment and a *they* sentiment; *insiders* and *outsiders*. A greater degree of empathy and sympathy exists among insiders than between insiders and outsiders. Indeed, the notion of *insiders* and *outsiders* derives from the concept of a community living closely together within a physical boundary, e.g. an encampment or settlement enclosed by a fence or ditch. A nation's boundary markers are more often cultural and perceptual than physical.

One of the most important things that binds a nation together is the fact or perception of insiders sharing a common history and ancestry. The members of a nation usually have real ancestral links, but even in those instances where the links are weak, the illusion of common ancestry is possible because insiders share certain physical characteristics that make it possible for them to believe in a shared ancestry. As is so often the case, perception is more important than fact but pretence has its limits. For example, it would be difficult for a Japanese to pretend to be a Zulu because whatever clothes that person wore or the language they spoke, their appearance would remain so different from that of Zulus that any claim to share a common ancestry would obviously be doubtful.

That we have mental images of Zulus, Swedes and Japanese indicates that the linked factors of common physical characteristics and common ancestry are important considerations in determining membership of national communities. Despite the instinctive links we make, some ideologues are outraged by the idea that common ancestry has any part in determining nationality, not because it is untrue but because it is ideologically inconvenient. The very people who deny a link between kinship and nationality when defining, for example, Swedish nationality, nevertheless think it relevant when, for example, determining membership of North American Indian nations. An instance of this is the procedure used when the US government granted the remnants of certain Indian nations various land rights in a belated attempt to compensate them for the loss of their homelands. The financial benefits for members of those nations can sometimes be great, and there are many claimants. The method used to establish membership of an Indian nation is ancestry, which has to be proved.[1] In other words, that which determines membership of a North American Indian nation is judged to be *in the blood*, hence, for example, the term full-blooded Navajo. A similar blood-line procedure is used by the US government for determining who are indigenous Hawaiians. Place of residence or birth or the expression of a firmly held belief by the applicant that they are a member of the appropriate tribe/nation counts for little. Nationality is not, therefore, taken to be a matter of personal choice.[2]

---

[1] North American Indian nations find the process acceptable because blood ties play an important part in their cultures.

[2] It is to be noted that states generally confer citizenship on the children of their citizens and demand as of right certain things from their citizens, including loyalty. It is a sort of protection racket – you pay the state taxes and the state will protect you. Refusal to co-operate results in punishment.

Other factors that help identify a nation are myths and folklore that throw light on its origins and ancestry. Mythology is important even when it is only loosely based on fact or is a complete invention, as is the case with the various legends of King Arthur.[3] Folklore and history help to unite a nation and give it a distinct identity but it need not be one hundred percent *true* in order to fulfil that function.

Religions and political ideologies are powerful bonding factors that sometimes cut across national identity but they more often compliment and re-enforce national identities and promote alliances of nations and their states. For example, the conflict in Bosnia re-enforced various alliances of states based on common religion. Turkey and other Moslem states supported the Bosnian Moslems, and the Greeks supported their fellow Orthodox Christians, the Serbs. States with large Catholic populations supported the Catholic Croats. Another feature of the war was the way Moslems in Bosnia used, or had imposed on them, a religious identity as an ethnic identity. In other words, *Moslem* became an ethnic identity.

Individuals tend to feel more secure when they are in the company of persons with whom they have much in common; birds of a feather flock together. Common values, experiences, attitudes and perceptions help make up the glue that binds together both small, face-to-face, local communities and large national communities. A nation is organic; it lives; it is more than the sum of its parts; it repairs and renews itself; it has a memory; it evolves. Its personality is to be found in its culture, its institutions and the attitudes and behaviour of its parts. Each member of a nation is a link between its past and its future. As with all living things a nation has to renew itself if it is to survive. It is the communal duty of each generation to preserve and renew the national culture. In doing so, it in turn becomes part of the nation's present, past, and future.

When a nation ceases to renew itself it dies and the memory of those that have gone before and the culture they helped to weave dies with it: it is a loss to all mankind. A dead nation leaves behind it artefacts, buildings, a history, language - the threads of a culture - but nothing to weave those things together and give them life. The parts remain as curiosities, the preservation and interpretation of which lies with outsiders. Nationalism is the expression of a will to avoid communal extinction.

A nation is a reference point for individuals, it is a community where individuals can feel comfortable and at ease. A nation provides physical and cultural surroundings that are familiar and unthreatening. A nation is a home, and for many individuals it is such an important part of their being that they are prepared to endure hardships and to fight and die in its defence.

---

[3] The invented tales of a King Arthur were promoted by the Normans and Plantagenets in place of English history. It was part of a policy that can be called *ethnocide*. The aim was to impose on the English a history of Britain in which the English played little part except as villains. This fictional account served the dual purpose of providing the Britons with a glorious history that made them feel better about themselves, and undermining English national identity, thus making the English more accepting of Norman rule. The legends took on a life of their own and as they developed they came to represent an ideal of chivalrous behaviour which influenced real knights and kings.

Nationality and Citizenship

Nationality

Nationality is the condition, or fact, of belonging to a body of people sharing a common descent, culture, history and language. Nationality is acquired at birth; individuals are born into a community. It is the reality and perception of a common ancestry and shared communal experiences that binds a nation together.

At the heart of nationality is a feeling of belonging and oneness that marks out a communal boundary. The *we sentiment* is not, as many wish us to believe, evil and deserving of eradication. On the contrary, it is at the heart of any community anywhere in the world, and usually gives rise to positive communal thoughts and deeds.

It is difficult to frame exact rules for determining who is a member of a given nation but a useful guide, which can be used for any nation, is as follows: I am English if I believe[4] that I am English *and* if I am accepted as being English by the members of that group of people who are commonly recognised as being English. It is a two-way instinctive relationship between individual and community. I could, for example, assert that I am Japanese but if I have physical and cultural characteristics that are not Japanese, as determined by the Japanese, I will not be accepted as part of the Japanese community. No amount of law-making, sulking or haranguing will alter that.

The two-way process of selection for inclusion or exclusion helps provide an answer to the question often thrown at nationalists, "What does it mean [for example] to be English?" The aim of the questioner is to draw out a list of characteristics that identify the English. Those asked are usually stumped for an answer, which is not surprising because the process of inclusion and exclusion is not a conscious one and does not work in the way implied by the question. The English, like all other nations, first see characteristics that exclude people because that is a more efficient way of working when analysing vast amounts of information.[5] Most of the Earth's population can be quickly excluded from membership of any given nation on the basis of appearance and language. If necessary, other tests of varying degrees of sophistication can be used until we are satisfied that the person is either an *insider* or an *outsider*.

If the person is accepted as an insider, the instinctive assessment process goes on and makes other judgements about the person, including such things as their social class. At this *insider* level of assessment, the filtering process can make finer distinctions because we have far more experience of dealing with insiders and can make better use of small amounts of information. For example, if a

---

[4] The word *believe* is hardly adequate to convey the emotional feeling of identity with and concern for a nation that is at the heart of nationality.

[5] It is usual when processing a large amount of information to set markers, and exclude information that falls outside the set boundaries. Alan Turin applied this principle when devising the system known as the Bombe, which automated and speeded up the daily processing of information for the purpose of breaking the German Enigma code during World War II.

Russian gives me his home address it will tell me little, if anything, about him because my knowledge of Russia and things Russian is poor. An address in my hometown will tell me far more about the person who lives there.

Nationality is a total experience that starts in the family, which is the smallest community. Children are born into both a family and the wider communities of which that family is part. They are immersed in and soak up like a sponge the language, culture and history of the communities to which they belong.[6] That experience helps mould children and gives them an identity and sense of belonging. They pick up habits of behaviour and thought that are part of what is meant by national character. That character-building process, if that is what it can properly be called, works best when there is cultural immersion and socialisation from a very early age. Once a national identity has been absorbed, it is embedded for life. It shapes values and perceptions in a way that makes it impossible for a member of one nation to completely shake off that identity and take on another. Learning another nation's customs, history and language is not enough because the new information is laid on old foundations.

The link between kinship, identity and loyalty can be illustrated as follows. An adopted child reared from a baby by loving adopted parents is likely to feel love and affection for those parents. When the child learns of its adoption it will normally want to seek out its biological parents.[7] If they are found, the child is likely to feel an attachment to them that is different from that felt for the adopted parents, who it will probably continue to love as before. This need to know our origins is instinctive and essential to our sense of identity and belonging. It is therefore understandable that when a child learns that its real parents belong to a nation different from the one it has been raised in, it is likely to be drawn to that other nation's culture, and identify with it. This can cause difficulties that are made worse when differences of race are added to those of nationality. The experience of many children involved in cross-race adoptions is one of confusion in adulthood due to the draw of conflicting communal identities and loyalties. Having been immersed in one culture from birth and having had that identity imprinted on them they find it difficult, if not impossible, to feel totally part of another culture to which they are subsequently drawn. They cannot overcome the fact that the first all-important immersion in a communal identity is a one-off experience.

---

[6] Young children naturally absorb cultural information from those around them. This instinct enables them to learn up-to-date survival strategies that can be laid over their long-term survival instincts. This ability to quickly adapt to the requirements of the immediate environment has evolved over millions of years, and under conditions where cultural information and skills helped individuals and communities survive and reproduce. We now have conditions where children are subject to the influence of a culture which promotes values and perceptions that are harmful to both individual and communal survival and reproduction. The result is a high proportion of young adults with attitudes and behavioural habits that make them well suited for life in the virtual-reality world promoted by the global me-culture but ill-equipped for survival in the real world. Natural selection ruthlessly weeds out those with unsuitable survival strategies.

[7] Children who learn that they are the product of an arrangement involving an anonymous sperm donor also feel the need to find their roots and establish their identity.

In a similar way, children with parents of the same race but different nationality have to deal with conflicting attractions and loyalties. However, the problem is usually not so great for these children because they are generally drawn to, and accepted by, at least one of the nations to which they are linked by kinship. A child raised in the national homeland, culture and language of one parent is likely to be drawn to that nation and be accepted by it. However, physical appearance can sometimes play a more important part than upbringing in determining which community a person is drawn to and which community accepts them. A child brought up in a community where s/he is the physical odd-one-out, is likely to be drawn to and identify with the members of another community that shares *odd-one-out* characteristics. The other side of this is that if a person's physical or cultural characteristics differ greatly from the norm for a particular nation, that person is unlikely to seek acceptance in it or to be accepted by it.

Liberals feel the need to put a positive slant on these things and suggest that children with parents of different nationality or race have the advantage of two identities and two cultures.[8] But is it really possible to immerse oneself in two cultures, identify with two histories, feel an insider in two communities, and, more difficult still, be accepted as a full member of two communities? The answer is probably, no. To feel an insider and be accepted as an insider it is usually necessary for a person to be immersed in the culture of that community from birth and to be free of traits that would cause that person to be seen as an outsider.

A nation is an extended family and like a family it has a life greater than that of any single member. Nations, like families, are bound together by the bonds of empathy and loyalty that come from a shared identity. Those bonds are not only with the living but also with those who have gone before and those who are yet to come. That link between past, present and future encourages the living members of a national community to protect the memory of earlier generations and safeguard the position of future generations. That sentiment is not something that can be learned or feigned.

Citizenship

Using *nationality* as a synonym for *citizenship* can cause confusion and misunderstanding. Nationality denotes membership of a particular community, while citizenship denotes membership of a civic-society. The two identities are sometimes complementary (in nation-states) and sometimes they conflict or have no close association (in multi-nation-states).

A civic identity is like a national identity in that it is usually acquired at birth with no opportunity available for opting out or negotiating terms. Those who were born in the Soviet Union usually acquired Soviet citizenship and, like other Soviet citizens, became a part of Soviet society and were subject to the rules of the Soviet state, which like other states deemed that it had the right to demand obedience and loyalty in certain things. Soviet citizens also belonged to a

---

[8] Multi-culturalism is an ideology (a very recent one) and should be subject to the same tests as any other. It is not, as many of its followers believe, derived from an unchallengeable universal truth.

nation (e.g. Russian, Latvian, Armenian) and a family, both of which are communities that endure despite the coming and going of states. In a similar way, a British citizen (more properly called a British subject[9]) might be English, Scottish, Welsh, Nigerian, Bangladeshi, Jamaican, Italian or a member of any nation you care to mention.[10] Citizenship indicates a person's relationship with a state (political structure) and is usually defined in a legalistic form of words that is embodied in the state's constitution. Nationality indicates a person's relationship with a nation (community and its culture) and cannot be formally defined.

Each state determines who are its citizens and how non-citizens can qualify for citizenship. The acquisition of citizenship is a legal formality that gives an individual civic rights and obligations. It is a legal procedure and because of that it is possible to be a citizen of two or more states and have dual citizenship, which is often inaccurately termed, dual-nationality. Some states permit their citizens to hold dual citizenship but others do not.

Afterword

If you equate nationalism with conservatism, you should look at the history of nationalist movements throughout the world. Ho Chi Minh, Abdul Nasser, Fidel Castro, and Gerry Adams all carry the label *nationalist* – all have sought national self-determination. Those who are opposed to nationalists and nationalism often wear the label *internationalist* (individualism and loyalty to a globalist political and economic ideology) or *statist* (loyalty to the state and its ideology) – statists often call themselves *patriots* – as do George Bush and Tony Blair. It is of course open to debate whether either of these men has greater loyalty to *their* state or to a globalist ideology which sees all states as tools in an ideological war.

---

[9]   A subject is a person who lives under (is subject to) the rule of a monarch. The term is technically correct but will cease to be so if the UK is absorbed into the European Union. *Subject* is probably no longer appropriate in the UK because although the monarch is Head of State he or she does not rule in any real sense and, in effect, acts as an unelected president. *Citizen* seems to be the more appropriate term.

[10] British subjects in the province of Northern Ireland who are Republicans or members of the *Nationalist Community*, consider themselves to be Irish. The position of the *Loyalist Community* is more complex but they can, with justification, claim to be a nation with a homeland called Ulster. They are Ulstermen. *Protestant* describes their religion and *Loyalist* is a political stance.

English frogs go 'croak'

Mak Norman

The English frog is in threat of Americanisation. It appears that the English frog in children's books and television programmes no longer goes croak but *ribbit*.

This has been creeping in for sometime through TV and films from the States. Now it's come into my home via my 3 year old daughter because that's what her teacher at nursery school says.

I hope this doesn't sound petty because I actually find it quite upsetting. Even children's television presenters are saying *ribbit*.

Ribbit is an accurate impersonation of American bullfrogs and that's fine with me. However (and I will not budge from this), English frogs go croak.

I have tried to correct my little girl but obviously she likes saying what all the children say.

One day my daughter said to me (plainly see my torment), "I know daddy! I have an idea; frogs go *ribbit* and they go *croak*".

And I suppose they will have to. Until that is the last croak, *croaks*.

Croak!

Afterword
Tony Linsell

What is happening in England today is not a game or the plot of a film or soap opera, although if it were it is likely that more people would take it seriously. It is actually happening, it is reality, and those who have eyes to see are witnessing something of immense historical importance.

The English need to quickly learn ethnic and diaspora politics because if we do not, and existing trends continue, we will perish. Essential to success is a widespread and celebrated sense of origins and identity. We have to defend and promote our communal culture and our communal space. Our chance of success will be improved if we join with other members of the Anglo-Saxon diaspora, all of whom, to varying degrees, are faced with threats to their identity and way of life. Each part of the diaspora can learn from the experience of the others. We should support and learn from all nations that are struggling to govern themselves in their homelands. We are all suffering at the hands of an aggressive globalism that is vandalising our physical, economic, political, and cultural environments. We should together seek a form of democracy that gives us control over these aspects of our lives.

Those responsible for denying us the power to manage our lives want us to feel despair and resign ourselves to the inevitability of it all. It is for each of us to rise to the task in ways that suit our aptitudes, abilities, and the opportunities that present themselves. It is a big task but a start has to be made somewhere and at sometime. The first step occurs in your head; you must stop being afraid. They use fear to control you. It is fear of what others may think, say, or do, that prevents you confronting those who wish to control your thoughts and actions. You have to be able to say to yourself each day, *I am not afraid of them and I will not be intimidated – they will not control me*. When you can say that and mean it you will be free. When they have lost the ability to control your mind, they will be afraid of you.

Come join the shieldwall and stand shoulder-to-shoulder with us. Fate has given each of us an opportunity to play a part in a heroic struggle. May he grieve forever who flees the fight.

wæs þa hæl

Some of our other titles

The English Dragon
T.P. Bragg

The English Dragon is a story of loss of innocence; a search for identity; of what it means to be English. The narrative gives the flavour of a culture obsessed with image and dogma. There is a juxtaposition of the new and often violent urban society with the rural, traditional community.

The author does not shy away from difficult subjects - the treatment and housing of asylum-seekers being crucial to the novel's structure.

£5-95 A5 ISBN 1-903313-02-3 232pp

An English Nationalism
Tony Linsell

In this handbook of modern nationalism the author investigates the origins of the English and England. This is followed by a critical look at modern liberalism, multiculturalism, and the way public opinion is manipulated. "Our political institutions deny us meaningful choice." A democratic system should aim to give us the ability to govern ourselves, which involves the management of our economy and physical environment. Yet the trend in modern politics is to deny us this control. Instead, we are increasingly in the thrall of the unelected and unaccountable.

£16-90 248 x 170mm ISBN 1-903313-01-5 430pp

The Deculturalisation of the English People
The Rev. John Lovejoy

In Australia the author witnessed the sad fate of Aborigines who have had their culture and communal life shattered. On his return to England, he saw the English facing a similar process of deculturalisation but lacking the will to resist or reverse it.

The young have no sense of who they are or where they are from. Deculturalisation is revealed in the inability of many, and especially the young, to be able to answer the questions, Who am I? What do I believe? Where do I belong? Who am I loyal to?

Everywhere we see the loss of communal values and perceptions. John Lovejoy gives reasons for the deculturalisation of the English and points to the remedy.

£4-95 A5 ISBN 1-903313-00-7 80pp

For details of other titles see our web site www.athelney.org or ask for details –
Athelney, 1 Providence Street, King's Lynn, Norfolk, PE30 5ET

Our aim is to publish good books at a reasonable price.

Organisations

Campaign for an English Parliament
The CEP is campaigning for an English Parliament with at least the same powers as the Scottish Parliament. It is a non-party-political organisation which draws its support from across the political spectrum.

Members receive a quarterly newsletter – *Think of England*

1 Providence Street, King's Lynn, Norfolk, PE30 5ET
www.thecep.org.uk

Steadfast – Voice of the English Community
A quarterly journal which gives English people the opportunity to express their views on events and ideas affecting the English community.

Steadfast, 27 Old Gloucester Street, London WC1N 3XX

www.wearetheenglish.com
Merchandise – clothing – news – views.
Stocks a wide assortment of products that have an English flavour.
Flags, mugs, clothing, car number plates, and much more.

www.theanglo-saxons
A web and DVD magazine for the Ethnic English, i.e. persons of Anglo-Saxon descent or origin, providing coverage on news; entertainment, festival activities; art, book, film, music and other cultural sources, community and charity activities; education; legal thought and very much more.
For more details see web site www.theanglo-saxons.co.uk

The Steadfast Trust
A registered charity whose main objectives are to relieve poverty among the ethnic English and to promote the health, welfare and education of that community. In short, the aim is to improve the conditions of life for the Anglo-Saxon population of England.

Donations should be made payable to The Steadfast Trust.
Write to Steadfast, 27 Old Gloucester Street, London WC1N 3XX
Please mark the back of the envelope 'TST'.